COMMUNITIES

 Harcourt Brace Jovanovich, Inc.

Holt, Rinehart and Winston, Inc.

Orlando · Austin · San Diego · Chicago · Dallas · Toronto

SENIOR EDITORIAL ADVISER

Dr. Phillip Bacon is a professor Emeritus of Geography and Anthropology at the University of Houston. Dr. Bacon has also served on the faculties of Columbia University and the University of Washington. Formerly Dean of the Graduate School of Peabody College for Teachers at Vanderbilt University, Dr. Bacon began his career in education as a teacher of elementary and secondary social studies. He is the author or editor of more than 36 books, including the *Life Pictorial Atlas of the World*. For 18 years, Dr. Bacon served as a member of the Editorial Advisory Board of the *World Book Encyclopedia*.

Among his numerous honors and awards, Dr. Bacon holds the distinguished titles of Fellow of the Explorers Club and Fellow of the Royal Geographic Society of Great Britain. He is a three-time recipient of the Teaching Excellence Award at the University of Houston. His biography appears in *Who's Who in America* and *American Men and Women in Science*.

ACKNOWLEDGMENTS

For permission to reprint copyrighted material, grateful acknowledgment is made to the following sources:

Greenwillow Books, a division of William Morrow & Company, Inc.: From *Goodbye, My Island* by Jean Rogers. Text copyright © 1983 by Jean Rogers.

Harcourt Brace Jovanovich, Inc.: "Buffalo Dusk" from *Smoke and Steel* by Carl Sandburg. Copyright 1920 by Harcourt Brace Jovanovich, Inc., renewed 1948 by Carl Sandburg.

Harper & Row, Publishers, Inc.: "Rudolph Is Tired of the City" from *Bronzeville Boys and Girls* by Gwendolyn Brooks. Copyright © 1956 by Gwendolyn Brooks Blakely. "Ring Around the World" from *All Through the Year* by Annette Wynne. Copyright 1932 by Annette Wynne. Published by J. B. Lippincott.

Barbara A. Huff: From "The Library" by Barbara A. Huff. Copyright © 1972 by Barbara A. Huff.

Alfred A. Knopf, Inc.: From *In Coal Country* by Judith Hendershot. Text copyright © 1987 by Judith Hendershot.

Gina Maccoby Literary Agency: "The Folk Who Live in Backward Town" from *Hello and Goodby* by Mary Ann Hoberman. Copyright © 1959, renewed 1987 by Mary Ann Hoberman. Published by Little, Brown and Company.

Macmillan Publishing Company: From "Whistles" in *Poems* by Rachel Field. Published by Macmillan Publishing Company, 1957.

Morrow Junior Books, a division of William Morrow & Company, Inc.: The House on Maple Street by Bonnie Pryor. Text copyright © 1987 by Bonnie Pryor.

Rand McNally & Company: "Our History" by Catherine Cate Coblentz from *Child Life* Magazine. Copyright by Rand McNally & Company.

Scholastic, Inc.: From "Face to Face" by Anita E. Posey in *Poetry Place Anthology*. Copyright © 1983 by Scholastic, Inc.

Printed in the United States of America
ISBN 0-15-372622-9

PROGRAM ADVISERS

John F. Barbini, Ed.D.
Assistant Superintendent
School District 54
Schaumburg, Illinois

Willard Bill, Ph.D.
Chair, Social Sciences
International and Multicultural
Division
North Seattle Community College
Seattle, Washington

Frank de Varona
Associate Superintendent
Dade County Public Schools
Miami, Florida

Paul S. Hanson
Principal
North Miami Beach Senior
High School
Miami, Florida

William D. Travis, Ed.D.
Curriculum Director
Pittsfield Public Schools
Pittsfield, Massachusetts

Donald P. Vetter
Supervisor of Social Studies
Carroll County Public Schools
Westminster, Maryland

CONTENT SPECIALISTS

Irving Cutler, Ph.D.
Chairman Emeritus, Geography
Department
Chicago State University
Chicago, Illinois

Donald O. Schneider, Ph.D.
Professor and Head of
Social Science Education
University of Georgia
Athens, Georgia

Wm. Doyle Smith, Ph.D.
Associate Professor of Economics
University of Texas at El Paso
El Paso, Texas

Peter J. Stein, Ph.D.
Professor of Sociology
William Paterson College
Wayne, New Jersey

CHILDREN'S LITERATURE ADVISERS

Meredith McGowan
Children's Librarian
and Consultant
Tempe, Arizona

Thomas McGowan, Ph.D.
Associate Professor
Curriculum and Instruction
Arizona State University
Tempe, Arizona

CLASSROOM CONSULTANTS

Nancy Anderson
Teacher
Cookson Elementary School
Troy, Ohio

Ellen Bach
Teacher
Southside Elementary School
Livingston Parish, Louisiana

Donna M. Bosman
Librarian
Emerson Elementary School
Everett, Washington

Joyce Buckner, Ed.D.
Director of Elementary Education
Omaha Public Schools
Omaha, Nebraska

Howard Faber
Teacher
Miller Park Elementary School
Omaha, Nebraska

Diane Loughlin
Teacher
Antioch C. C. School District 34
Antioch, Illinois

Cynthia V. McKinney
Teacher
Public School 233
Brooklyn, New York

Betty Martindale
Teacher
Hillis Elementary School
Des Moines, Iowa

Kay Psencik
Director of Curriculum/
Staff Development
Temple Independent School District
Temple, Texas

Mary Lou Purpura
Librarian
H. B. Whitehorne Middle School
Verona, New Jersey

Sally E. Reed
Teacher
Foster Elementary School
Ludington, Michigan

Cynthia Rogers
Coordinator for Elementary Social
Studies
Minneapolis Public Schools
Minneapolis, Minnesota

Mary Simpson
Teacher
Eastwood Elementary School
Salt Lake City, Utah

Lester John Szabo
Supervisor of Social Studies
and Staff Development
Kenmore—Town of Tonawanda
Union Free School District
Kenmore, New York

Kaye Tague
Director of Elementary Education
Emporia Unified School District
No. 253
Emporia, Kansas

Kathy G. Walker
Assistant Principal
Longan Elementary School
Richmond, Virginia

CONTENTS

Introduction   ◇   1

Using Your Textbook   ◇   2

Geography: Review and Practice   ◇   4

UNIT ONE
PEOPLE AND COMMUNITIES
16

CHAPTER ONE
How Communities Are Alike   ◇   18

SECTION ONE   Why People Live in Communities   ◇   19

PEOPLE MAKE HISTORY: **Arthur Mitchell**   ◇   22

SECTION TWO   Communities Help People Meet Needs   ◇   23

IN FOCUS: **Second Harvest** ◇ 28

SKILLS IN ACTION: **Using the Library** ◇ 30

SKILLS IN ACTION: **Using Dictionaries and Encyclopedias** ◇ 32

Review   ◇   34

CHAPTER TWO
How Communities Are Different   ◇   36

SECTION ONE   Communities Are in Different Places   ◇   37

IN FOCUS: **Amish Communities** ◇ 39

SECTION TWO   Communities Are Different Sizes   ◇   **41**

HISTORY CONNECTION: **Skyscrapers**   ◇   **43**

PEOPLE MAKE HISTORY: **Frank Lloyd Wright**   ◇   **48**

SKILLS IN ACTION: **Using Maps to Show Your Address**   ◇   **49**

Review   ◇   **54**

from **Goodbye, My Island**
by Jean Rogers

56

UNIT REVIEW

61

Exploring Your Community   ◇   **63**

UNIT TWO

COMMUNITIES USE NATURAL RESOURCES

64

CHAPTER THREE

Farming Communities   ◇   **66**

SECTION ONE   Natural Resources and Our Farms   ◇   **67**

GEOGRAPHY CONNECTION: **Greenhouses**   ◇   **70**

IN FOCUS: **Anasazi Indians**   ◇   **72**

SKILLS IN ACTION: **Using Resource Maps**   ◇   **74**

SECTION TWO   Merced, California   ◇   **76**

SKILLS IN ACTION: **Using Climate Maps**   ◇   **82**

SECTION THREE   Tomatoes at the Cannery   ◇   **84**

SKILLS IN ACTION: **Using Lists and Tables**   ◇   **86**

SECTION FOUR   Independence, Iowa   ◇   **88**

SECTION FIVE   Milk at the Creamery   ◇   **91**

PEOPLE MAKE HISTORY: **Chan Hong Tai**   ◇   **93**

Review   ◇   **94**

CHAPTER FOUR
Mining Communities   ◇   **96**

SECTION ONE   Mineral Resources and Our Communities   ◇   **97**

IN FOCUS: **Crater of Diamonds**   ◇   **100**

SKILLS IN ACTION: **Saving Resources**   ◇   **102**

SECTION TWO   Pikeville, Kentucky   ◇   **104**

PEOPLE MAKE HISTORY: **Molly Brown**   ◇   **110**

SKILLS IN ACTION: **Reading Landform Maps**   ◇   **111**

SECTION THREE   Midland, Texas   ◇   **113**

SKILLS IN ACTION: **Using Bar Graphs**   ◇   **120**

Review   ◇   **122**

CHAPTER FIVE
Port Communities   ◇   **124**

SECTION ONE   Water and Our Communities   ◇   **125**

SECTION TWO   Chicago, Illinois   ◇   **130**

PEOPLE MAKE HISTORY: **Jean Baptist Pointe du Sable**   ◇   **135**

SECTION THREE   Trains, Trucks, and Planes   ◇   **136**

SKILLS IN ACTION: **Finding Routes**   ◇   **139**

SECTION FOUR   Seattle, Washington   ◇   **141**

IN FOCUS: **Lighthouses**   ◇   **145**

SECTION FIVE   Lumber and Fishing in Seattle   ◇   **147**

GEOGRAPHY CONNECTION: **Salmon Ladders**   ◇   **150**

SKILLS IN ACTION: **Using Flow Charts** ◇ **152**

Review ◇ **154**

Why People Work ◇ 156

UNIT REVIEW

161

Exploring Your Community ◇ **163**

UNIT THREE

COMMUNITY GOVERNMENTS AND SERVICES

164

CHAPTER SIX
Communities Have Rules and Governments ◇ **166**

SECTION ONE Rules in Communities ◇ **167**

IN FOCUS: **Laws and Rules of Long Ago** ◇ **170**

SECTION TWO How Governments Work ◇ **172**

SECTION THREE Newfane, Vermont ◇ **175**

HISTORY CONNECTION: **Town Crier** ◇ **177**

SKILLS IN ACTION: **Making Choices** ◇ **179**

SECTION FOUR Governments for Our States and Country ◇ **182**

PEOPLE MAKE HISTORY: **Wilma Mankiller** ◇ **185**

SKILLS IN ACTION: **Finding the Information You Need** ◇ **186**

Review ◇ **188**

CHAPTER SEVEN
Communities Provide Services ◇ **190**

SECTION ONE Community Services Protect Us ◇ **191**

vii

SECTION TWO   A Fire Department in Orlando, Florida   ◇   **195**

SKILLS IN ACTION: **Using Maps and Grids**   ◇   **199**

SECTION THREE   More Community Services   ◇   **201**

PEOPLE MAKE HISTORY: **Anne Carroll Moore**   ◇   **205**

SECTION FOUR   Libraries, Parks, and Museums   ◇   **206**

IN FOCUS: **Golden Gate Park**   ◇   **210**

SECTION FIVE   Taxes Pay for Community Services   ◇   **212**

SKILLS IN ACTION: **Being a Responsible Citizen**   ◇   **215**

Review   ◇   **218**

The San Diego Zoo   ◇   220

UNIT REVIEW

225

Exploring Your Community   ◇   **227**

UNIT FOUR

COMMUNITIES OF YESTERDAY, TODAY, AND TOMORROW

228

CHAPTER EIGHT

Communities Grow and Change   ◇   **230**

SECTION ONE   How Communities Begin   ◇   **231**

SECTION TWO   Denver, Colorado—The Early Years   ◇   **234**

PEOPLE MAKE HISTORY: **"Buffalo Bill" Cody**   ◇   **238**

SECTION THREE   Mining in Denver   ◇   **239**

IN FOCUS: **Denver Mint**   ◇   **242**

SECTION FOUR   Modern Denver   ◇   **244**

SKILLS IN ACTION: **Using Pictures to Tell a Story**   ◇   **247**

Review   ◇   **250**

CHAPTER NINE

Our Country Has a History   ◇   **252**

SECTION ONE   Early Years in America   ◇   **253**

SECTION TWO   Settlers Come to America   ◇   **257**

IN FOCUS: **Plimoth Plantation**   ◇   **260**

SECTION THREE   A New Country Is Born   ◇   **262**

SKILLS IN ACTION: **Reading Calendars and Timelines**   ◇   **266**

SECTION FOUR   The New Nation Grows   ◇   **268**

PEOPLE MAKE HISTORY: **David Farragut**   ◇   **273**

SECTION FIVE   Modern America   ◇   **274**

GEOGRAPHY CONNECTION: **Submersibles**   ◇   **277**

SKILLS IN ACTION: **Using Timelines to Show History**   ◇   **278**

Review   ◇   **280**

The House on Maple Street
by Bonnie Pryor

282

UNIT REVIEW

287

Exploring Your Community   ◇   **289**

UNIT FIVE
AROUND THE WORLD

290

CHAPTER TEN
Meeting Needs Around the World ◇ 292

SECTION ONE Foods Around the World ◇ 293
IN FOCUS: **Seaweed** ◇ 297

SECTION TWO Clothing Around the World ◇ 299
PEOPLE MAKE HISTORY: **Levi Strauss** ◇ 304

SECTION THREE Shelters Around the World ◇ 305
SKILLS IN ACTION: **Time, the Earth, and the Sun** ◇ 309
Review ◇ 312

CHAPTER ELEVEN
Living in Communities Around the World ◇ 314

SECTION ONE Communities Use Natural Resources ◇ 315
IN FOCUS: **World's Fairs** ◇ 322
SKILLS IN ACTION: **Reading Population Maps** ◇ 324

SECTION TWO Governments and Services Around the World ◇ 326
PEOPLE MAKE HISTORY: **Mother Teresa** ◇ 330

SECTION THREE The Histories of Two Cities ◇ 331
HISTORY CONNECTION: **Windmills** ◇ 333
SKILLS IN ACTION: **Using Intermediate Directions** ◇ 335
Review ◇ 336

Celebrations Around the World   ◇   338

UNIT REVIEW

341

Exploring Your Community   ◇   **343**

FOR YOUR REFERENCE

R1

Symbols of America   ◇   **R2**

Facts About the States   ◇   **R6**

Geographic Dictionary   ◇   **R19**

Atlas   ◇   **R22**

Glossary   ◇   **R28**

Index   ◇   **R40**

PEOPLE MAKE HISTORY

Arthur Mitchell	**22**	Anne Carroll Moore	**205**
Frank Lloyd Wright	**48**	"Buffalo Bill" Cody	**238**
Chan Hong Tai	**93**	David Farragut	**273**
Molly Brown	**110**	Levi Strauss	**304**
Jean Baptist Pointe du Sable	**135**	Mother Teresa	**330**
Wilma Mankiller	**185**		

IN FOCUS

Second Harvest	**28**	Golden Gate Park	**210**
Amish Communities	**39**	Denver Mint	**242**
Anasazi Indians	**72**	Plimoth Plantation	**260**
Crater of Diamonds	**100**	Seaweed	**297**
Lighthouses	**145**	World's Fairs	**322**
Laws and Rules of Long Ago	**170**		

xi

CONNECTIONS

Skyscrapers	43	Town Crier	177
Greenhouses	70	Submersibles	277
Salmon Ladders	150	Windmills	333

SKILLS IN ACTION

Using the Library	30	Making Choices	179
Using Dictionaries and Encyclopedias	32	Finding the Information You Need	186
Using Maps to Show Your Address	49	Using Maps and Grids	199
Using Resource Maps	74	Being a Responsible Citizen	215
Using Climate Maps	82	Using Pictures to Tell a Story	247
Using Lists and Tables	86	Reading Calendars and Timelines	266
Saving Resources	102	Using Timelines to Show History	278
Reading Landform Maps	111	Time, the Earth, and the Sun	309
Using Bar Graphs	120	Reading Population Maps	324
Finding Routes	139	Using Intermediate Directions	335
Using Flow Charts	152		

READINGS

Goodbye, My Island	56	The House on Maple Street	282
Why People Work	156	Celebrations Around the World	338
The San Diego Zoo	220		

MAPS AND GLOBES

Map (of a model)	6	North America	52
Albuquerque, New Mexico	8	The World	53
New Mexico	9	Kansas	74
Wyoming	11	California	78
Globe (illustration)	12	Climate Map of California	82
Globe (illustration)	14	Iowa	89
Joanie's Street	49	Kentucky	105
Michigan Street Neighborhood	49	Landform Map of Kentucky	111
Indianapolis	50	Texas	114
Indiana	50	Illinois	131
The United States (Boundaries and Capitals)	51	The Great Lakes and the St. Lawrence Seaway	134
		Route Map	139

Travel Routes in Illinois 140
Washington 142
Finding Routes in Texas 162
Vermont 176
Florida 196
Map Grid 199
Centerville (Grid Map) 200
North Carolina 208
Green Hill (Grid Map) 226
Colorado 235
The English Colonies 263

Picture Map of Harbor City Area 324
Population Map of Harbor City Area 325
Central Amsterdam 334
Mexico City 335
Louisiana 342
United States of America R22
Landform Map of the United States R24
The World R26

CHARTS, GRAPHS, DIAGRAMS, AND TIMELINES

Using a Distance Scale 7
Compass Rose 10
Tomato Harvesting 81
Some California Crops (List) 86
Some State Capitals (List) 86
Some Things That Make Up Climate (List) 86
Table of Facts About Three States 87
Some Goods Made from Mineral Resources 98
Inside a Coal Mine 108
Drilling for Oil 118
Different Shapes (Bar Graph) 120
Some Important Places in Midland (Bar Graph) 121
Washing a Dog (Flow Chart) 152

Catching Fish (Flow Chart) 153
Producers and Consumers (Flow Chart) 160
Government in Santa Rosa 174
How We Get Our Water Supply 202
Taxes and Services 213
How Denver Has Grown (Bar Graph) 241
Calendar 266
Timeline of Matt's Life 267
Timeline of a Century 278
Timeline of American Firsts 279
Day and Night Around the World 310
Seasons on the Earth 311
Facts About the States R6

Introduction

CITIZENS IN THE COMMUNITY

You might know someone who is just like Martin. Martin is the boy you see in all of these pictures.

Martin likes doing things on his own. He likes to read and listen to music. He likes to ride his bicycle. But Martin also likes doing things with other people. He likes playing with friends. He likes talking with his family at the dinner table. These other people make up groups who share Martin's needs and interests.

Martin's family is just one of the many **groups** he belongs to. Martin plays soccer on a team. He sings in a church choir. He studies with his class at school.

Martin also belongs to some groups that are very large. One of these large groups is the **community** (kuh•MYOO•nuht•ee) where he lives. Martin's community includes his home and his neighborhood.

Martin also belongs to the larger communities of his city and state. His country, the United States of America, is a very large community. The members of these large communities are often called **citizens** (SIHT•uh•zuhnz).

This book is about citizens and communities. You will discover ways that citizens live in different communities. You will learn how good citizens help their communities.

Like Martin, you are a citizen of many communities. This book is for you.

USING YOUR TEXTBOOK

Books are special tools. You need to take care of them. You should keep books clean. You should not mark in books. You should open and close books carefully so you do not tear the pages.

Open your textbook to the **Contents** in the front of your book. This table of contents shows parts of the book in the order in which they appear in the book. Each **unit** in the book tells about one large subject. Each unit has two or three **chapters.** Each chapter tells about one part of the unit subject.

Reading Your Textbook

Each chapter in your book is divided into two or more **sections.** Each section has a title in large capital letters and a number.

Each section starts with a part called **Reading for a Purpose.** This part is made up of a list of important words and questions.

The list of words is divided into **Key Words, People,** and **Places.** When you first meet these words in your reading, they appear in thick, dark type called **boldface.** Sometimes a boldface word is followed by a different spelling. An example of this is **business** (BIZ•nuhs). The spelling tells you how to say the word.

The sections are divided into smaller parts. The smaller parts have titles, such as **Reading Your Textbook** on this page. The titles help you find the main ideas in the section.

Kelly looks at an atlas map of the United States.

Each section finishes with **Reading Check** questions. When you answer a Reading Check question, look only in that section for the answer.

Special Parts of Your Textbook

If you do not remember the meaning of a key word, look in the **Glossary** at the back of the book. There you can find out what the word means and also how to pronounce it.

While you are reading your book, you will look at a lot of maps. You can also find maps in the **Atlas** in the back of your book.

To find information, look at the **Index** in the back of the book. The Index lists in ABC order all the important items talked about in the book. The index gives the page numbers where information about that item may be found.

Your book has three other special parts. The **Geographic Dictionary** describes different kinds of land and water. **Facts About the States** and **Symbols of America** help you learn more about your country.

GEOGRAPHY: REVIEW AND PRACTICE

There are many ways to find out about different communities. You read about Martin and looked at pictures of his community. Reading and looking at pictures are good ways to find out about a person or a place.

Look at the picture below. It shows a **model** of a place. A model is a small copy of something. What things can you see in this model?

The model below shows part of a community. There are houses, streets, trees, a mountain, and a railroad.

Now look at another picture of the same model. The picture on this page is of the same place. It is taken from a different view, though. If you were standing above the model, looking straight down, the picture shows what you would see. Where are the trees in the picture? What do the houses in the picture look like?

This picture shows the model on page 4. How does the model look different when seen from above?

Looking at Maps

We can show this same model in another way. We can show where things are in the model by making a **map** of it. A map is a drawing of a place. Most maps show a place as it would look from above.

Here is a map of the model you saw in the pictures. How is the map different from the pictures of the model? If a map showed every tree, bush, and blade of grass, it would be too crowded. So maps use **symbols** (SIM•buhlz). A symbol is a picture that stands for something that is real on the Earth. Some symbols do not look like the things they stand for.

Look at the box to the left of the map. This box is called the **map key.** A map key tells what each of the symbols on the map stands for. Look at the map key. What symbol stands for a road? What symbol stands for a railroad?

A map key shows what symbols in a map stand for.

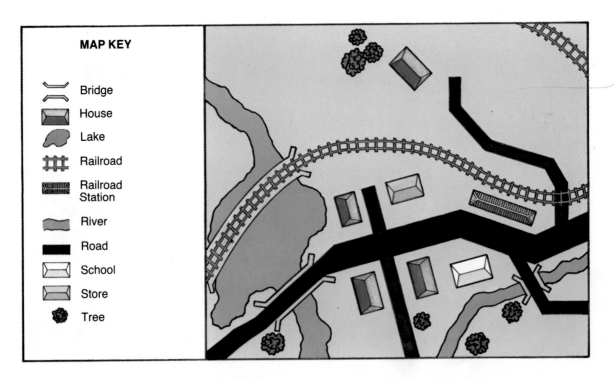

MAP KEY

Bridge

House

Lake

Railroad

Railroad Station

River

Road

School

Store

Tree

6

Colors in a map can be symbols, too. Usually lakes, rivers, oceans, and other things that stand for water are blue. Different colors may be used to show land.

Using a Distance Scale

Names and symbols on a map show real things and places. However, maps cannot show things in real-life sizes. The maps would have to be too big. So mapmakers made up a different way to measure. They have a small length stand for a longer, real length. For example, one inch on a map might show one mile on the real land. We call this the **distance scale** of a map.

Most maps have a distance scale. The distance scale lets you find out how far one place really is from another. To use the distance scale, you can use a ruler or a piece of paper.

The picture below shows you how to use a distance scale.

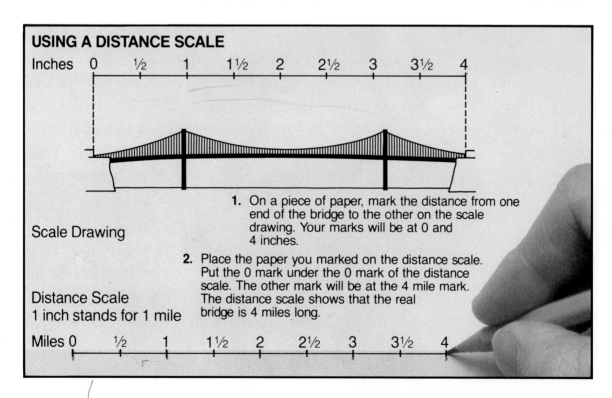

USING A DISTANCE SCALE

Inches 0 ½ 1 1½ 2 2½ 3 3½ 4

1. On a piece of paper, mark the distance from one end of the bridge to the other on the scale drawing. Your marks will be at 0 and 4 inches.

Scale Drawing

2. Place the paper you marked on the distance scale. Put the 0 mark under the 0 mark of the distance scale. The other mark will be at the 4 mile mark. The distance scale shows that the real bridge is 4 miles long.

Distance Scale
1 inch stands for 1 mile

Miles 0 ½ 1 1½ 2 2½ 3 3½ 4

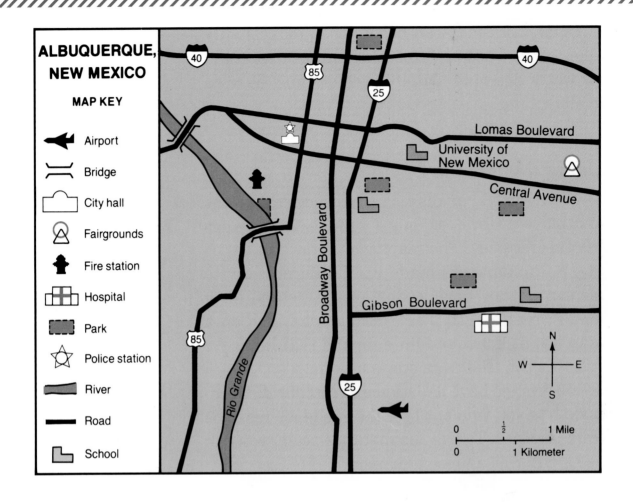

ALBUQUERQUE, NEW MEXICO

MAP KEY

Airport
Bridge
City hall
Fairgrounds
Fire station
Hospital
Park
Police station
River
Road
School

Lomas Boulevard
University of New Mexico
Central Avenue
Broadway Boulevard
Gibson Boulevard
Rio Grande

0   ½   1 Mile
0   1 Kilometer

Look at the map of Albuquerque, New Mexico on this page. Mark on a piece of paper the distance from the airport to the hospital. Put your paper on the distance scale at the bottom of the map. The distance should be one inch. That means that there is really one mile between the airport and the hospital.

Look at the map again. How far is it from the hospital to the University of New Mexico? How far is it from the fire station to city hall? How far is it from the fairgrounds to the Rio Grande on this map? Could you walk that distance? How far is it from the University of New Mexico to I-25? How much of I-25 can you see on this map?

Look at this map of New Mexico. New Mexico is a big state. Only Alaska, Texas, California, and Montana are larger. Use the distance scale at the bottom of the map to learn some things about distances in New Mexico.

How far is it from Gallup to Las Cruces? How far is it from Santa Fe to Carlsbad? Albuquerque is New Mexico's biggest city. People like to come to Albuquerque. How far do they have to travel from Farmington? How far is it from Las Cruces?

Distance scales often use the metric system. You find distance in the same way. The only difference is that you use the kilometer part of the scale to measure the distance between places.

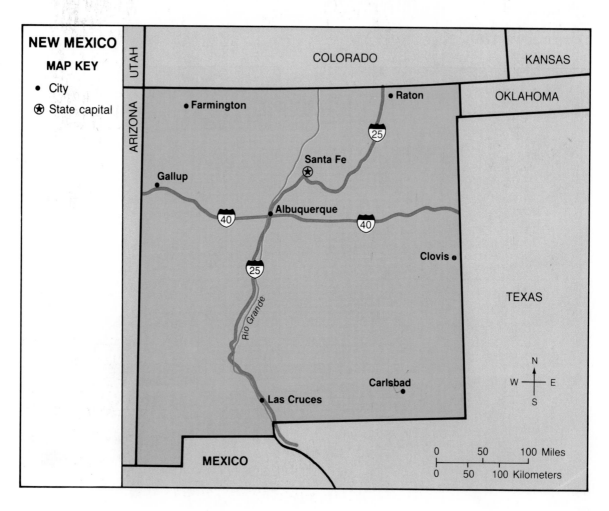

Learning About Directions

Look at the drawings below. The lines on each of the drawings look something like the petals of a rose. That is why we call each of these symbols a **compass rose.**

A compass rose tells you **directions,** or which way to go. Each of the arrows on the compass rose points to one of the four main directions. The main directions are north, south, east, and west. On a compass rose, **N** means north, **S** means south, **E** means east, and **W** means west.

When you face north, south is behind you. What direction is on your right? What direction is on your left?

The compass rose on the right was used on a map made in 1787.

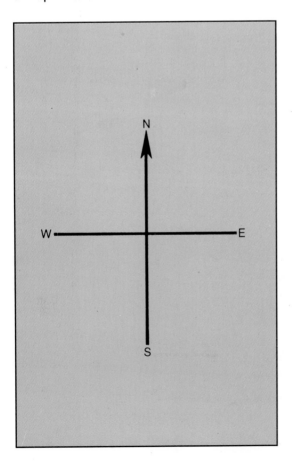

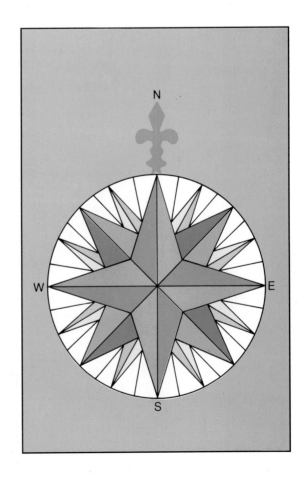

Find the compass rose on the map of Wyoming. This compass rose can help you find places in Wyoming. It could also help you show someone how to get from one place to another.

How could you show someone how to get from Saratoga to Buffalo? Find Saratoga. Now move your finger toward Buffalo. The compass rose tells you that your finger is moving north. Now move your finger from Casper to Pinedale. In what direction did your finger move?

What is the name of the state that is north of Wyoming? If you are in Wyoming facing north, what are the two states behind you? In what direction are they from Wyoming?

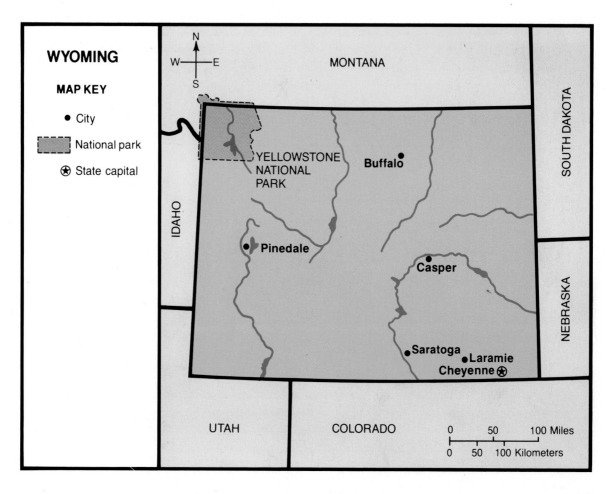

You now know the four main directions, north, south, east, and west. What do these directions really tell you? To answer that question it is helpful to look at a **globe.** A globe is a model of the Earth. Look at the picture of a globe on this page.

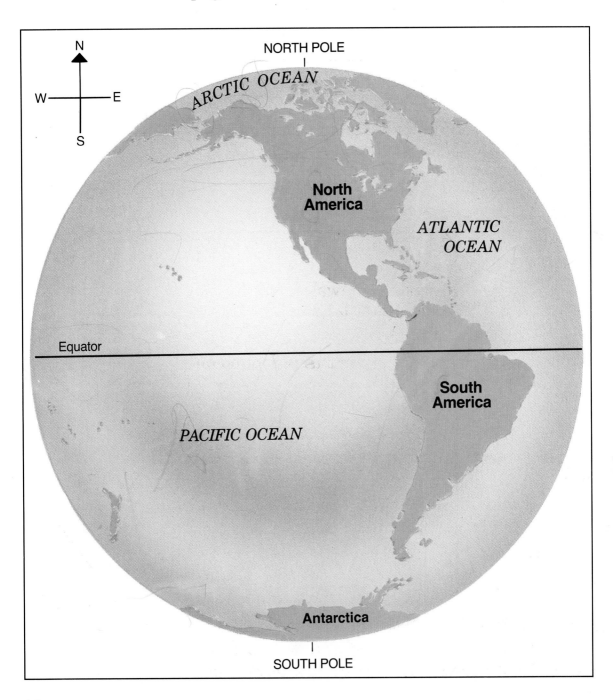

You can find directions on a globe. The North Pole is a good place to start. It is as far north as you can go on Earth. When a compass rose is pointing to **N,** it is really pointing toward the North Pole. Place your finger in the middle of the picture of the globe. Move your finger toward the North Pole. Your finger is moving toward the north. It is moving in the same direction that the compass rose is pointing.

Next move your finger toward the South Pole. The South Pole is as far south as you can go on Earth. When your finger is moving toward the South Pole it is moving in the direction south.

You can find the North Pole and the South Pole on every globe. However, maps do not always show the poles. On a map the compass rose shows you the direction of the North and South poles, even if you cannot see them.

Now look at the globe halfway between the North Pole and the South Pole. You will find a line. It is called the **equator** (ee•KWAY•tur). The equator is a make-believe line. It is not found on the real Earth. It is useful on globes because it divides the globe into a northern half and a southern half.

Place your finger on the area of land marked North America. Is it north or south of the equator? Now find South America. Is more of South America north of the equator or south of the equator?

Looking at Land and Water

Globes show you the land and water of the Earth. The large water areas are called **oceans.**

Our world has four oceans. The smallest ocean is the Arctic Ocean. The Pacific Ocean is the largest. Find the two other oceans on the globes on pages 12 and 14.

Put your finger on North America again. Move it toward the Atlantic Ocean. You are moving east.

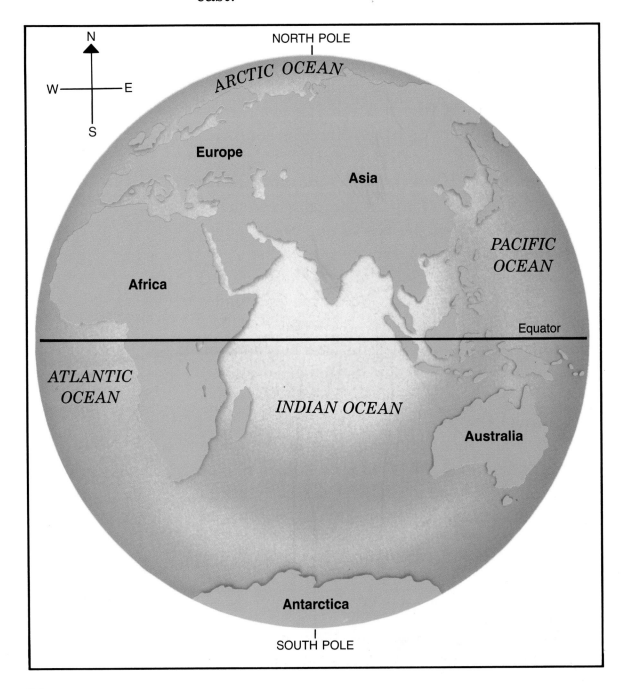

Now move your finger toward the Pacific Ocean. In what direction is your finger moving?

The large land areas on Earth are called **continents** (KAHNT•uhn•uhnts). Some continents are joined. Find North America again. It is joined to South America. The two continents separate most of the Atlantic and Pacific oceans. Can you find where these oceans meet?

Two other continents that are joined are Asia and Europe. Together they make up a huge area of land. The continent of Asia is on the eastern side. Europe is on the western side.

Africa is south of Europe. A small part of it is joined to Asia. The Atlantic Ocean is west of Africa. Which ocean is east of Africa? What direction is Asia from Africa?

Two continents, Australia and Antarctica, are not joined to other continents at all. Find these continents on the globes. Which oceans are near Australia? Which pole is in Antarctica?

The equator can help you find continents. Two of the continents are north of the equator. What are their names? Three other continents, South America, Africa, and Asia, are crossed by the equator. Find where the equator crosses Asia. Find and name the two continents which are completely south of the equator.

Questions to Answer

1. What is a map symbol?
2. What are the four main directions?
3. What is the smallest ocean? What is the largest ocean?
4. Where is North America on the globe?
5. What two continents are joined to Asia?

UNIT
1
PEOPLE AND COMMUNITIES

Community Facts and Figures

Location	New York City, New York	Cape Canaveral, Florida	Sun City, Arizona
Population (estimated)	7,263,000	8,400	42,405
Landmark	Statue of Liberty	Kennedy Space Center	The Sundome
Nickname/Motto	The Big Apple	Space Hub	Forerunner in American Retirement Communities

Our country is made up of many kinds of communities. There are large communities and small communities. Communities are known for different things.

Yet all communities are made up of people. Communities everywhere are places where people can belong. All communities have things for people to see and do.

In this unit we will look at how people live in communities across the United States. We will see how communities are alike and how they are different.

Think Beyond   Why it is important for your family to live in a community?

Location	Spring, Texas	Boonesboro, Kentucky
Population (estimated)	3,000	100
Landmark	The Blimp	Fort Boonesboro
Nickname/Motto	Old Town Spring	Kentucky's First Settlement

CHAPTER 1

How Communities Are Alike

"Mid pleasures and palaces though
   we may roam,
Be it ever so humble, there's no
   place like home;
A charm from the sky seems to
   hallow us there,
Which, seek through the
   world, is ne'er met with
   elsewhere.
Home, home, sweet, sweet home!
There's no place like home,
   oh, there's no place
   like home!"
—from the poem "Home, Sweet Home"
   by John Howard Payne

Look for these important words:

Key Words
- business center
- banks

Look for answers to these questions:
1. Why do people live in communities?
2. What places are in the business center of a community?
3. What are banks?

1 WHY PEOPLE LIVE IN COMMUNITIES

If you are like most people, you live in or near a community. A community is a town, city, or other place where people live and work.

Communities are alike in many ways. For one thing, all communities have names. What is the name of your community?

Have you ever wondered why people choose to live in communities? One reason is that people like each other's company. People want to live near each other. Many people like to belong to some group. You belong to your family. You are a part of it. You do things together. In the same way, people belong to a community. They have a place in it. People do things together in a community.

All communities—large, small, or medium-sized—are places where people can belong. All communities are places where people carry on their lives.

Working in Communities

People often live in certain communities because of their work. Most communities have a downtown. We call this a **business** (BIZ·nuhs) **center.** Most of the office buildings where people work are in the business center. There are usually many stores in the business center of a community. You can also find many **banks** in a business center. Banks are places where people keep money.

People shop and go to work in business centers.

People have fun at a community parade.

Having Fun in Communities

People in a community can do many things together for fun. Sports teams, Brownie Scouts, Cub Scouts, and 4-H clubs are all community activities for people your age.

Communities have many places where people can go to have fun. Most communities have parks where people can picnic, play games, and enjoy the outdoors. People can also go to places such as movie theaters and zoos. People in a community share all of these places.

Reading Check

1. Name two ways in which all communities are alike.
2. What is a business center?

Think Beyond Why do you think communities provide places for people to have fun?

People MAKE HISTORY

Arthur Mitchell sits in a room that was once a garage. He looks carefully at the dance students. Sometimes he jumps up to show them how to do a step. He smiles and laughs often. Arthur Mitchell is proud of these young people. They are students in his ballet school, the Dance Theatre of Harlem. The school is very important to this New York City community.

When Mitchell was 21 years old, he was asked to join the New York City Ballet. He was the company's first African-American dancer. The dance director wrote ballets just for him. After leaving the New York City Ballet, Mitchell helped start a dance company in Brazil.

When Mitchell returned to New York, a friend asked him to give dance lessons to children in Harlem. No one had ever given ballet lessons in Harlem before. Mitchell opened a ballet school in a garage. At first he had only 30 students. After four months he had 800.

Today Mitchell's dance school continues to grow. He and his students give talks to the community. They travel all over the world dancing for others. Many of Mitchell's students thank him for making their dreams of being dancers come true.

Think Beyond What other kinds of schools might your community have?

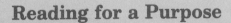
Look for these important words:

Key Words
- shelters
- needs
- hospital

Look for answers to these questions:
1. What needs do people have?
2. What people in a community help meet our need for safety?
3. Why are schools and libraries important to the people in a community?

2 | COMMUNITIES HELP PEOPLE MEET NEEDS

In order to live, we need food to eat. Food makes us strong so we can play hard and do our work well. We need clothes to wear. We need sweaters and other heavy clothes to stay warm on cold days. We need light-weight clothes for very hot days. People also need **shelters** to live in. Shelters are homes, stores, and buildings where people work. Shelters protect us, or keep us safe, from the weather. Shelters keep out the rain and the snow. In very warm or hot weather, shelters protect people from the sun.

We need love and safety, too. Food, clothing, shelter, love and safety are our **needs.** Needs are things we must have to live. People working together in communities can help one another meet all these needs. That is another way communities are alike.

23

Sam must keep very busy to meet her needs. What is she doing in each of the pictures?

Think how busy you would be if you had to meet all your needs by yourself! You would have to grow your own vegetables. You would have to raise animals to get meat, eggs, and milk. You could not turn on a faucet and get water. Instead, you would have to dig a well or go to a river or lake for water.

You would have to build your own house, too. Remember, you would not be able to go to a store to buy nails or boards. You would have to make your own nails and boards.

You would have to make your own clothing, too. First, you would have to make cloth. Then you would have to sew it.

In a community, some people grow food. Others sell this food. Some people make clothes. Others sell them. Some people build houses. Others get the materials from which houses are made. Nobody has to do all these jobs. People in communities share their learning. Living in a community helps people save time.

How is this picture different from the one on page 24? How are people helping one another meet needs?

Mr. Sanchez reported a fire that was burning in an empty building in his community. Fire fighters came quickly to put it out.

People Depend on One Another

People in a community depend on one another for safety. Police officers work to keep us safe. Fire fighters also protect us. Fire fighters put out fires everywhere in your community. However, fire fighters need you and others to report fires to them. By reporting fires, people help one another meet their need for safety.

People need good care when they are sick. Doctors and nurses are taught to take care of sick people. They work for the whole community.

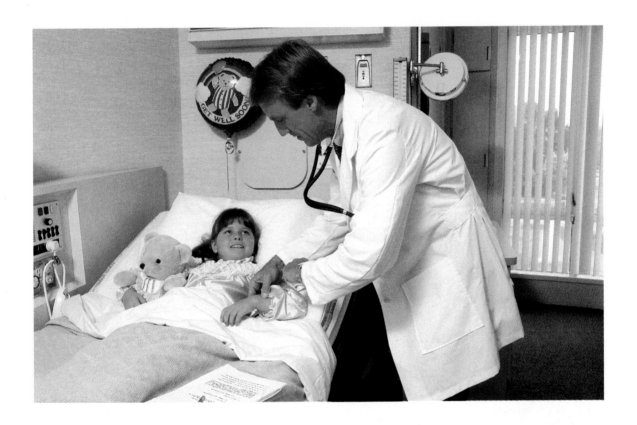

A community often has a **hospital,** too. A hospital is a place where hurt or sick people can go for special care. Doctors, nurses, and hospitals meet people's need for good health.

Schools and libraries are also important to the people of a community. Schools are places where people of all ages can learn about things. A library keeps books for the people of a community to use. Libraries are also good places where people can go to learn things.

Maria went to the hospital when she became ill. With the doctor's help, she is feeling much better.

 Reading Check

1. Why do we need food?
2. What need do doctors and nurses in a community help us meet?

Think Beyond Why is it important for people to share their learning?

27

SECOND HARVEST

In every country there are people who do not have enough to eat. Even in the United States there are people who have trouble meeting the need for food. They might be out of a job, too ill to work, or homeless. They need help. A group called Second Harvest is working to help feed the hungry in the United States.

Sometimes food companies make too much food. Sometimes grocery stores have more food than they can sell. Second Harvest asks the companies and stores for this extra food. This food includes everything from meat to fruit juice and crackers.

Second Harvest keeps the food in special places called food banks. Different places in a community receive food from the food banks. These places might include soup kitchens, shelters for the homeless, and day-care centers. Workers at these places prepare the food and serve it to the hungry people.

Most of the people who work for Second Harvest are unpaid.

Second Harvest helps to make sure that children in day-care centers have healthful food to eat.

Workers sort the food into different boxes. The boxes will be given to people who need food.

They share their free time for the good of the community. These workers help set up the food banks. They ask local businesses for donations. They also help collect, sort, and label donated food items. Computers help the workers keep track of the donated food.

In one year Second Harvest and its food banks were able to collect more than 400 million pounds (1,816,000 kg) of food. With the help of caring citizens in many communities, Second Harvest helps feed people who have no food.

Think Beyond What can you and your family do to keep from wasting food?

A Second Harvest worker will take the donated food to the closest food bank.

29

SKILLS IN ACTION

USING THE LIBRARY

A **library** is a place where you can find books, newspapers, and magazines. Some libraries have records and films. You can learn about many things at the library.

A **librarian** is a person who works in the library. Librarians keep the books in order. They can help you find what you are looking for. Some librarians are now helped by computers. Computers can help check out books. A computer may even charge you an overdue fine!

The librarian helps children find the books they want.

Libraries Have Rules

Most books may be checked out of the library and taken home. Before you can take books out, you must know the rules of the library. Here are a few of them.

- In most libraries, you need a library card to take books home. You must show the card to the librarian.

- The librarian stamps a "due date" in each book you want to take out. You must bring the books back by that date.

- You must not mark in the books. You should take good care of them.

A due date card tells you when to return a library book.

30

Books at the Library

You can find two kinds of books at the library. One kind is called **fiction.** Fiction books are make-believe stories. A story about a boy who meets a community of six-foot-tall talking lizards is fiction. Fiction books can also be stories that seem real but that are about made-up people and animals.

Nonfiction books are about real people, animals, places, and things. A book about lizards, where they live, what they eat, and how they grow, is nonfiction. A book about the life of a real American Indian long ago is nonfiction.

To find books in the library, you have to know the alphabet, or ABC's. Fiction books are arranged in alphabetical or ABC order by the **authors'** last names. Authors are people who write books. Most of the time you have to put more than the first letter in order. A book

by Caroline **Haywood** comes before a book by Felice **Holman,** because **Ha** comes before **Ho** in alphabetical order.

CHECKING YOUR SKILLS

Tell or write the answers to these questions.

1. You want to find a book by Pamela Rogers in the library. Does this book come before or after a book by Barbara Reynolds?

2. Is a book about a real girl who becomes a skating champion fiction or nonfiction?

3. Is a story about a boy who makes friends with a talking horse fiction or nonfiction?

4. When you borrow a book from a library, the librarian stamps a date in it. Why do you need to look at the date?

31

SKILLS IN ACTION

USING DICTIONARIES AND ENCYCLOPEDIAS

Suppose you are reading about a community in Florida. You read that **mangos** grow there. How can you find out what a mango is?

Suppose you want to read about New York City. Where can you look for information?

You can find this information in **dictionaries** (DIK•shuhn•air•eez) and **encyclopedias** (en•sy•cloh•PEE•dee•uhz). These two kinds of books can give you a whole world of information.

Using a Dictionary

Dictionaries are full of facts about words. A dictionary tells you how to say a word. It tells you what a word means. Sometimes a dictionary will show you a picture of the thing the word names. A dictionary often gives a sentence using the word, too.

Here is what a dictionary might tell you about the word "mango."

- **man•go** (mang′gō) *n.* A juicy fruit with a slightly sour taste. Many mangos grow in Florida where the weather is warm.

The letters in parentheses tell you how to say the word. The dictionary might also show a picture of a mango.

Sometimes dictionaries give more than one meaning for a word. It is important to read all the meanings listed for a word.

How can you find a word in the dictionary? It is as easy as ABC. All the words in a dictionary are listed in ABC order.

The top of a dictionary page shows two **guide words.** These words tell you the first and last words on the page. All the words that come between these two words will be on the page. For example, "mango" comes after "make" but before "map." Notice that the first two letters of these words are the same. You must look at the third letter of the words.

32

Using an Encyclopedia

An encyclopedia does not tell you about words. Instead it gives facts about a great many subjects. It tells you about people, places, things, and events. These are listed in alphabetical order, just as words are in a dictionary.

Most encyclopedias have many **volumes,** or separate books. Each book has one or two letters of the alphabet on the cover. If you want to find out about New York City, you should look in the volume that has "N" on the cover.

Here is what an encyclopedia might say about New York City.

- **New York City** (population 7,263,000) has more people than any other city in the United States. It is an important center of business.

The encyclopedia tells you more about New York City. It tells you what the city looks like and what goods are made there. It tells you about the people and the ways they meet their needs. It tells you the history of the city. There might also be maps of New York City.

CHECKING YOUR SKILLS

Tell whether you would find the answers to the following questions in a dictionary or in an encyclopedia.

1. What is the meaning of the word "dependence"?
2. What is the community of Atlanta, Georgia, like?
3. How do you say the word "university"?
4. What kinds of shelter do people in South America have?

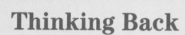
Thinking Back

- People live in communities to be near other people. In most communities there is a business center with offices and stores. Communities also have banks where people can keep their money safely.

- People in a community can join many groups to have fun. In a community there are parks, zoos, movie theaters, and other places to go to have fun.

- People have needs for food, clothing, shelter, love, and safety. In communities, people do different jobs to share the work. They save time by sharing their learning.

- Police officers and fire fighters protect everyone in the community. Doctors and nurses in hospitals help those who are sick or hurt. Teachers and librarians work with people of all ages who want to learn.

Check for Understanding

Using Words

Use one of the words in parentheses to complete each sentence.

1. Most of the office buildings where people work are in the ____ . (business center, banks)

2. People keep money in ____ . (needs, banks)

3. Homes, stores, and buildings where people work are called ____ . (hospitals, shelters)

4. ____ are things we must have to live. (Needs, Banks)

Reviewing Facts

1. How are communities alike?

2. What happens in the business center of a community?

3. What places do people in a community share?

4. How do communities help people meet needs?

5. How do people in a community depend on police officers and fire fighters?

Thinking Critically

1. What kinds of work do people in your community do? Why is the business center in your community important?

2. Why do communities have places like parks and zoos? Who may visit them?

3. How do people in a community depend on one another?

Writing About It

Imagine you have two friends, Jack and Molly, who live far away. Write a letter to them describing your city or town.

Practicing Study Skills

Using the Library
Answer these questions.

1. Tell whether each of these books is fiction or nonfiction.
   a. a book about growing food
   b. a book about a talking cat
2. Tell whether you would find the information below in a dictionary or in an encyclopedia.
   a. the meaning of community
   b. how the Brownie Scouts started

On Your Own

Social Studies at Home

Ask five people what they like best about your community. Write down their answers. Did they name the same things or did they name different things? Write a paragraph telling what people like about living in a community.

Read More About It

Building a House by Byron Barton. Greenwillow. In this book you will find out how to build your very own house.

Come to Town by Anne Rockwell. T. Y. Crowell. Visit the school, supermarket, office, and library in the Bear family's community.

Fire! Fire! by Gail Gibbons. T. Y. Crowell. Follow fire fighters as they provide an important community service.

The Hospital Book by James Howe. Crown. This book tells about a hospital like the one Maria goes to.

Theater Magic: Behind the Scenes at a Children's Theater by Cheryl Walsh Bellville. Carolrhoda Books. Look at the work and fun that go into putting on a play.

CHAPTER 2

How Communities Are Different

"The folk who live in Backward town
Are inside out and upside down.
They wear their hats inside their heads
And go to sleep beneath their beds.
They only eat the apple peeling
And take their walks across the ceiling."

—"The Folks Who Live in Backward Town"
by Mary Ann Hoberman

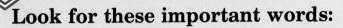
Look for these important words:

Key Words
- river
- lake
- ocean
- mountains
- deserts

Look for answers to these questions:

1. What are some kinds of places communities can be near?
2. What are deserts?
3. What makes communities special?

1 COMMUNITIES ARE IN DIFFERENT PLACES

Communities are different in several ways. For one thing, communities are in different places. Some are near water. They may be near a **river, lake,** or **ocean.** A river is a long, flowing body of water. A lake is a body of water with land all around. An ocean is a huge body of salt water. Remember there are four oceans on Earth. They are the Pacific, Atlantic, Indian, and Arctic oceans.

Some communities are near **mountains.** Mountains are large, raised parts of land. They rise high above the land around them. There are many mountains in our country.

Other communities are in very dry lands called **deserts.** Few kinds of plants grow there. There is not enough water. Water must sometimes be brought to deserts from somewhere else.

The top picture shows the mountain town of Silverton, Colorado. Below is Chicago, Illinois, a city on the shores of Lake Michigan.

Communities are known for different things, too. Some are known for growing food, like wheat or potatoes. Others are known for making things, like clothes or cars. Still others are known for their beauty. Many people like to visit those beautiful places.

 Reading Check

1. How are communities different?
2. Name two kinds of land found near communities.

Think Beyond How might being near water make a community special?

38

IN FOCUS

AMISH COMMUNITIES

The Amish are a religious group that came to the United States from Switzerland in 1728. They are part of a group called the Pennsylvania Dutch. They have communities in 23 states. Most of them live in Indiana, Pennsylvania, Ohio, Iowa, and Illinois. The Amish people are sometimes called the Plain People. They are called this because they like to live plain and simple lives. They live just as their relatives did more than 200 years ago.

Because of their beliefs, the Amish do not live in big cities. They have their own communities, and most live on farms. They do all the farmwork themselves, using simple tools and horses. They do not own or drive cars. Instead they drive and ride in horse-drawn buggies. They seldom travel far from home.

Amish children work with other family members on their farms.

An Amish man and woman use horse-drawn machinery to bale hay.

The Amish grow or make all their own food and clothing. They use windmills or waterwheels instead of electricity for power. This means the Amish do not have telephones, televisions, or electrical tools. They live this way so they can spend time with each other.

Sharing is an important part of Amish community life. If one Amish family has a problem, the rest of the Amish community helps the family solve it. If one Amish family's barn burns, all the other Amish families help rebuild it. If one Amish person has medical bills, the other Amish families help pay them. All communities share some things. In an Amish community, however, sharing is a way of life.

Think Beyond   What are some activities you and your family might enjoy doing together?

Barn raising and quilt making are two activities Amish people enjoy doing together.

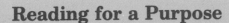
Look for these important words:

Key Words
- suburb
- rural
- capital
- President
- pastures

People
- George Washington

Places
- New York City, New York
- Washington, D.C.

- Cape Canaveral, Florida
- Sun City, Arizona
- Spring, Texas
- Boonesboro, Kentucky

Look for answers to these questions:
1. What are some good things about living in a city?
2. What are some good things about living in a suburb?
3. What are some good things about living in a town?

2 COMMUNITIES ARE DIFFERENT SIZES

Communities are different sizes. A town is a small community. A city is a large community. A community that is close to a city is a **suburb** (SUB•urb). A community that is near forests or farms is a **rural** (RUR•uhl) community.

Living in Cities

A city is the largest kind of community. A city has many, many people in it. Because there are so many people, there are a lot of schools, stores, and libraries. There are also many places to have fun, like parks, museums, and movie theaters. A city offers a lot of choices of things to do.

41

Large cities are working to solve their traffic problems.

There are many different jobs in a city, too. A city person might have a job fixing pianos. In a smaller community, there would not be as many pianos. So fixing pianos might not be a full-time job in a small community.

City people usually work at jobs that do not take much land. There is no room for farming in most cities. Often, there is not much room for trees, lawns, or gardens.

A city often has more problems than a smaller community. Sometimes a city is very crowded or very noisy. Sometimes there is too much traffic. The people of a city try to work together to solve these problems.

New York City, New York

New York City is very big. It has more people than any other city in the United States. New York City is in the eastern part of our country. It is right by the Atlantic Ocean.

The elevator door closes. In seconds you are 110 floors above the ground. You are in one of the world's tallest skyscrapers, the Sears Tower in Chicago. Can you imagine what it would be like to climb 110 flights of stairs?

Before 1852 few buildings could be more than five stories high. People did not want to climb more than five flights of stairs. Elisha Otis solved this problem with his invention of the safe passenger elevator.

The next problem to be solved was how to support the great weight of a many-storied building. The American invention of the iron frame allowed tall buildings to be built without using thick, heavy walls.

Today, frames of steel and concrete support the skyscrapers that have changed the landscape of cities across America and around the world.

New York City has many tall buildings. They are very close together. Some of them are office buildings where people work. Some of the buildings are apartment houses where many people live. Other buildings are huge stores.

There is a lot to see and do in New York City. There are parks, museums, and restaurants. People can watch New York teams play football, hockey, baseball, and other sports. There are interesting and different neighborhoods. Many different groups of people live in these neighborhoods. Some of them come from different parts of our country and from other countries.

People enjoy a buggy ride in Central Park, New York City's largest park.

Rules for our country are made in Washington, D.C. This picture shows the White House. It was designed by James Hoban in 1792.

Washington, D.C.

There are also other large cities in our country. **Washington, D.C.,** is in the eastern part of our country. It is a very famous city. It is the **capital** of the United States. A capital is a place where rules for a state or country are made. There are fifty states in our country.

The **President,** the leader of our country, lives and works in Washington, D.C. The White House is the President's home and office. Washington, D.C., is named after **George Washington,** our country's first President. Americans are proud of this beautiful city.

Cape Canaveral, Florida

There are small cities in our country, too. One small city is **Cape Canaveral** (kuh•NAV•ruhl), **Florida.** Florida is next to the Atlantic Ocean. It is in the southern part of our country.

44

Cape Canaveral is famous for one thing. It has a space center. Rockets and other spaceships blast off from there. Many of the people who live in Cape Canaveral work at the space center. It is called the John F. Kennedy Space Center.

A spaceship blasts off from Cape Canaveral, Florida.

Sun City, Arizona

Sun City, Arizona, is another special kind of small city. Mostly older people live there. A lot of them worked for many years in other places. Then they decided to stop working. They moved to Sun City. They like the dry, sunny weather. They like the things they can do there.

Living in Suburbs

Many cities have suburbs. Suburbs are communities that are close to large cities. Suburbs usually have their own schools. Some have their own business centers. The stores and offices in the community are in these business centers. A suburb usually has a lot of places to shop.

People often move to suburbs because they do not want to live in big cities. They might think that cities are too crowded. They might want more open space for their families. They might like to live closer to land that has not been built upon.

People enjoy walks in the suburbs.

Spring, Texas

Spring, Texas, is a suburb of the big city of Houston, Texas. Most of the people of Spring work in Houston. Some of them lived in Houston before moving to this suburb.

A blimp is a large airship. To fly, blimps must be filled with gases lighter than air. The crew rides in a tiny cabin below the gasbag.

You may not have heard of Spring, Texas, before. You may know about something famous that comes from there, though. Spring is the home of a blimp called "America." A blimp is like a giant balloon. It looks like a huge silver football. It has a tiny engine so its crew can make it fly.

Many new houses have been built in Spring. It is a growing community. Spring used to be mostly woods. Today there are still a lot of pine and oak trees. You can still see many birds and some small animals, like raccoons.

Living in Towns

Very small communities are called towns. Most of the people in a town know one another. Everyone in the town is a neighbor. People in towns often help one another. Sometimes they all get together to have fun.

In towns, people often work at something that has to do with the land nearby. They may cut trees for boards. They may farm the land or raise animals for food.

Boonesboro, Kentucky

Boonesboro, Kentucky, is a small town. Boonesboro is in an area called "bluegrass country." Bluegrass is a special kind of grass. When breezes blow across the fields, this grass looks more blue than green.

The bluegrass country is famous for its horses. Many of the people from that area raise racing horses. The people take good care of the horses. They often keep the horses in **pastures.** A pasture is a field of grass and other kinds of plants that animals eat.

These horses eat the thick grasses that grow in Kentucky's pastures.

Reading Check

1. What city in the United States has the most people?
2. Why do most people in a town know each other?

Think Beyond How do you think a person from a small town would feel in a big city?

People MAKE HISTORY

Frank Lloyd Wright
1867–1959

▶▶▶▶▶▶▶▶▶▶▶▶▶▶▶▶▶

Even as a young boy in Wisconsin, Frank Lloyd Wright dreamed of becoming an **architect** (AHR•kuh•tehkt). An architect is a person who designs buildings. As a boy, Wright spent hours arranging blocks and strips of colorful paper into different shapes.

In Wright's day a person did not have to go to college to become an architect. People learned by working with other architects. Wright moved to Chicago to find work. He took a job with first one architect and then another. He learned all that he could. Soon Wright was designing buildings on his own. He used a lot of wood and glass. He wanted to fill his buildings with sunlight.

The buildings that Wright designed not only looked good, they were also strong. One of his designs was for a hotel in Tokyo, Japan. When a terrible earthquake hit Tokyo, Wright's hotel was one of the few buildings that remained standing.

Wright became popular for the way he used different shapes and colors in his designs. Many people think he was the greatest American architect who ever lived. His designs changed the look of many communities. Those communities are proud of their Frank Lloyd Wright buildings.

Think Beyond If you were an architect, what colors and shapes would you use in designing a building?

SKILLS IN ACTION

USING MAPS TO SHOW YOUR ADDRESS

Joanie lives in Indianapolis (in·dee·uh·NAP·uh·luhs), Indiana. Her **address** tells where she lives. Here is her address.

> Joanie Hermann
> 5240 Michigan St.
> Indianapolis, Indiana 46219
> United States of America
> North America
> Northern Hemisphere
> Earth

Of course, we do not usually include all this when we write an address. Usually we write the person's name, the house or apartment number, street name, and the city, state, and **ZIP code.** ZIP codes are numbers that are used to get mail to places faster. If we are writing a letter to someone in a different country, we use the name of that country too.

The information that tells where Joanie lives can be seen on a map. The first map on this page shows Joanie's street.

Find the house with the number 5240. That is Joanie's house.

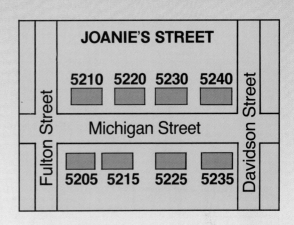

The map below shows streets in the neighborhood where Joanie lives. Her neighborhood includes the streets shown on the map. A neighborhood is usually larger than just one street.

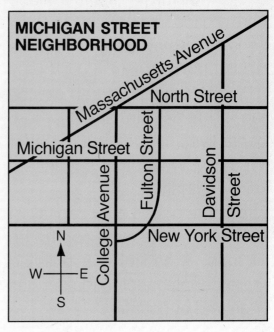

49

Joanie's neighborhood is in the city of Indianapolis. The map below shows the city of Indianapolis.

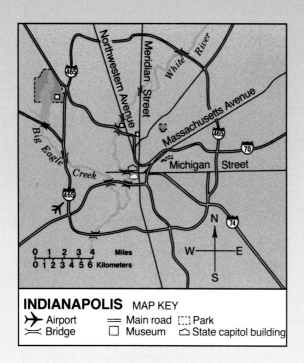

INDIANAPOLIS MAP KEY
✈ Airport   ═ Main road   ▢ Park
⋈ Bridge   ▢ Museum   ⌂ State capitol building

The map of Indianapolis does not show all the streets in the city. There are too many streets to show in one small map. The map shows only the main streets.

Find Michigan Street on the map. That is the street where Joanie lives. It is near the center of the city. What other streets are near Michigan Street?

Indianapolis is the capital of Indiana. Find the state **capitol** on the map. A capitol is a building where people meet to make rules for a state or country.

Now look at the map below. It shows the state of Indiana.

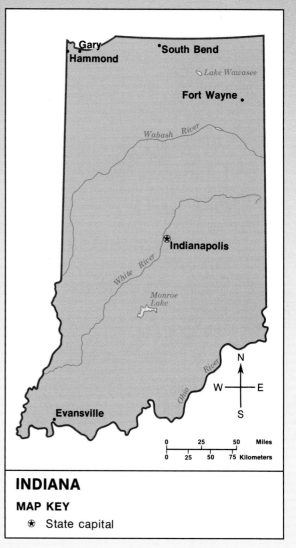

INDIANA
MAP KEY
✹ State capital

The symbol of the star with a circle around it tells you that Indianapolis is the capital of Indiana.

The map also shows some of the biggest cities in Indiana. What city is south of Indianapolis? What cities are to the north?

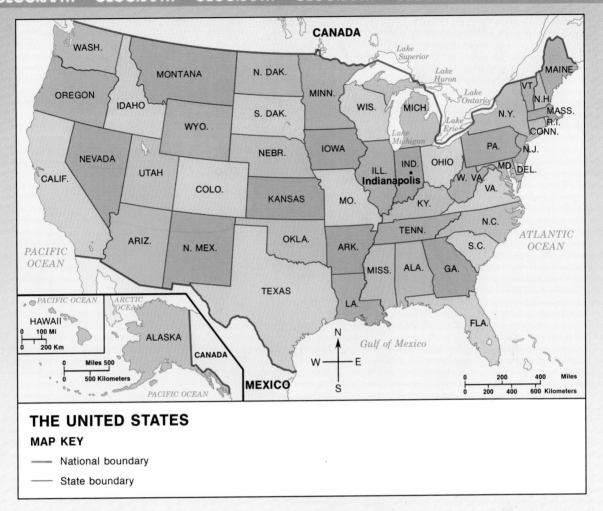

THE UNITED STATES

MAP KEY

—— National boundary

—— State boundary

A Map of Our Country

The map above shows the 50 states that make up the United States.

Indiana is one state in the United States. Find Indiana on the map. Point to Indianapolis.

This map shows the **borders** of Indiana. Borders are lines that are drawn on the map to show where one place ends and another begins. Borders are also called **boundaries** (BOWN•duh•reez). The

state north of Indiana is Michigan. What state is east of Indiana?

Our Country Is in North America

The map on the next page shows an even larger area. It shows the continent of **North America.** A continent is one of the main land areas in the world. The North American continent has a number of countries.

51

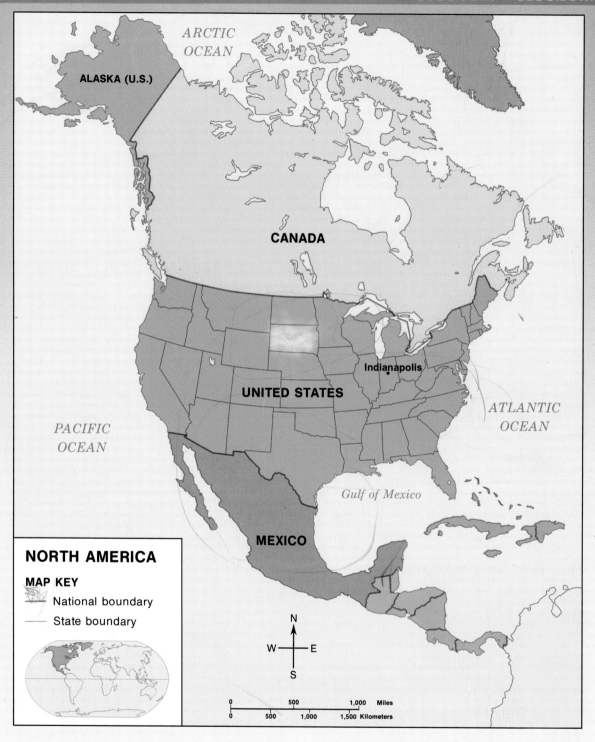

ARCTIC
OCEAN

ALASKA (U.S.)

CANADA

Indianapolis

UNITED STATES

PACIFIC
OCEAN

ATLANTIC
OCEAN

Gulf of Mexico

MEXICO

NORTH AMERICA

MAP KEY

National boundary

State boundary

N
W　E
S

0　　　500　　　1,000　Miles
0　　500　　1,000　　1,500　Kilometers

The United States takes up a big part of the continent. What two other large countries do you see on the map of North America? Alaska is close to Canada. Yet it is part of the United States.

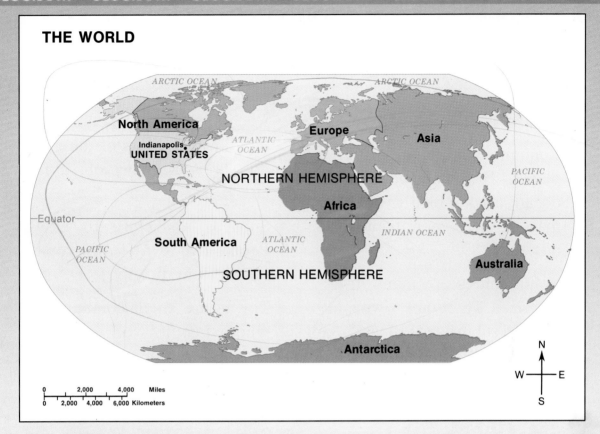

The Equator and the Hemispheres

The map above shows all the lands and oceans in the world. Map-makers draw an imaginary line around the Earth, halfway between the North Pole and the South Pole. This line is the equator.

The equator divides the Earth into two halves. These halves are called **hemispheres** (HEM•uh•sfeerz). North America is in the Northern Hemisphere. Find Indianapolis in the Northern Hemisphere. Now find Asia. In which hemisphere is it?

Of course, this map does not show the true shape of the Earth. The map is very flat, and the Earth is almost round.

CHECKING YOUR SKILLS

Use the maps to help you answer these questions.

1. What community do you live in? What state do you live in?

2. Is Texas a state or a country?

3. What countries share borders with the United States?

4. In which hemisphere is the continent of Europe?

53

Thinking Back

- Communities are in different places. They may be near an ocean, a lake, or a river. They may be near mountains or a desert.

- Communities are many different sizes. There are towns, cities, and suburbs of cities. There are also rural communities.

- A city has many people, tall buildings, and lots of things to do. There are many jobs in the city.

- Suburbs are close to cities. People live away from crowds but work in the city.

- Towns are small communities where people work and play closely together.

Check for Understanding

Using Words

Use one of the words in parentheses to complete each sentence.

1. A ____ is a long, flowing body of water. (lake, river)

2. A community that is close to a large city is a ____ . (capital, suburb)

3. A community that is near forests or farms is a ____ community. (pasture, rural)

4. A ____ is a place where rules for a state or a country are made. (capital, hospital)

5. A ____ is a field of grass and other plants that animals eat. (pasture, mountain)

Reviewing Facts

1. Why are communities different from one another?

2. What are four different kinds of communities?

3. What kinds of things can people do in a large city?

4. Where does the President of our country live and work?

5. For what is Cape Canaveral, Florida, famous?

Thinking Critically

1. How is life in a city different from life in a town?

2. Is your community a city, a suburb, a town, or a rural community? How is it like or different from a nearby community?

3. How is the work people do in a rural community different from the work people do in a city? Which kind of work would you rather do? Why?

4. Boonesboro is special because of its horses. What makes your community special?

Writing About It

Imagine you live in a large city called Grandville. Write a travel booklet telling about all the interesting places, people, and things to do in your city.

Practicing Geography Skills

Using Maps to Show Your Address

Write down your address. Tell which parts of the address are the house or apartment number, street, city, and state.

On Your Own

Social Studies at Home

Make a "Where Am I?" game to play with your family or friends. Write sentences describing places in your community. Use two to three sentences for each place. Read each of the descriptions out loud. Have your family or friends try to guess the places you have described.

Read More About It

Block City by Robert Louis Stevenson. E. P. Dutton. A boy uses his blocks to build interesting structures.

Efan the Great by Roni Schotter. Lothrop, Lee & Shepard. Efan gives his entire New York neighborhood a surprise gift.

The Inside-Outside Book of Washington, D.C. by Roxie Munro. E. P. Dutton. Read about twelve landmarks to visit in our nation's capital.

When I Was Young in the Mountains by Cynthia Rylant. E. P. Dutton. A young girl remembers her grandparents who live in the mountains of the rural South.

Goodbye, My Island

by
Jean Rogers

*Esther Atoolik and her brother Lewis have a new
friend from school. They are helping him learn
about their home, King Island. King Island is in
the Bering Sea. The Eskimos who live on the
island spend their summers in Nome, Alaska.
There they sell their ivory carvings and buy the
supplies they need to live through the winter on
the island. This is the last winter Esther will spend
on King Island. The only school on the island is to
be closed. Many families will have to move, ending
a way of life that has not changed for many years.*

Lewis brought Dixon to see where we live. Dixon
is the teacher's nephew. He is the same age as Lewis,
but he is much broader and taller. He talks as much
and asks as many questions as Mary's friend Vicky.
His speech sounded full of funny sputters because
he talked so fast and kept saying, "What's this?
What's that?"

"Uncle Roger says you and Lewis speak the most English," he said to me. "So I can ask you everything I want to know. It is so different here I want to know everything." We all laughed, Mother, too. She does not speak English much, but she understands. In our house it is our father who speaks English. He spent many years in the hospital when he was a boy. He was flown from Nome to the Alaska Native Hospital in Anchorage, where the doctors kept him until he was a young man. But he never forgot his home on King Island, and he has never gone away again. The other men who speak English learned it in the army or in the hospital like Father. Some of the women, too, have learned English, especially Etta, who works at the school and translates for the children what the teachers are saying. Lewis and I do that, too. We learned English from Father. He told Mother that in these days to speak Eskimo is not enough. He says that often. Mother can speak English, too, when she wants to, but she is shy and does not like to do it when others are present.

Dixon is nice, and I did not mind that he asked us about everything.

"Why is your door only sort of a window?" he asked as he stepped into our house. "Why does it open only at the top half?" True, our doors are not

like the doors in the schoolhouse or church. Our doors start halfway up the house wall, and there is only one door, not like at school.

"To keep out the cold," Lewis explained. "It gets very, very cold in the winter." I could tell by the look on Dixon's face that he didn't understand.

"See," I said. "We have no chairs. We sit on the floor in our houses. If our doors opened all the way down, the cold would creep in under the door."

"Sure," said Dixon. "I see." Mother was lighting the Coleman stove to make tea. Lewis offered some to Dixon. "Is that your only stove?" he asked. "Do you do all your cooking on that?"

Lewis nodded, passing the sugar to Dixon. "We are lucky to have a stove like this," he said. "We used to cook over a seal-oil lamp. Now most of us on King Island have Coleman stoves. The lamp gives us light and keeps us warm."

"Where are your beds?" asked Dixon. He looked all around the small room that is our house with his eager, searching eyes, asking and asking. Ours was the very first house he had been in on King Island. Lewis showed him our furs and blankets on the racks along one wall, our tea and sugar and kettles in the boxes, our water can with its dipper, our clothes hanging on their pegs, everything.

Dixon turned to me. "Can I ask you a question?" We all laughed at that. Even my mother, who is so polite, laughed behind her hand. What had Dixon been doing but asking questions so fast that Lewis barely had time to answer? Dixon laughed, too, as I nodded. "All you girls are wearing print dresses. I thought Eskimos wear fur parkas like Marie and Roger do."

"We do, but they are kept for special occasions, Dixon. See, this is our father's hanging here." Lewis took Father's fur parka from its hook and showed Dixon the fur strips that made the design, the wolf fur that trimmed the parka hood. "These take a lot of time to sew," Lewis explained. "Special fur has to be collected to make the pattern come out just right. If you have a parka as fine as this one, you don't go hunting or fishing in it; for that, you wear your everyday parka with the skin side out. Show him, Esther."

I put on my reindeer skin parka and put my blue parka cover over it, the one Mother made new for

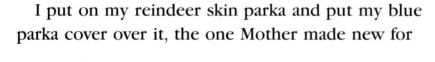

me just before we went to Nome. She would make me another one soon of the calico we had ordered from the catalog while we were there. The skin was tanned so that it was soft and white; the fur side turned in kept me warm as warm. Lewis showed Dixon Father's white parka cover that he wore hunting. We girls and women never go hunting, so our parka covers can be the brightest colors and patterns that we can find.

I knew why Dixon wanted to know about everything because that is the way we are when we go to the schoolhouse. We want to see and touch everything that is so different—the glass windows that look out over the sea, the stove in teacher's room that is big and black and so hot all the time. It has an oven where Teacher Marie can make bread and cookies; she has let me help her do this. At our house we have pilot bread from the store to dip in our stew or our tea.

"When the shore ice freezes hard enough," Lewis told Dixon, "I will take you to the big ice cave where we store our meat all winter long. Big Peter says the cave is so long it goes all the way through our island and comes out on the other side.

"Wow, really?" Dixon said. "Really?"

"Well, I've never been all the way through it, but that's what Peter says," Lewis said. He was proud to be the one to tell Dixon about our King Island.

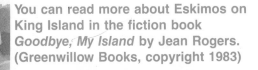

You can read more about Eskimos on King Island in the fiction book *Goodbye, My Island* by Jean Rogers. (Greenwillow Books, copyright 1983)

Unit Review

WORDS TO REMEMBER

Number your paper from 1 to 10. Use the words below to fill in the blanks. Use each word only once.

banks   needs
business centers   pastures
capital   rural
deserts   shelters
hospitals   suburb

1. _____ are places where people keep money.

2. Communities have stores and offices in their _____ .

3. Homes, stores, and buildings where people work are called _____ .

4. Food, clothing, and shelter are _____ .

5. Doctors and nurses often work in _____ .

6. _____ are very dry lands.

7. There are often farms near _____ communities.

8. Washington, D.C., is our country's _____ .

9. Spring, Texas, is a _____ of Houston.

10. Horses eat grass and other plants in _____ .

FOCUS ON MAIN IDEAS

1. Why do people like to live in communities?

2. How are some communities alike?

3. What groups can you belong to in a community?

4. How do people in a community meet needs?

5. How do people in a community depend on each other?

6. What are some places that every community has?

7. What are three main things that make communities different from one another?

8. How does a community affect the kind of work people do? What kind of work might people who live in a town do?

9. How is living in a city different from living in a town?

10. Why do people live in suburbs? How is a suburb different from a city?

THINK/WRITE
Find or draw pictures of your community. Write a paragraph telling how your community is like other communities. Write a paragraph telling how it is different.

ACTIVITIES

1. **Maps** Draw a map of your neighborhood. Show some places that help people meet their needs.

2. **Research/Writing** Use a telephone book to look up the address of a store. Write down the name and address.

SKILLS REVIEW

1. **Using the Library** Name three rules you must obey in order to use the library. Explain why they are important.

2. **Using Dictionaries and Encyclopedias** Number your paper from 1 to 5. Then write these words in the order that you would find them in a dictionary or an encyclopedia.

   pasture ZIP code bank
   map suburb

3. **Using Maps** Use the map on page 51 to answer the following questions.
   a. What two countries share a border with the United States?
   b. If you were in Kansas, in which direction would you go to reach Utah? Which direction is Tennessee from Kansas?
   c. If you traveled from Missouri to New York, in which direction would you be going?
   d. Which states share a border with Texas?

4. **Reviewing a World Map** Use the map on page 53 to answer the following questions.
   a. What divides the northern and southern parts of the globe?
   b. Which continents are in the Southern Hemisphere?
   c. The equator crosses which three continents?
   d. What ocean is between Africa and Australia?
   e. Which continent is south of Africa?

EXPLORING
YOUR COMMUNITY

As you read about other communities, you can compare them with your own community. At the end of each unit you also will find "Your Community." The activities here will help you find out more about your community.

MAKING A SCRAPBOOK

1. Make a scrapbook out of construction paper. Write "My Community" on the cover. On the first page, draw a map showing five places in your community that you like. Put a compass rose on your map. During the year, add pictures and stories about your community to your scrapbook.

DESCRIBING YOUR COMMUNITY

2. Write a paragraph describing how the land around your community looks. Tell about any hills, lakes, deserts, or rivers that may be near your community. Add your paragraph to your scrapbook.

3. On a map of your state, find the state capital, two large cities, and your community. Trace your state on a sheet of paper. Add the cities you found and your community to your map.

LEARNING ABOUT NATIVE AMERICANS

4. Many ideas for food, shelter, and art came to us from Native Americans. Find out about the Native Americans who live or used to live in your community. Do you eat any of the foods they ate? Does your community use any of the same materials for buildings? Choose one thing that the Native Americans gave to your community that is still used today. Share your choice with the class.

5. Imagine Native Americans once lived where your school is now. Draw a picture showing Native Americans and how you think your community might have looked.

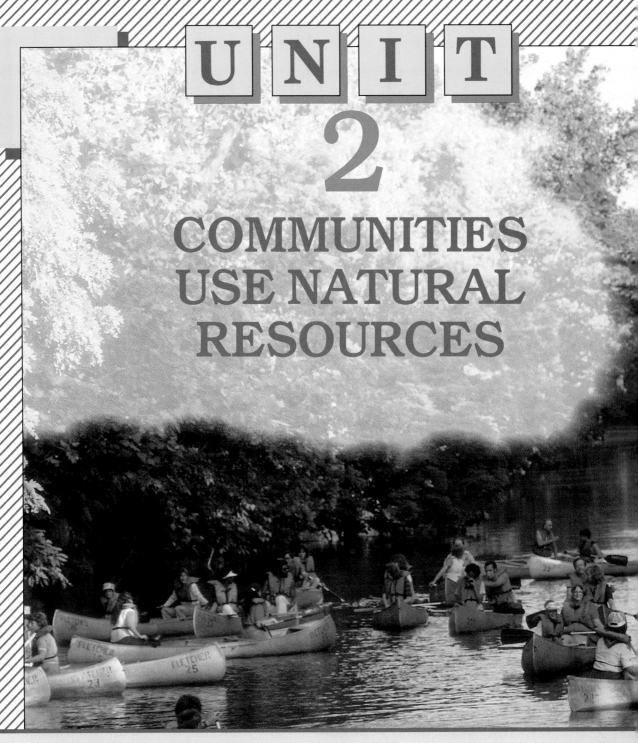

UNIT
2
COMMUNITIES USE NATURAL RESOURCES

Community Facts and Figures

	Merced, California	Independence, Iowa	Midland, Texas
Location	Merced, California	Independence, Iowa	Midland, Texas
Population (estimated)	53,550	6,392	100,249
Landmark	Courthouse Museum	Wapsipinicon Mill	Permian Basin Museum
Nickname/Motto	The Gateway to Yosemite	Proud People Promoting Progress	City of Surprises

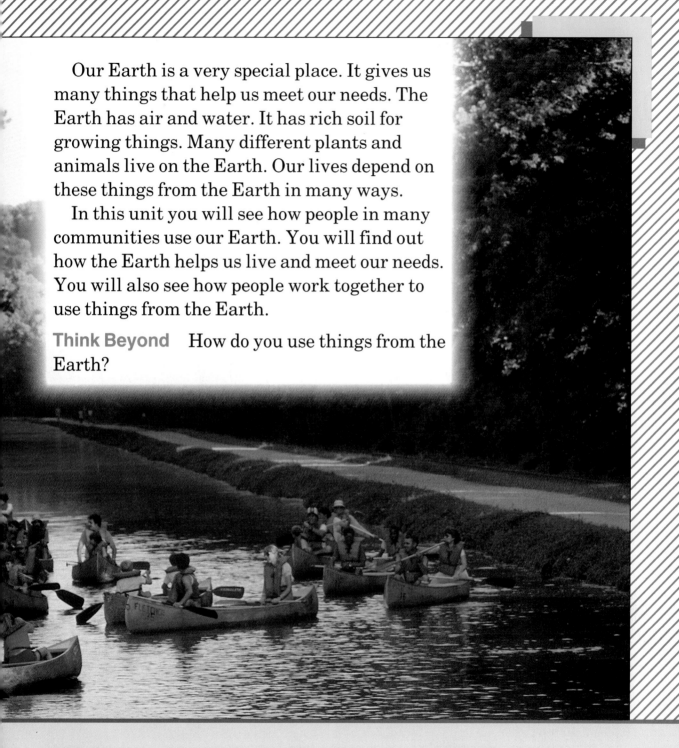

Our Earth is a very special place. It gives us many things that help us meet our needs. The Earth has air and water. It has rich soil for growing things. Many different plants and animals live on the Earth. Our lives depend on these things from the Earth in many ways.

In this unit you will see how people in many communities use our Earth. You will find out how the Earth helps us live and meet our needs. You will also see how people work together to use things from the Earth.

Think Beyond How do you use things from the Earth?

Location	Pikeville, Kentucky	Chicago, Illinois	Seattle, Washington
Population (estimated)	5,600	3,010,000	486,000
Landmark	Pikeville College	Sears Tower	Space Needle
Nickname/Motto	Marketplace of the Mountains	The Windy City	The Emerald City

CHAPTER 3

Farming Communities

"These buildings are too close to me.
I'd like to PUSH away.
I'd like to live in the country,
And spread my arms all day.

I'd like to spread my breath out, too—
As farmers' sons and daughters do.

I'd tend the cows and chickens.
I'd do the other chores.
Then, all the hours left I'd go
A-SPREADING out-of-doors."

—"Rudolph Is Tired of the City"
by Gwendolyn Brooks

Look for these important words:

Key Words
- natural resources
- goods
- climate
- crop
- fertilizer
- harvest
- growing season
- irrigation

Look for answers to these questions:
1. What are natural resources?
2. What can we make from natural resources?
3. How are farms alike and different?

1 NATURAL RESOURCES AND OUR FARMS

The Earth and the sun give us everything we need to meet our needs. They give us our **natural resources** (REE•sohr•suhz). Resources are things that people can use. Natural resources are resources found in nature. Natural resources are not made by people.

Clean air, soil, and fresh water are natural resources. So are trees and fish.

We use natural resources to make food and **goods.** Goods are people-made things. We use the natural resource of trees to make paper. We use the natural resource of sand to make glass.

Farmers use natural resources, too. Farmers raise plants or animals to sell. To raise things, farmers need the natural resources of good soil, enough water, and the right **climate.** Climate is the usual weather in a place. Climate means how hot or cold it is year after year. Climate is how much rain or snow falls during the year.

How Farms Are Alike and Different

There are many different kinds of farms in the United States. Some farms are large. Some farms are small. Farmers give us different things. Some raise animals, such as chickens, hogs, and cows.

Other farmers grow food. Some raise a single **crop,** or kind of plant. For example, a farmer might raise only wheat.

Joe feeds his family's chickens. These chickens are being raised for eggs and meat.

Some farmers raise vegetables. Others grow trees that produce fruits or nuts. In the United States, one farmer can grow enough food for hundreds of people.

Although farms are different from one another, they are the same in some ways. All farms must have soil, the right climate, and enough water for the animals or crops.

Above, a farmer harvests fields of wheat. Below, Susan and her friend pick apples from high in a tree.

From the soil, plants get a lot of what they need to grow. However, many farmers make the soil even better for growing plants by adding **fertilizer** (FUR•tuhl•eye•zur) to it. A fertilizer feeds the plants. It helps plants to grow.

Plants also need enough time to grow. Most crops will die or stop growing when the weather gets too cold. That is one reason farmers plant most crops in the spring, when the winter weather is over. Farmers **harvest,** or pick their crops, in the summer or fall, before the colder weather comes again.

GEOGRAPHY CONNECTION

Long ago in Italy a ruler wanted to eat cucumbers all year round. He used a special type of building to grow his cucumbers. The building let in light but kept out the cold weather.

People in other countries borrowed this idea. In Holland a doctor used a greenhouse to grow plants used for medicine. Many people in England became interested in using greenhouses to grow tropical plants brought back by English explorers. The English built very large greenhouses to grow palms and other exotic plants. From England greenhouses came to

America. Our first greenhouses were used to grow oranges and were called orangeries.

Today people in Israel use greenhouse farming to save water. They have built huge greenhouses in the desert. The greenhouses help keep the water used to irrigate crops from evaporating into the dry desert air.

Water from lakes, rivers, or wells irrigates plants. Narrow ditches carry the water between the rows.

The months in which crops can grow are called the **growing season.** Growing seasons depend on the climate of a place. In places with long, cold winters, the growing season is short. In places where the winter climate is warmer, the growing season is long.

Crops also need water. Most water comes from rain. If there is not enough rain in a farming area, water must be brought from another place. This is called **irrigation** (eer•uh•GAY•shun).

 Reading Check

1. What are four natural resources?
2. How does fertilizer help plants?

Think Beyond Why are apples grown in the North and oranges in the South?

ANASAZI INDIANS

In 1888 two cowhands were looking for stray cattle in the canyons of Colorado. As they rode up to the edge of a canyon cliff, they were startled by what they saw. Rising many stories high in the side of the canyon wall were the ruins of an American Indian community. This community was built by the **Anasazi** (ahn•uh•SAH•zee), who lived in the Southwest about 700 years ago. The Anasazi were skilled farmers.

The area where the Anasazi lived received little rainfall. When it did rain, the water on the ground flowed so fast that it often carried away topsoil. The Anasazi needed to catch as much of the rainwater as possible for their crops. They also needed to protect the soil.

The Anasazi built this community on a plateau called the Mesa Verde.

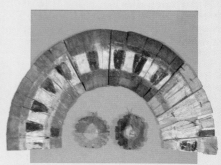

Head ornament and
earrings

Pottery bird pot

The Anasazi built small dams
to slow the speed of the water.
This gave the water time to soak
into the ground. The dams also
helped stop the topsoil from
washing away. The soil would
back up against the dams, form-
ing new growing fields. The
Anasazi also dug canals and irrigation ditches to catch and re-
route the rushing water. The canals and ditches directed the
water to the fields where corn,
beans, and cotton were planted.

Although the Anasazi were
good farmers, they did not stay in
the area. Some scientists think
that the rainwater picked up
harmful minerals as it flowed over
the land. Over time, too many of
the minerals may have soaked
into the Anasazi's fields, keeping
crops from growing well. Other
scientists think that a long dry
period forced the Anasazi to
leave. No one really knows why
they left.

Think Beyond   Why should you
be concerned about water use in
your community?

Scientists are still studying the symbols
drawn by the Anasazi on the rocks near
their communities.

73

SKILLS IN ACTION

USING RESOURCE MAPS

Resources are things that people can use. Resources include crops and animals. They include trees and land. You can show resources on **resource maps.**

Resource maps show where you can find resources. They can also show **factories.** Factories are big buildings. People use resources to make things in factories. They use resources to make goods.

You will be looking at many resource maps in this book. Look at this resource map of Kansas.

Find Topeka on the map. That is the capital of Kansas. There are some symbols near this city. One is a building. Now look at the map key. The map key shows you that the building is a symbol for factories. There are a lot of factories near Topeka.

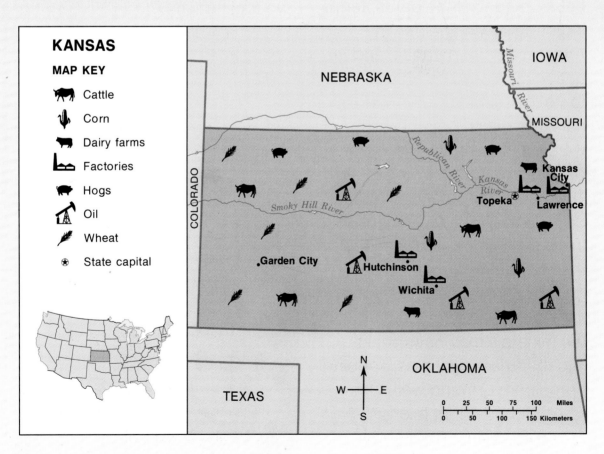

People in factories make goods.
There are many factories in our country.

Ranchers often use horses to round up
cattle.

There is another symbol north and to the east of Topeka. It is a picture of a cow. The map key shows you that the cow stands for the dairy farms near Topeka. Farmers get milk from cows on dairy farms.

Another symbol on the map stands for **cattle.** Cattle are cows, bulls, and steers. People raise these animals for their meat. Much of the meat that we eat comes from cattle raised in our country. Look at the map key. What other animal is raised in Kansas?

A lot of the food that we eat comes from Kansas. Look at the resource map again. Wheat and corn are two very important crops grown in Kansas. Many large farms in Kansas grow these crops.

The resource maps in this book name the states that share borders with the state you are reading about. They also show you a small map of our country with the state in color.

CHECKING YOUR SKILLS

Use the resource map to help you answer these questions.

1. What are two important crops grown in Kansas?

2. What are most factories in Kansas close to?

3. What are some resources near Garden City?

4. Oil is one resource people get from the Earth. Near what cities can oil be found?

75

Look for these important words:

Key Words
- factories
- valley
- farming community

- irrigate
- ripe

Places
- Merced, California

Look for answers to these questions:
1. How is climate important to the kinds of vegetables grown in a place?
2. Why is Merced called a farming community?
3. How do machines help farmers in Merced?

2 MERCED, CALIFORNIA

What is your favorite vegetable? Some people like sweet corn best, and others like fresh peas. Eating vegetables helps keep you healthy.

Different vegetables need different climates to grow best. Vegetables such as tomatoes and corn need lots of hot sun. Other vegetables, such as broccoli, grow best where the climate is wet. Farmers need to know what soil and climate are good for their vegetables. They must know how much water their vegetables need, too.

There are small vegetable farms near many cities. Sometimes people in the cities buy fresh vegetables from these farms. Sometimes they buy fresh vegetables at the store.

There are also large vegetable farms far from cities. Here, most farmers grow just one kind of vegetable. Then trucks, trains, or planes carry some of these vegetables to different places.

Many of the vegetables go to **factories.** A factory is a big building where goods are made. There are many big machines in factories. Vegetables are frozen or canned at the factories. These frozen or canned vegetables are shipped to stores all across the country.

The next pages tell you how a farmer in the state of California raises tomatoes. You will find out how tomatoes are made into special foods in factories, too.

The Garcias' Vegetable Farm

Merced (mur•SED) is a small city in the middle of **California.** Merced is in a big **valley** that is rich in natural resources. A valley is low land between hills or mountains.

The picture below shows the city of Merced. Huge fields and farms surround Merced.

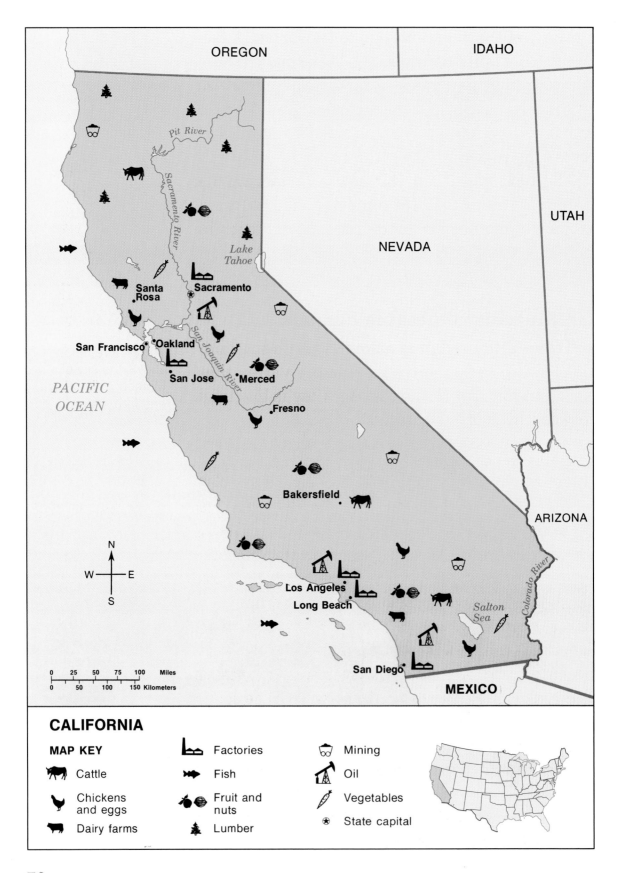

CALIFORNIA

MAP KEY

- 🐂 Cattle
- 🐔 Chickens and eggs
- 🐖 Dairy farms
- 🏭 Factories
- 🐟 Fish
- 🍎🌰 Fruit and nuts
- 🌲 Lumber
- ⛏ Mining
- 🛢 Oil
- 🥕 Vegetables
- ✹ State capital

The Garcia family enjoys an outdoor picnic during the long, hot California summer.

Many of the jobs in Merced have to do with farming. Because of this, Merced is called a **farming community.** Almost half of the people in Merced work on farms. Merced also has canning factories for vegetable and fruit crops.

Merced is a good place to grow tomatoes. Tomatoes need warm summers to grow well. Summers in Merced are long and very warm. Winters in Merced are mild and rainy. The soil is good for growing crops.

Mr. and Mrs. Garcia have a large farm near Merced. They raise only tomatoes. Most of their tomatoes are brought to factories. Anita Garcia is eight years old. She and her brothers and sister help with the farm work.

Planting and Harvesting Tomatoes

Raising tomatoes does not begin with planting seeds. The Garcias must first choose the kind of tomato they want to grow. The Garcias must choose tomato plants that will be strong and healthy. They must also grow a kind of tomato that fits the needs of the canning factory.

Early in the spring Anita's father gets the soil ready for planting. He uses a plow to turn over the soil. Next, he uses a special machine to plant the seeds. This machine also adds weed killer to the soil and puts fertilizer below the seeds.

As the plants grow, Mr. Garcia uses another machine. This machine kills weeds by turning them into the soil.

In Merced, little or no rain falls during the growing season. This means Mr. Garcia must **irrigate,** or water, his tomatoes. He does this about every other week.

To ready the soil for planting, a machine loosens the soil and destroys weeds. After the plants are growing, sprinkling machines irrigate the tomatoes.

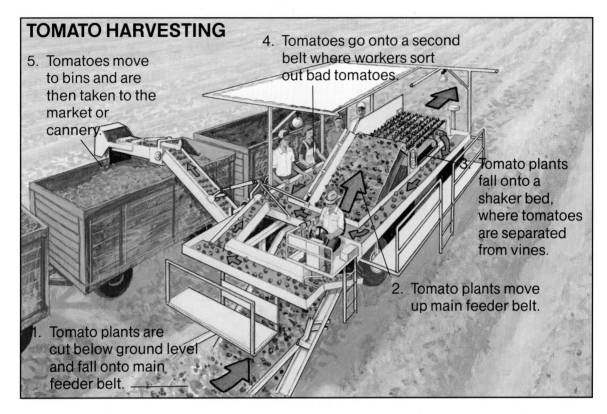

TOMATO HARVESTING

5. Tomatoes move to bins and are then taken to the market or cannery.

4. Tomatoes go onto a second belt where workers sort out bad tomatoes.

3. Tomato plants fall onto a shaker bed, where tomatoes are separated from vines.

2. Tomato plants move up main feeder belt.

1. Tomato plants are cut below ground level and fall onto main feeder belt.

The tomatoes are **ripe,** or ready to be eaten, when they are very red. This is when the Garcias harvest them for the canning factory.

A machine does the harvesting. It shakes the tomatoes off the plants. Then the machine moves the tomatoes up to the workers who are on the machine. The workers pick out rocks, dirt, and bad tomatoes. All the good tomatoes go into huge metal boxes. Then trucks take these boxes to the canning factory.

These pear-shaped tomatoes are good for canning.

 Reading Check

1. Where can people get fresh vegetables? Name two places.
2. How do machines help farmers in Merced?

Think Beyond   Why do you think the Garcias grow only tomatoes on their farm?

81

SKILLS IN ACTION

USING CLIMATE MAPS

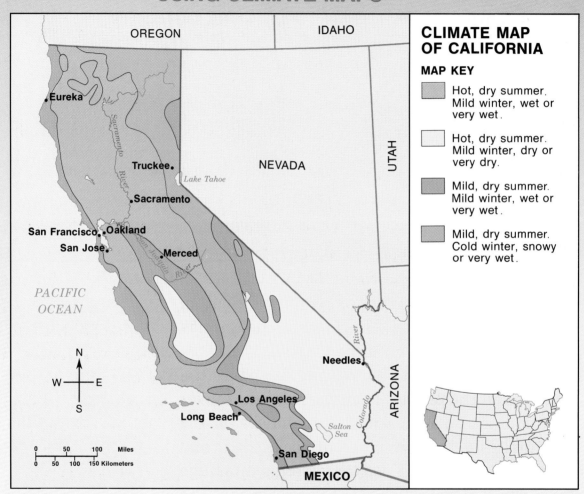

CLIMATE MAP OF CALIFORNIA

MAP KEY

- Hot, dry summer. Mild winter, wet or very wet.
- Hot, dry summer. Mild winter, dry or very dry.
- Mild, dry summer. Mild winter, wet or very wet.
- Mild, dry summer. Cold winter, snowy or very wet.

Climate is the usual weather in a place. Climate maps show what the weather in a place is like all year long. Climate maps show how much rain or snow falls in a place during the year. They show what the winters and summers in that place are like.

The map on this page shows climates in California. Each climate is shown by a color on the map. Look at the map key at the side of the map. How many climates does the map show? What colors are used on the map to show these different climates?

82

Different parts of California have different climates. In some parts of California, it snows a lot during the winter. In other parts, the winter is very dry.

Farmers Need Good Climates

Some areas in California have climates that are very good for growing crops. In other parts of California, it is hard to grow a lot of crops.

Merced is in the part of California colored green. Look at the map key. It tells you that the green area has mild, dry summers and mild, rainy winters.

The climate in the green area is very good for growing fruits and vegetables. During the dry summers, farmers irrigate the soil. Then crops can grow well. You have read about how well tomatoes grow in Merced.

Now look at the parts of California colored pink. These parts of the state are good for growing food, too. Find Sacramento in the pink area. There are many farms near Sacramento. The area around the city is famous for all the crops grown there.

Now find Needles in the southern part of the state. Needles is in the part of California colored yellow. Like the pink area, the yellow area has hot, dry summers. Winter in the yellow area, however, is dry, too. Very little rain falls in Needles. Needles is in a big desert. In a desert, few crops can be grown. There is not enough water for many plants to grow.

Find Truckee on the climate map. What color is the map there? Summers in Truckee are usually mild and dry. Winters in Truckee are very cold and snowy. It is much too cold in Truckee to grow certain kinds of crops.

CHECKING YOUR SKILLS

Use the climate map to help you answer these questions.

1. Find Los Angeles on the map. Is the area around there good for growing crops?

2. What are winters like in Eureka?

3. Most trees need a lot of rain to grow. Do you think there are more trees near Truckee or near Needles? Why?

4. Name at least two communities in areas where the climate is good for growing crops.

5. What is the climate like in San Jose?

83

Look for these important words:

Key Words
- cannery
- tomato paste
- pulp

Look for answers to these questions:

1. What is a cannery?
2. Why are tomatoes canned and bottled?
3. How are canned tomatoes taken away from factories? Where are they taken?

3 TOMATOES AT THE CANNERY

Many goods are made from tomatoes at the canning factory, or **cannery.** Some tomatoes are boiled and then canned. Other tomatoes are used to make ketchup. Still others are used to make tomato soup and tomato juice.

Tomatoes are canned and bottled for many reasons. One important reason to can food is so that you can use it longer. Fresh vegetables and fruit are often good only for a few weeks after the harvest. People can enjoy these healthful foods all year long in cans and bottles.

The Garcias' tomatoes are perfect for making **tomato paste.** Tomato paste is a thick, rich sauce. Cooks use tomato paste on top of pizza. They use it to make spaghetti sauce, too.

In the cannery, the Garcias' tomatoes are put into a long bin. Workers inspect and sort the tomatoes in the bin.

At the cannery, machines fill small cans with tomato paste.

The tomatoes that are good for tomato paste are chopped by a machine. Then the tomatoes are cooked. Cooking the tomatoes helps make sure no harmful germs enter the food. Germs can make people sick. The seeds and peels are then taken out of the tomatoes. What is left is called **pulp.**

The pulp goes to a machine that takes some water out of it. The machine cooks the pulp so that it becomes thick like paste. The pulp has now become tomato paste.

After it is cooled, the tomato paste is put in small cans. These cans are closed, cooked, and cooled. Machines close and seal the cans tightly. That way, no air gets in. Germs can grow when air is in cans. Labels are put on the cans. Later trucks bring them to our stores.

 Reading Check

1. How is tomato paste used?
2. Why are tomatoes cooked in canneries?

Think Beyond What might happen to a cannery that let germs get into the food?

SKILLS IN ACTION

USING LISTS AND TABLES

A **list** is a way to order things. Lists can help you learn facts or remember things. For example, a grocery list helps you remember what you need to buy at the store.

Look at the three lists shown on this page.

The lists show some California crops, some state capitals, and some things that make up climates. As you can see, lists usually do not have sentences. When you write a list, you use only words or groups of words.

Some California Crops	Some State Capitals	Some Things That Make Up Climate
cotton	Tallahassee	amounts of rain or snow
grapes	Austin	summer weather
oranges	Boise	winter weather
vegetables	Sacramento	wind
nuts	Salem	
rice	Des Moines	
grains		

TABLE OF FACTS ABOUT THREE STATES

State	Capital	Important Crops	Climate
California	Sacramento	cotton, grapes, oranges, grapefruits, vegetables, nuts, rice, grains, hay	hot or warm summers; mild, rainy winters
Iowa	Des Moines	corn, oats, soybeans, hay	wet, hot summers; cold, snowy winters
Florida	Tallahassee	oranges, grapefruits, lemons, sugarcane, nuts, cotton, watermelons, vegetables	wet, hot summers; mild winters

Lists of facts can be put together in **tables.** You can see information quickly on a table. Tables let you compare things easily.

Now look at the table on this page. You can find out what crops are grown in California by looking at the table. Put your finger on the word "California." Then move your finger to the right across the table until you reach the column that says "Important Crops." Now read the list of crops.

If you want to find out what the climate of Florida is, find the box on the left that says "Florida." Then find the column that says "Climate." The words across from "Florida" in the "Climate" column tell about the usual weather in Florida. They tell how much rain falls in Florida and what the winters and summers are like.

CHECKING YOUR SKILLS

Use the table to help you answer these questions.

1. What is the capital of Iowa?
2. Which crops are grown in both California and Florida?
3. How is the climate of Iowa different from the climate of Florida?
4. What crop does Florida have that California and Iowa do not?
5. Which two states have wet, hot summers?

Look for these important words:

Key Words
- dairy farms
- yogurt
- dairy products

Places
- Independence, Iowa

Look for answers to these questions:
1. What is a dairy farm?
2. What kind of community is Independence, Iowa?
3. How do machines help dairy farmers?

4 INDEPENDENCE, IOWA

Farms where cows are raised for their milk are called **dairy farms.** Most dairy farms are in places where grass grows thick and green. Rain falls often enough to keep the grasses growing. Cows eat a lot of grass.

In the United States, a good dairy cow can give about 64 quarts (61 L) of milk a day. Some of this milk is used for drinking. Many things that we eat are made from milk, too. Cheese, butter, and **yogurt** are made from milk. Yogurt is thicker than milk and has a slightly sour taste. All things made from milk are called **dairy products.**

Cows graze in Iowa's pastures.

The Swansons' Dairy Farm

Independence, Iowa, is a town. Like Merced in California, Independence is a farming community. There are about 1,500 large farms in the area. Many of them are dairy farms.

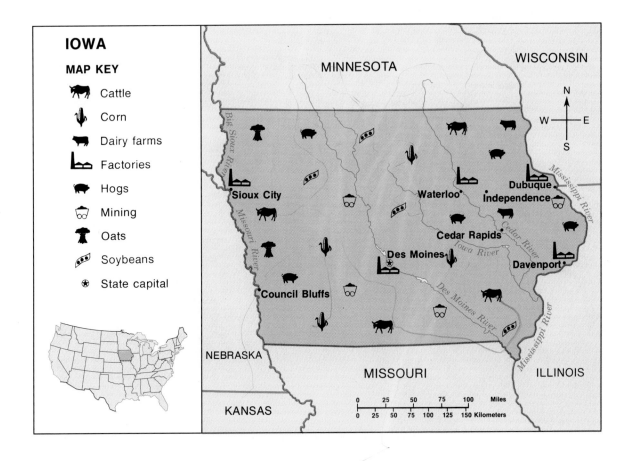

The dairy farm of the Swanson family is about five miles from Independence. Mr. and Mrs. Swanson live and work there. They have two children. Laura is 12, and Carl is 9. The children help milk and feed the 150 cows on the farm.

The Swansons' cows are milked very early every morning. They are milked again in the late afternoon. In the Swansons' barn, 16 cows can be milked at the same time.

The children line the cows up. Then they clean them for milking. They brush and wash the cows. Milking machines make the work go fast. A pump pulls milk from the cows into hoses. The milk goes through the hoses into a large tank. It is kept cool there.

Milking by hand used to take several hours. Now, many cows can be milked at one time using milking machines.

Getting the cows' milk is just part of the work on the dairy farm. The Swansons must check their cows to make sure they are healthy. They keep track of how much milk each cow gives. They also make sure the cows eat well in the pastures.

 Reading Check

1. Why do dairy farms need grassy places?
2. Name three dairy products.

Think Beyond Why do you think cows are washed before they are milked?

Look for these important words:

Key Words
- creamery
- butterfat
- pasteurized
- homogenized
- skim milk

Look for answers to these questions:
1. How does milk get to a creamery?
2. What kinds of jobs do machines do in a creamery?
3. What products are made in a creamery?

5 MILK AT THE CREAMERY

Every day a truck picks up milk from the Swansons' farm. The truck keeps the milk cool in a special tank. Then the truck takes the milk to a **creamery.** A creamery is a factory that makes milk ready for people to buy.

At the creamery, machines do most of the work. The milk is weighed and checked for **butterfat.** Butterfat is the cream that rises when milk is left standing.

Next the milk is **pasteurized** (PAS•chuh•ryzd). This means that the milk is quickly heated and then cooled. Heating the milk kills any harmful germs that might be in it.

Some of the milk is **homogenized** (hoh•MAHJ•uh•nyzd). To make homogenized milk, a machine mixes the butterfat with the rest of the milk. The butterfat in homogenized milk stays mixed. The butterfat that is mixed in gives homogenized milk a rich taste.

Machines working at high speed fill containers with milk, and cap the containers after they are filled.

Some milk is not homogenized. Instead, the cream is taken off the top of the milk. The **skim milk** that remains is sold. Some of the rich cream is sold, too. Some of it is made into butter.

At the creamery, milk is put into cartons or containers. Then the containers are put into boxes. The creamery keeps the milk cool until trucks can take it to our stores.

 Reading Check

1. What is a creamery?
2. Why is milk pasteurized?

Think Beyond Which is more healthful, skim milk or homogenized milk? Tell why.

People MAKE HISTORY

Chan Hong Tai
1864–1942

▶▶▶▶▶▶▶▶▶▶▶▶▶▶

Chan Hong Tai (CHAN HAWNG TY), also known as Ah Lung, came to California from China in the early 1880s. He wanted to be a farmer. Ah Lung's first job was helping drain wet land so that crops could be planted. This work was so hard that Ah Lung's hands and feet would be bloody at the end of the day.

Ah Lung did not give up his dream of having his own farm. He kept working hard. Except for food and shelter, he spent less than a dollar a month on himself. He saved the rest of his pay.

By the early 1890s, Ah Lung rented farmland all over the Sacramento-San Joaquin area. He hired other Chinese to help him farm. He became known as the Potato King because he grew mostly potatoes.

By 1912 Ah Lung had saved enough money to buy his own farm. Unfortunately, California passed a law to keep Chinese from owning American land.

Soon this law was changed to keep them from renting land as well. With no chance left to rent or buy land, Ah Lung returned to China. However, his hard work had paid off. He used the money he had saved to buy land and buildings in China. Ah Lung was satisfied. He had set a good example in California and in his homeland.

Think Beyond What are some reasons you might need to save money? What steps could you take to save the money you need?

Thinking Back

- Natural resources are things in nature that people can use to grow food and to make goods.

- The growing season for food depends on the climate of a place. In dry places farmers must irrigate their crops.

- Tomatoes grow especially well near Merced, California, because the soil is good and the climate is warm.

- The tomatoes are planted and harvested by large machines.

The crop is taken to a factory called a cannery. At the cannery tomatoes are sorted, cooked, and canned before being sent to stores.

- Cows are raised on dairy farms near Independence, Iowa. The climate is right for growing the grass cows need.

- The cows are milked by machine. At the creamery milk is heated and cooled to pasteurize it. Some milk is sold for drinking. The rest is made into other dairy products.

Check for Understanding

Using Words

Number a piece of paper from 1 to 5. Match the words with their meanings.

1. **ripe**

2. **natural resources**

3. **dairy farms**

4. **factories**

5. **climate**

a. things found in nature that people can use

b. the usual weather in a place

c. big buildings where goods are made

d. ready to be eaten

e. places where cows are raised for their milk

Reviewing Facts

1. What three natural resources are important to farmers?

2. What is a "growing season"?

3. What must tomato farmers do before they plant seeds?

4. Where are most dairy farms found? Why?

5. What are three things that happen to milk in a creamery?

Thinking Critically

1. What are some ways that farms are alike? What makes farms different from one another?

2. How is a cannery like a creamery? How is it different?

3. Would you rather live on a tomato farm or a dairy farm? Tell why.

Writing About It

Write two paragraphs telling how machines have helped dairy farmers like the Swansons. You may want to go to the library to find out how dairy farms operated long ago.

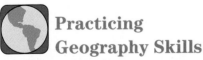 **Practicing Geography Skills**

Using Resource Maps Name three resources that are found in or near your community. Go to the library if you need help. Make up and draw symbols for the three resources you chose.

 On Your Own

Social Studies at Home

Make a farming-community song or poetry book. In the library, find songs or poems about farm life. Ask your family if they know any songs or poems about farm life. Copy each song or poem neatly onto a sheet of paper. Fasten your pages together to make a book. Draw a picture of a farm for the cover.

Read More About It

Family Farm by Thomas Locker. Dial Books. A farm family works hard to keep their farm going during a difficult year.

Farming Today Yesterday's Way by Cheryl Walsh Bellville. Carolrhoda Books. A Wisconsin dairy farmer uses old methods in a new way.

Natural Resources by Caroline Arnold. Franklin Watts. Learn about natural resources through many easy-to-do projects.

Town and Country by Alice and Martin Provensen. Crown. Even though they are different, both the country and city are nice places to live.

CHAPTER 4

Mining Communities

"Papa dug coal from deep in the earth to earn a living. He dressed for work when everyone went to bed. He wore faded denims and steel-toed shoes and he carried a silver lunch bucket and had a light on his miner's hat. It was important work. He was proud to do it."

—from the book *In Coal Country* by Judith Hendershot

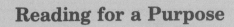
Look for these important words:

Key Words
- mineral
- coal
- oil
- mines
- wells
- energy

Look for answers to these questions:
1. What is a mineral?
2. How do we use mineral resources?
3. What are some of the jobs that people in a coal-mining community do?

1 MINERAL RESOURCES AND OUR COMMUNITIES

A **mineral** (MIN·uh·ruhl) is a natural resource found in the earth. **Coal** and **oil** are minerals. Coal is a dark brown or black mineral. It is like a dark rock. Oil is a dark, thick liquid found deep in the ground. Copper, gold, iron, and silver are also minerals.

We use mineral resources to meet our needs. We must dig deep into the ground to get most mineral resources. Workers dig large holes and tunnels, called **mines,** to get some mineral resources like coal. They dig narrow, deep holes, called **wells,** to get other mineral resources like oil.

We need many people to get minerals out of the earth. We need workers inside a mine or at a well for many different jobs. We need workers outside the mine or well, too. They take the minerals to factories. After that, we need workers in factories to make the minerals ready to use.

Silver (above) and coal (below) are two minerals found under the ground.

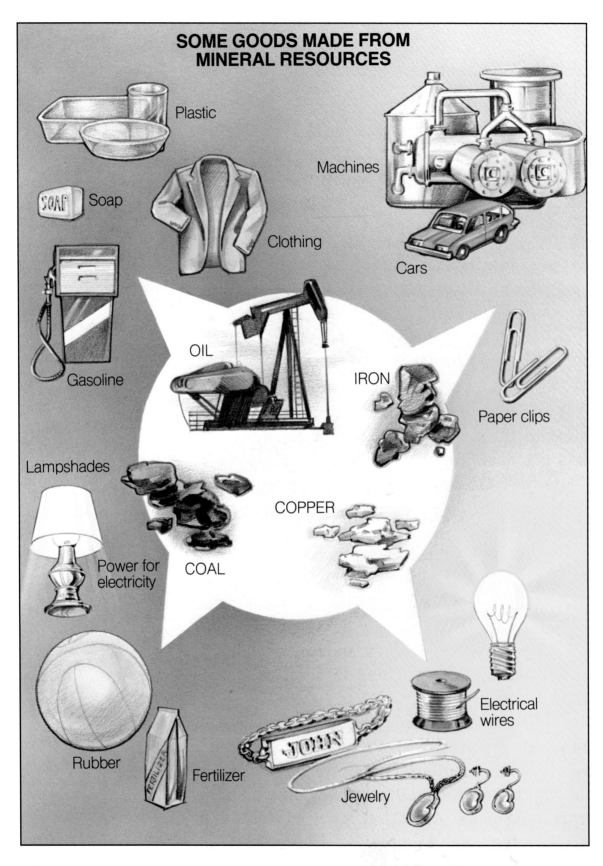

SOME GOODS MADE FROM MINERAL RESOURCES

Plastic

Machines

Soap

Clothing

Cars

Gasoline

OIL

IRON

Paper clips

Lampshades

COPPER

COAL

Power for electricity

Rubber

Fertilizer

JOHN

Jewelry

Electrical wires

Communities near mines or wells are usually called mining communities. Many of the people in mining communities do jobs using the mineral resources nearby.

A mining community has many jobs. For example, some workers might dig coal from a mine. Others work in a factory to clean and prepare the coal. A bank might lend coal miners money to buy more machines for the mines.

People in the stores sell the coal workers clothes and food. The workers pay with the money they get from their mining jobs.

How We Use Mineral Resources

People in the United States use many mineral resources. They use them in lots of different ways. Oil is used to make plastic dishes and to pave roads. Iron is used to make big machines.

Mineral resources are used for **energy,** too. Energy is power that makes things work. Factories burn oil and coal to make energy. Energy can make our cars go and heat our homes. Energy gives us power for our lights.

Some scientists think that we may run out of some mineral resources. Most people agree that we should be very careful not to waste mineral resources. Everyone wants there to be enough coal and oil for tomorrow.

Reading Check

1. Name five minerals.
2. How do we make energy from coal and oil?

Think Beyond How can we be careful not to waste natural resources?

IN FOCUS

CRATER OF DIAMONDS

It was a hot day in Arkansas in 1906. A farmer saw something glistening in the soil. The specks were unlike anything he had ever seen. They sparkled in the sunlight. He dug in the soil and picked up two shiny stones.

Diamonds have been used for spacecraft windows.

The farmer decided to test the stones on a grinding wheel. He was surprised. The grinding wheel did not even scratch the stones. Instead the stones put a groove into the wheel. The farmer stared at the stones in disbelief. What could they be? John Huddleston learned he had discovered diamonds!

The place where Huddleston found the diamonds became North America's only successful diamond mine. Diamonds were mined there, off and on, until 1963. Around 1950 the mine's owners turned the area into a

The most common colors of diamonds are white, yellow, and brown.

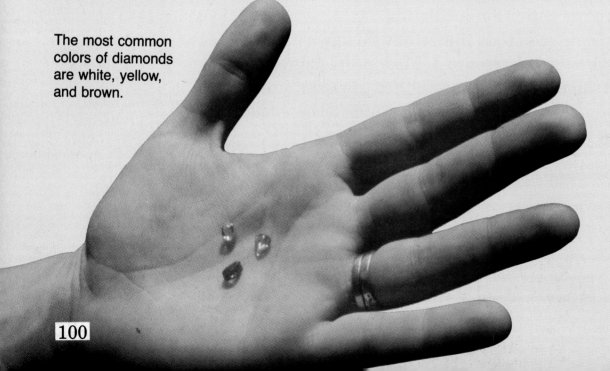

tourist attraction. They called it Crater of Diamonds. For a small fee, tourists could search for diamonds. They were allowed to keep any stones they found.

In 1972 the state of Arkansas bought the Crater of Diamonds. It was turned into a state park. Tourists are still finding more than a thousand diamonds a year there. Most of the diamonds are no larger than a match head. People can spot them because they sparkle like dew.

Most people think of mines being underground. The Arkansas diamond mine is on top of the ground. Probably, the diamonds were first brought to the surface of the Earth by a volcano long, long ago. Once a month, park officials plow the land in the Crater of Diamonds mine area. They hope that will bring to the surface more diamonds for tourists to find.

Think Beyond Why do you think diamonds are so valuable?

The largest diamond found at Crater of Diamonds is called the Uncle Sam.

Tourists find about 1,400 diamonds a year.

SKILLS IN ACTION

SAVING RESOURCES

Coal and oil are natural resources that we burn to make energy. Energy makes televisions, record players, lights, and air conditioners work. We use energy when we heat our homes. It takes a lot of energy to run our cars and to heat our water.

Not every community has coal and oil nearby. Most communities use energy from coal and oil, though. We must all be careful not to waste energy.

Ways to Save Energy

There are many ways you can save energy. Here are some of them.

- Open the refrigerator door less often. Get everything you need out at once. It takes energy to keep refrigerators cold.

- If you are cold, put on a sweater. If you turn on the heat, make sure the windows and doors are closed. This will keep the warm air inside.

102

- Close the curtains or shades at night when the weather is cold. This will help keep the heat in the house. On cold, sunny days, open the curtains and shades. That way, the warm sun can shine through the windows.

- Air conditioners cool the air. If you turn one on, close the shades and curtains. This will keep the hot sunlight out.

- Turn off the lights when you leave a room.

- Do not leave the radio, TV, or record player on when no one is listening or watching.

- Walk, ride a bike, or take a bus instead of going in a car. You save gasoline this way.

Ways to Save Resources

You can do things to save other resources. You can save water by taking short showers and turning off dripping faucets.

People in some schools and communities save old newspapers, cans, and bottles. These are collected at **recycling** (ree•SY•kling) **centers.** To recycle something means to use it again. Companies make recycled things into new paper, cans, and bottles. Recycling things saves resources.

When you use our resources wisely, you help your community. You help make sure that there will be enough resources for the future. If you are careful about using energy and other resources, you also help your family to save money.

What are some of the things being recycled at this recycling center?

CHECKING YOUR SKILLS

Tell or write the answers to these questions.

1. What are two resources that are burned to make energy?

2. What should you turn off when you leave a room?

3. How can you save water?

4. Why do people save old newspapers, cans, and bottles?

103

Look for these important words:

Key Words
- electricity
- by-products
- fuel

Places
- Pikeville, Kentucky
- Appalachian Mountains
- Levisa River

Look for answers to these questions:

1. How do we use coal?
2. How do many people in Pikeville, Kentucky, make their living?
3. Where does coal go after it is mined? What happens to coal at the factory?

 2

PIKEVILLE, KENTUCKY

Pikeville is a small town in **Kentucky.** The town is near the **Appalachian** (ap•uh•LAY•chuhn) **Mountains.** These mountains stretch north and south in the eastern part of our country.

This picture shows downtown Pikeville. You can see the mountains near the town.

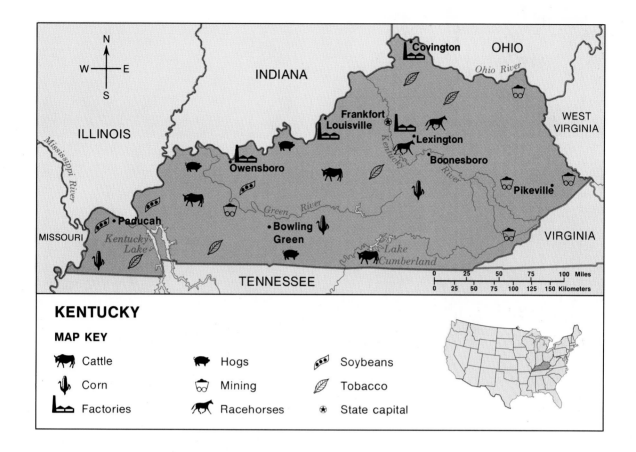

KENTUCKY

MAP KEY

Cattle		Hogs		Soybeans	
Corn		Mining		Tobacco	
Factories		Racehorses		State capital	

The mountains near Pikeville are rich in coal. Coal makes energy when it is burned.

Many people in Pikeville work in the mines or at coal factories. Almost all other work in Pikeville has something to do with coal, too.

We Americans count on coal from communities like Pikeville, Kentucky. Coal is used to make **electricity** (i•lek•TRIS•uh•tee). Electricity gives us power for lights, heating, and machines.

Coal is used to make many other things, too. Parts of coal, called **by-products,** are used to make many goods. Coal by-products are used in plastics and medicines. Coal by-products are used to make lampshades, window screens, and airplane parts. The soles on your shoes may once have been part of a lump of coal!

105

Pikeville is in the mountains of eastern Kentucky. This picture shows a view of Pikeville from the air. Can you see how the path of the Levisa River has been changed?

Pikeville used to have a problem. There was not enough empty land in town to build homes for new workers. To solve this problem, people in Pikeville changed the path of a river. They made the **Levisa River** go around Pikeville instead of through it. By moving the river, the people of Pikeville gave themselves more flat land to build on.

Coal and the Miners

Now you will find out more about work in Pikeville. You will read a letter from Loretta Sommers, who lives in Pikeville. Loretta is telling her pen pal how coal is mined and used.

Dear Marty,

I will try to tell you what my community, Pikeville, is like. To do this, I must tell you about coal.

Coal is a **fuel.** Fuels give off heat when they are burned. This heat is energy. We use the energy from coal to heat buildings and for electricity. We use it to make things, too.

Some scientists think coal was made from layers of plants and mud packed together for many years. The earth's weight changed them into thick layers of coal called coal beds.

When coal is first found in a hill, workers dig two tunnels into the hill. Miners go in and out one tunnel. Machines carry coal out the other.

Miners dig tunnels that go back into the coal bed. Workers make some of the tunnels into bigger rooms. They leave some coal standing in the tunnels and rooms. The coal props up the mines. This keeps the mines safe. Then the workers mine coal from the rooms they have dug out.

Long ago, most coal mining was done with picks and shovels. Now, though, machines do most of the digging and carrying away of coal.

Loretta writes to her friend, Marty.

Miners working underground must be careful. Roof-bolts on the ceiling of the mine protect the workers from falling rock.

Machines dig the coal from the walls of the rooms. The coal is loaded onto small trains. These trains carry the coal out of the mines. The trains run on railroad tracks that workers have built.

My father drives one of the trucks that take coal away from the mines. The coal goes to a factory nearby that makes it ready for people to buy.

I hope you liked my letter about coal mining, Marty. Please write soon and tell me about your community.

Your pen pal,
Loretta

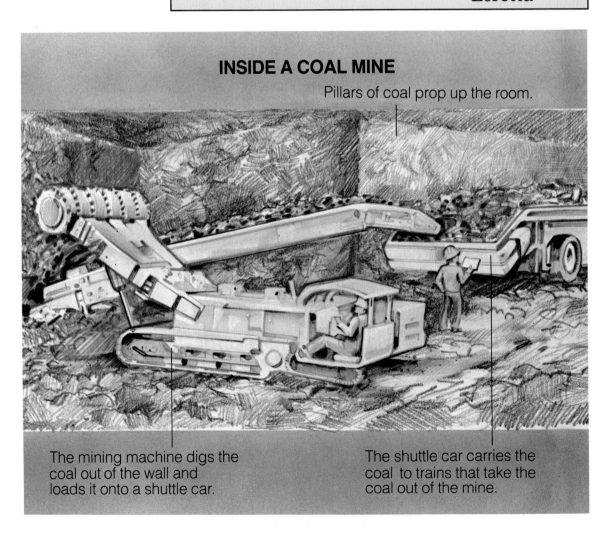

INSIDE A COAL MINE

Pillars of coal prop up the room.

The mining machine digs the coal out of the wall and loads it onto a shuttle car.

The shuttle car carries the coal to trains that take the coal out of the mine.

Coal at the Factory

When coal first gets to the factory, it is put on moving screens. These screens have holes of different sizes. They separate the coal by sizes. Then the coal is washed in water.

After all the coal is washed and sorted, it is dried. A machine dries the coal so it can be used. All this work is done for the different people who buy coal.

Trucks, trains, and boats move the coal from Pikeville. Trains do most of the work. They take the coal to other factories. In these factories, coal is used to make heat, electricity, and goods.

The picture on the left shows a computer being used at a coal processing factory. On the right, loaded trains take the coal from the factory.

Reading Check

1. How do we use electricity?
2. Name three things made from coal.

Think Beyond If you lived in Pikeville, what job would you choose to do? Tell why.

People MAKE HISTORY

Molly Brown
1867–1923

▶▶▶▶▶▶▶▶▶▶▶▶▶▶▶▶▶▶

The "Unsinkable Molly Brown" was the nickname of Margaret Tobin Brown. Maggie, as she liked to be called, was born in Hannibal, Missouri. At age 13 she left school to go to work. Later she moved to Leadville, Colorado, a busy mining town. There she met and married J. J. Brown, a mining engineer.

Maggie and her husband saved enough money to buy a part of the Ibex Mining Company. Soon afterwards the company struck a vein of gold so wide that it was called the world's richest gold strike.

The Browns moved to Denver. Molly became involved in her new community. She gave money to many charities. She gave freely of her time to work for the **Juvenile Court,** a law court that deals with cases involving children.

Maggie's unselfishness really became famous after she survived the sinking of the steamship Titanic. Using her knowledge of foreign languages, she comforted the many passengers who did not speak English. She helped prepare lists of survivors and raised money for them. Because of her good works during this time, she became known as the "Unsinkable Molly Brown."

Think Beyond Why are people sometimes given nicknames?

GRAPHY · GEOGRAPHY · GEOGRAPHY · GEOGRAPHY · GEOGRAPHY · GEOGRAPHY · GEOGRAPHY · GE

SKILLS IN ACTION

READING LANDFORM MAPS

A **landform map** tells you about the shape of the land. It tells you where the mountains and hills are. It tells you where the **plains** and **plateaus** (pla•TOHZ) are. Plains are low, flat lands. Plateaus are usually high, flat lands. Different colors and markings on the map show you where these landforms are.

Look at the landform map of Kentucky.

Find the brown box in the map key. The color brown is used to show mountains. Now find the brown area on the map. What are these mountains called?

Much of the coal in Kentucky is found in the mountains. You have seen how much coal there is in the mountains near Pikeville. People in many Kentucky communities mine coal for a living.

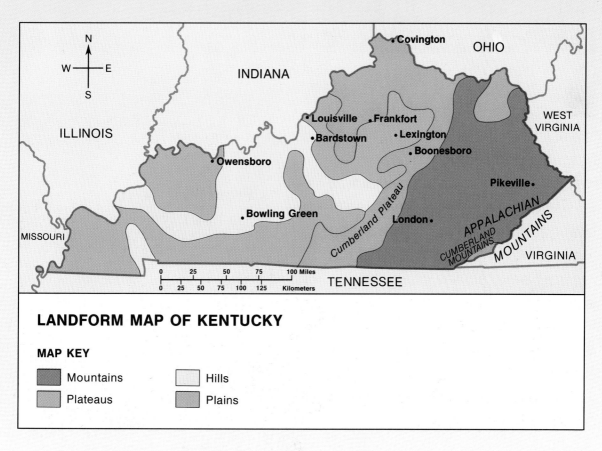

LANDFORM MAP OF KENTUCKY

MAP KEY

Mountains   Hills
Plateaus   Plains

111

Plains

Plateaus

Hills

Mountains

Hills are not as high as mountains. Look at the map key. What color is used to show hills?

Look at the map key again. It tells you that plateaus are colored orange. Plateaus often have steep sides. Their tops are flat. Find the orange area on the map. Which cities are on plateaus?

Look at the map key once more. What color is used for plains? Now find the plains on the map. Plains are lower than plateaus. Their land is flat, or gently rolling.

CHECKING YOUR SKILLS

Tell or write the answers to these questions.

1. Is Pikeville in the mountains or in the hills?

2. On what kind of land is Lexington?

3. What is the name of a plateau in Kentucky?

4. Which city is on higher land, Lexington or Boonesboro?

5. Which cities are in the plains?

112

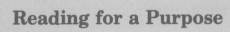
Look for these important words:

Key Words
- petroleum
- derrick

- drill
- valves
- refinery

Places
- Midland, Texas

Look for answers to these questions:

1. What are some of the jobs that people in an oil-drilling community do?
2. How do we use oil?
3. What happens in an oil refinery?

3 MIDLAND, TEXAS

Midland is a medium-sized city in Texas. It is a center for oil, ranching, and banking. The people in Midland enjoy living in their community. They like to use the many parks in Midland. People can swim, eat a picnic lunch, and play games at these parks.

Young people rehearse for a play at the Midland Community Theatre.

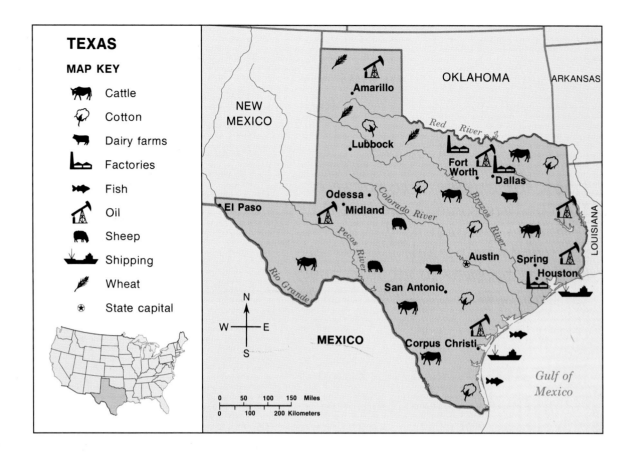

TEXAS

MAP KEY

Cattle
Cotton
Dairy farms
Factories
Fish
Oil
Sheep
Shipping
Wheat
State capital

The oil wells around Midland show you that this is an oil-drilling community. Oil was first found in Midland about 60 years ago. You know that oil is a mineral. Oil is also called **petroleum** (puh•TROH•lee•uhm).

Before oil was discovered, very few people lived in Midland. More people moved to Midland after oil was found. Many of these people went to work in the oil business. Some helped to drill for oil. Some found jobs at factories that make oil ready to use.

Many jobs in Midland depend on how much oil our country needs. If very little oil is needed, people in Midland may lose jobs. If a lot of oil is needed, new jobs will open up. Oil is important to Midland's future.

One interesting place to visit in Midland is the Petroleum Museum. The museum shows how oil was probably formed. It has some of the machines used to get oil long ago.

On the next pages you will meet a boy who lives in Midland, Texas. He knows a lot about oil and oil drilling. His mother works in the oil fields.

This picture shows the city of Midland. Midland is part of a large oil-producing area called the Permian Basin.

In front of the Permian Basin Petroleum Museum is an outdoor exhibit showing some of the machines used in oil drilling.

115

Al talks about oil.

At the Oil Museum

"Hi, my name is Al Kimball. I live in Midland. I want to tell you what I learned about oil at our museum.

"People at the museum said that oil, like coal, is a fuel. It makes energy when it is burned. In fact, petroleum gives us almost half the energy used in the world! We use oil to heat our homes. Oil is used to make gasoline for our cars. Oil is used to make the roads we drive on, too! We use oil to make many goods. Fertilizer, clothing, and plastic are just a few goods made with oil.

"One part of Midland's oil museum shows how scientists think oil began. Long ago, plants and animals lived in seas that covered much of the Earth. As they died, they fell to the bottom. Mud fell on them. Many years passed. More mud fell on them. Then the seas began to dry up. The heat and weight of the earth slowly changed the dead animals. Over a long time, they were changed into oil."

A guide shows Al and his class a museum exhibit. The exhibit shows layers of rock and sand from oil zones in the earth.

Drilling for Oil

"My mother drills for oil near Midland. I can tell you about her work.

"Mom works on a **derrick** in the oil fields. A derrick looks like a tall tower. It fits over an oil well. The derrick holds machines for drilling, lifting, and pumping oil.

"Once I went to see Mom at work. I saw her start the **drill.** A drill is made up of pieces of pipe. The drill makes a deep hole going down into the earth. The tip of the drill is called a drill bit.

"The bit turned as it went into the ground. The bit went down about 30 feet (9 m) each time. Then it stopped. I saw the workers pull the bit out. They added more pipe to make the drill longer. Then they started the drill again.

The machines and controls at an oil site must be checked often to make sure they are running smoothly.

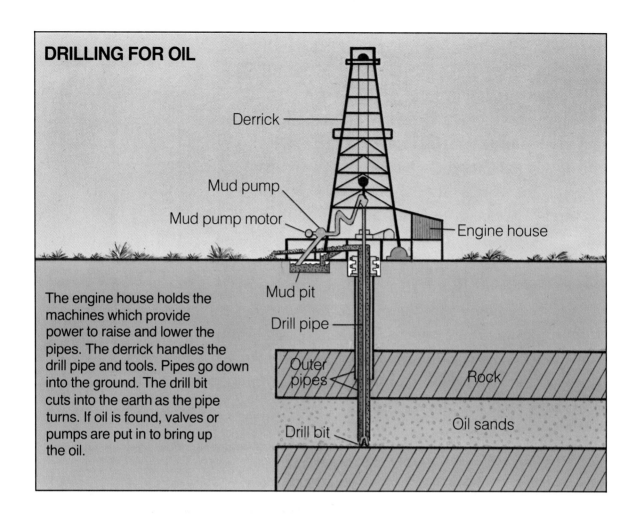

DRILLING FOR OIL

Derrick

Mud pump

Mud pump motor

Engine house

Mud pit

The engine house holds the machines which provide power to raise and lower the pipes. The derrick handles the drill pipe and tools. Pipes go down into the ground. The drill bit cuts into the earth as the pipe turns. If oil is found, valves or pumps are put in to bring up the oil.

Drill pipe

Outer pipes

Rock

Oil sands

Drill bit

"As the bit drilled down through rock, it got very hot. To cool the bit, the drillers pumped mud down the pipes and back up.

"No oil was found when I was there. Mom said the bit had to break through hard rock first. Then the drillers would have a good chance of finding some oil.

"Oil sometimes has water or gas mixed with it. Water or gas can make the oil come up too fast. Drillers put **valves** on the well to slow down the oil. A valve controls how fast a liquid flows.

"Oil sometimes does not come up fast enough. Then drillers use a pump. The pump pulls the oil up out of the well."

Oil at the Refinery

"I asked Mom what happens to oil after it is found. She said the oil goes through pipes or by trucks to a **refinery**. A refinery is a special kind of factory. Oil is made ready for different uses in a refinery. The refinery makes gasoline and motor oil for our cars. It makes heating oil for homes.

"Someday maybe I will drill for oil, too. It is not easy work, but I think it's exciting. It's like a science lesson and a treasure hunt, all in one."

There are many towers, tanks, and pipes at an oil refinery. Work at a refinery goes on day and night.

Reading Check

1. Why did a lot of people move to Midland?
2. How is a derrick used?

Think Beyond Why would a refinery keep working at night?

SKILLS IN ACTION

USING BAR GRAPHS

Sometimes you need to compare things quickly. Look at the shapes below.

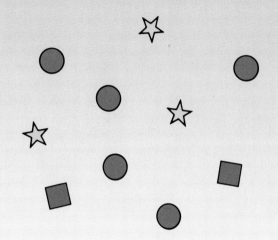

graph. The different shapes are shown across the bottom. The bars show how many of each shape there are.

Find the bar for the circles. Move your finger to the top of the bar. Then move your finger across to the number at the left. The bar comes up to the number 5. This tells you that there are five circles in the group.

Find the bar for the stars. How many stars are in the drawing?

Are there more circles than squares? How many stars are there? It is hard to answer these questions fast just by looking at the drawing.

One easy way to compare numbers of things is to look at a **bar graph.** A bar graph uses bars of different heights to show amounts of things. Look at the bar graph on the right.

The bar graph shows how many stars, squares, and circles are in the drawing. The numbers are shown along the left side of the

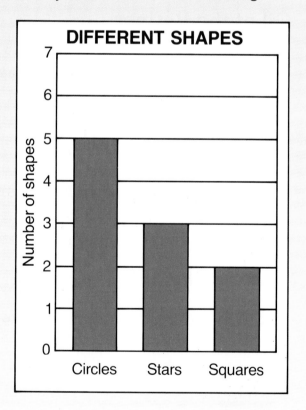

120

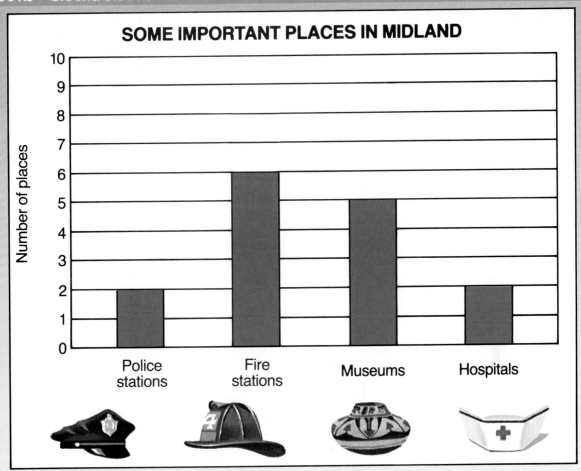

SOME IMPORTANT PLACES IN MIDLAND

A Bar Graph of Midland

Now look at another bar graph. This bar graph shows some important places in Midland. Most communities have these places.

Look at the bottom of the bar graph. It shows you police stations, fire stations, museums, and hospitals. The numbers on the left side of the graph show how many of each place there are in Midland.

What kind of place shown on the bar graph has the highest number?

CHECKING YOUR SKILLS

Use the bar graph to answer these questions.

1. Are there more fire stations or police stations in Midland?

2. How many hospitals are there in Midland?

3. How many museums are there in Midland?

4. How many fire stations are in Midland?

5. Are there more hospitals or museums in Midland?

121

Thinking Back

- The Earth gives us other natural resources called minerals. We use minerals in many different ways.

- Workers must dig mines to get solid minerals out of the ground. Workers drill wells for liquid minerals.

- Pikeville, Kentucky, is a coal-mining town in the mountains. Long ago, plants that lived there died and were pressed together to form coal under the ground.

- Miners in Pikeville use machines to dig tunnels to the coal and bring it out. The coal goes first to a factory to be washed and sorted. Then trains take it to other factories that use it to make energy and goods.

- Midland, Texas, is an oil-drilling community. Long ago, seas covered much of the surface of the Earth. Dead plants and animals became covered with mud and were pressed into oil, or petroleum.

- Workers in Midland drill deep into the ground for oil. The oil is taken to a refinery, where it is made ready for many different uses.

Check for Understanding

Using Words

Look at the words listed. Two tell about work in Pikeville. Two tell about work in Midland. One tells about work in both communities. Write the five words on a piece of paper. Write **P** beside each word that tells about Pikeville. Write **M** beside each word that tells about Midland. Write **B** beside the word that tells about both communities.

1. **mines**

2. **wells**

3. **derrick**

4. **factories**

5. **coal**

Reviewing Facts

1. Where do we find most of our mineral resources?

2. Why did the people in Pikeville change the path of the Levisa River?

3. How do coal miners make sure that tunnels and underground rooms are safe?

4. Why are valves important in oil drilling?

5. Name four products that are made from oil.

Thinking Critically

1. How are coal and oil important in your life? Think of three ways in which they help you meet your needs.

2. Pretend you are a store owner in an oil-drilling town. How do you depend on the oil workers in your community?

3. Machines are very important in mining. How do machines help make miners' jobs easier?

Writing About It

Write a description of a job that a person in an oil-drilling or coal-mining community might do.

 Practicing Graph Skills

Using Bar Graphs

Make a bar graph. Use it to show these things.

a. the number of chalkboard erasers in your classroom

b. the number of pencils you have in your desk

c. the number of books you have in your desk

 On Your Own

Social Studies at Home

Ask your family to name the things they did today that used energy. Now ask your family to name ways they could have saved energy.

Read More About It

About Garbage and Stuff by Ann Zane Shanks. Viking. Discover how much garbage can be recycled.

In Coal Country by Judith Hendershot. Alfred A. Knopf. A girl tells about life in a mining town.

See Inside an Oil Rig and Tanker by Jonathan Rutland. Warwick Press. Read about how people search and drill for oil.

CHAPTER 5

Port Communities

"I never even hear
The boats that pass by day;
By night they seem so near,
A-whistling down the bay,
That I can almost understand
The things their whistles say."

—from the poem "Whistles" by Rachel Field

Look for these important words:

Key Words
- salt water
- fresh water
- dam

- transportation
- harbor
- port

Look for answers to these questions:
1. Why do our water resources need to be protected?
2. How do people use water to make a living?
3. Why do people build communities near bodies of water?

1 WATER AND OUR COMMUNITIES

There are two kinds of water, **salt water** and **fresh water.** The water in oceans is salt water. People cannot drink salt water.

The water in most lakes and rivers is fresh. Rain water is also fresh. People must have fresh water to drink. The water people need in homes and businesses is fresh, too.

Often, people build cities and towns near bodies of water. Then they can use the water to meet their needs.

Using Water

How many ways do people use water at home? We use water for drinking and cooking. We use it to keep plants and gardens healthy. We wash clothes and dishes with water. We wash ourselves with water, too.

This water was ruined because people did not care for it.

People have cared for this water. It has stayed beautiful.

How much water do you think you use in a day? You may use more than you think. In the United States, each person uses about 70 gallons (260 L) a day. That much water would almost fill two bathtubs!

Water is a natural resource that we need to save. We need to use it wisely. We need to save water because some areas do not have enough. In other places the water has become dirty and cannot be used.

Our water resources also need to be protected. In the past, people have spoiled rivers and lakes. They threw things into them and did not care for them. In the last few years, government and citizens groups have formed. The groups work to protect our nation's rivers and lakes.

There are many important reasons to save and protect our water supply. One reason is that many people use water to make a living. In some areas farmers do not get enough rain to grow crops. In these areas farmers must irrigate. This water for irrigation comes from rivers, lakes, and wells. It is important that there is enough water for our crops. It is also important that the water used to grow our crops is clean. People might become sick if the water used for crops is unclean.

Factories need water, too. Factories in the United States use water more than any other resource. To make just one car, a factory uses 15,000 gallons (57,000 L) of water. That much water would fill about 400 bathtubs.

Water also gives us energy for our homes. Water from a **dam** can be used to make electricity. A dam is a wall built across a river or a lake. The wall lets water rush through it. The rushing water turns machines. These machines make electricity.

The High Gorge Dam goes across the Skagit River, in the Cascade Mountains of Washington.

People go river rafting on the Ocoee River in Tennessee. They wear helmets to protect themselves if the raft tips over.

It is also important to care about water because we use it to have fun. Some of our favorite times are on water. We can swim and fish in water. We can ice-skate on a frozen lake. We may enjoy going to an ocean beach.

Communities Near Water

For thousands of years people have chosen to live near water. Some communities have been built near the ocean so people could catch fish for food. Cities are often built near lakes or rivers so that factories can have fresh water to use.

Many towns and cities built near water have become **transportation** centers. Transportation means moving people or things from one place to another. Transportation centers are communities that depend on transportation for many jobs.

Why are cities near water transportation centers? The answer is that water makes it easy to move heavy loads. It takes many railroad cars to move a huge load of coal over land. It also takes a lot of fuel. Yet the same amount of coal can be moved on one ship, using less fuel.

A **harbor** is a protected place where ships or boats can stay. Ships are safe from high waves and strong winds in harbors.

A **port** is a community where ships dock. You will read more about some important port cities in the next pages.

Boats traveling along Alaska's coast often stop at the harbor of Petersburg, Alaska.

Reading Check

1. How can water give us energy for our homes?
2. Why are some cities built near water?

Think Beyond What would you do if you saw someone wasting water?

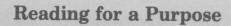

Look for these important words:

Key Words
- cargo
- containers
- canal

Places
- Chicago, Illinois

- Lake Michigan
- Great Lakes
- Mississippi River
- St. Lawrence Seaway

Look for answers to these questions:

1. What are some of the groups of people who live in Chicago?
2. What made Chicago grow?
3. What is the St. Lawrence Seaway?

2 CHICAGO, ILLINOIS

People have fun sailing their boats on Lake Michigan.

Chicago, Illinois, is a big, busy city. It is in the middle of a large farming area. Many of the crops grown nearby are moved through Chicago. Chicago is an important transportation center.

Chicago is a port city. Chicago is on the shore of **Lake Michigan.** Lake Michigan is one of the five large lakes called the **Great Lakes.** There are also several rivers in and near Chicago.

Goods can be shipped out of Chicago on many waterways. From Chicago, goods are shipped from the Great Lakes to the **Mississippi River.** They are shipped on the **St. Lawrence Seaway** to the Atlantic Ocean.

Chicago has almost 30 miles (48 km) of land along the shore of Lake Michigan. Much of the land next to the lake is parkland. People like to use the beaches and playing fields there.

Like other big cities, Chicago has many kinds of jobs for people. Many of them have to do with the water resources nearby. Some people work in shipping. Others work in different kinds of transportation. There are many other businesses in Chicago, too.

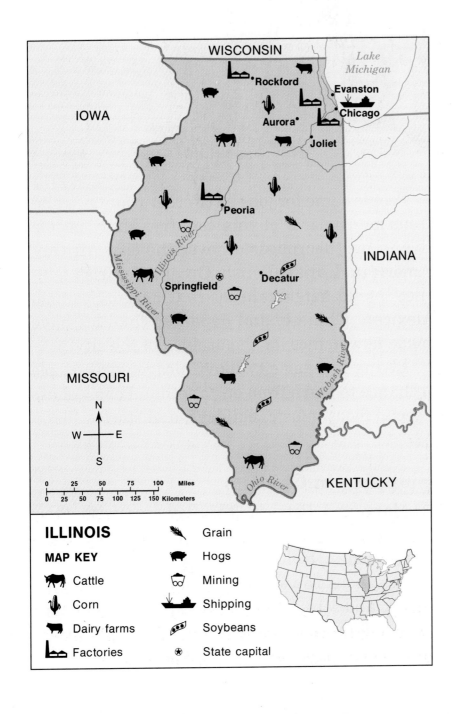

ILLINOIS

MAP KEY

🐂 Cattle
🌽 Corn
🐄 Dairy farms
🏭 Factories
🌾 Grain
🐖 Hogs
⛏ Mining
🚢 Shipping
🫘 Soybeans
✹ State capital

On the left, Polish Americans in Chicago dance in a parade. On the right, African-American students carry flags in a Columbus Day parade.

People came for jobs from other countries and from many parts of this country. Many people live in neighborhoods all over the city. African-American, Italian, Polish, Greek, and Irish families live in neighborhoods in Chicago. Spanish, Mexican, Chinese, and Japanese families have made new homes for themselves in the city.

Living in a big city like Chicago gives people a chance to learn from one another. People share special foods, music, holidays, and stories.

Shipping in Chicago

Mary and Patrick O'Malley live with their parents in Chicago. Mary and Patrick's parents were born in Ireland. They came to the United States about 15 years ago.

Mr. and Mrs. O'Malley work. Today, they took time off from work to show Chicago to their nephew Mike. Mike is visiting from Ohio.

"How did Chicago get to be so big?" asked Mike.

"Shipping and other kinds of transportation made it grow," said Mr. O'Malley. "We want to show you Lake Calumet. It is our biggest harbor."

Mrs. O'Malley told Mike about shipping today. "**Cargo** ships are important in Chicago. Cargo is goods carried on ships or planes. There has been a big change in cargo shipping. Instead of loading goods one at a time, shippers can now pack things into large steel boxes. These boxes are called **containers.** Containers are easily moved from a ship to a train or a truck."

"What is shipped from Chicago?" asked Mike.

"Crops are shipped from here. Steel is shipped from here. So are many goods made in our factories. Much of the cargo goes through Canada on the St. Lawrence Seaway."

At Lake Calumet, the O'Malley family saw containers being loaded onto cargo ships.

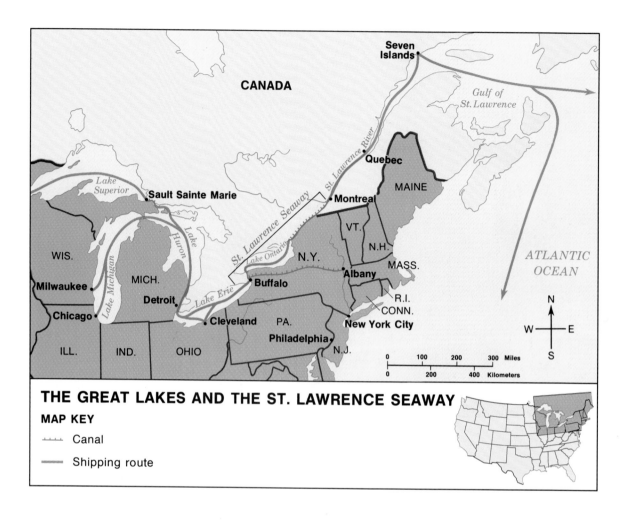

THE GREAT LAKES AND THE ST. LAWRENCE SEAWAY

MAP KEY

⊢⊢⊢⊢ Canal

——— Shipping route

The St. Lawrence Seaway

"Is the St. Lawrence Seaway a **canal**?" asked Mike. "I know that canals are people-made waterways. They are used by ships and boats."

"No, the St. Lawrence Seaway is not just a canal. The seaway is made up of the St. Lawrence River and lakes, canals, and dams. It helps join the Atlantic Ocean and the Great Lakes."

Reading Check

1. Name some waterways near Chicago.
2. Why are containers used in cargo shipping?

Think Beyond How did the opening of the St. Lawrence Seaway change Chicago?

People MAKE HISTORY

Do you collect stamps? The United States Post Office sold this stamp in 1987. The man on the stamp is Jean Baptiste Pointe du Sable (ZHAHN bap•TEEST PWANT du SAHB•luh). He was one of the first settlers to live in the area that became Chicago. Du Sable settled there about 200 years ago. He was an African American.

The site Du Sable chose for building his house and trading post was on a well-traveled route. Native Americans, trappers, and missionaries passed through the area. They often needed supplies. Du Sable knew his trading post could help meet their needs.

In 1800 Du Sable sold his property in Chicago and moved to Missouri. The list of his buildings and goods at this time showed he had become a very wealthy man. People who met him described him as honest and very well educated.

Today the city of Chicago remembers this early settler. The Du Sable Museum of African American History—the oldest museum of its kind in the country—honors his name.

Think Beyond   Why do you think a great city grew up around Du Sable's trading post?

Jean Baptiste Pointe Du Sable
22
Black Heritage USA

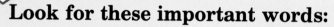
Look for these important words:

Key Words
- location

Places
- O'Hare International Airport

Look for answers to these questions:
1. What does "location" mean?
2. How do crops get from farms to Chicago?
3. What kinds of transportation make Chicago the busiest transportation center in our country?

3 TRAINS, TRUCKS, AND PLANES

"Shipping is important in Chicago. Yet that is only part of Chicago's story," Patrick O'Malley said to Mike. "Chicago is a center for other kinds of transportation, too. That is because of Chicago's **location** (loh•KAY•shuhn). Location means where something is. Chicago is located near the middle of our country.

"Goods go from the East through Chicago to the West. Goods also go from the West to the East through Chicago. Steel for building, foods, and goods made in factories are just a few of the things carried into and out of Chicago. These goods are carried by trucks, trains, and planes."

"How do crops get from the farms to Chicago?" Mike asked.

136

"Railroads are one way to carry food from the farms to Chicago. Railroads are an important kind of transportation," said Mr. O'Malley.

"Chicago is the biggest railroad center in the United States," said Mrs. O'Malley. "Trains carry all kinds of goods into and out of Chicago."

At the railroad station, the O'Malleys saw containers being taken off trucks and loaded onto railroad cars.

Trucking in Chicago

"I see a lot of trucks on the road here," said Mike as the O'Malleys drove along.

"That is because Chicago is the busiest trucking center in America. Many goods are sent by truck into and out of Chicago," said Mrs. O'Malley.

137

Containers are taken off trucks and loaded onto planes at O'Hare International Airport.

Planes in Chicago

Mike pointed to the sky. "Where are all the planes going?" he asked.

"They are landing at O'Hare," said Patrick. "Our **O'Hare International Airport** in Chicago is the busiest airport in the world. More people and goods go through O'Hare than any other airport."

 Reading Check

1. Where is Chicago located?
2. How did Chicago's location help the city become a transportation center?

Think Beyond Why do you think trucks and trains work together to move goods?

SKILLS IN ACTION

FINDING ROUTES

A **route** is a way to get from one place to another. A route can be a river, a road, a railroad, or even a bicycle path.

Look at the route map below. It shows routes between cities. The map key tells you what the symbols stand for. Find the symbol for railroads. It is ⊞⊞⊞. Find the railroad on the map. It connects Brownsville and Blue City.

Find the Snail River. Brownsville and Greenville are near this river. You could travel between these two cities by boat. What other route connects Brownsville and Greenville?

Find Red Rock. The only way to get to Red Rock is to take Highland Road north from Brownsville. How could you get from Greenville to Red Rock?

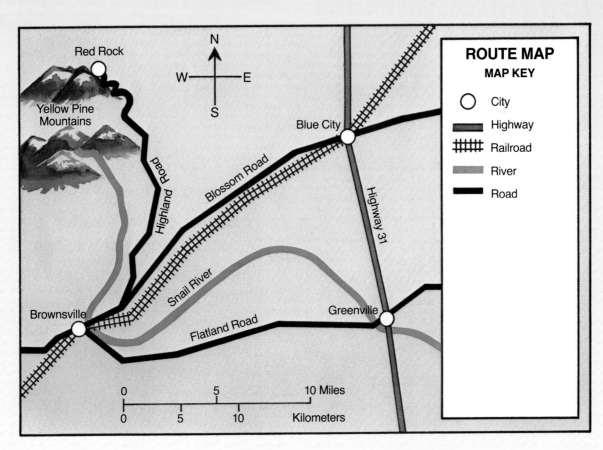

139

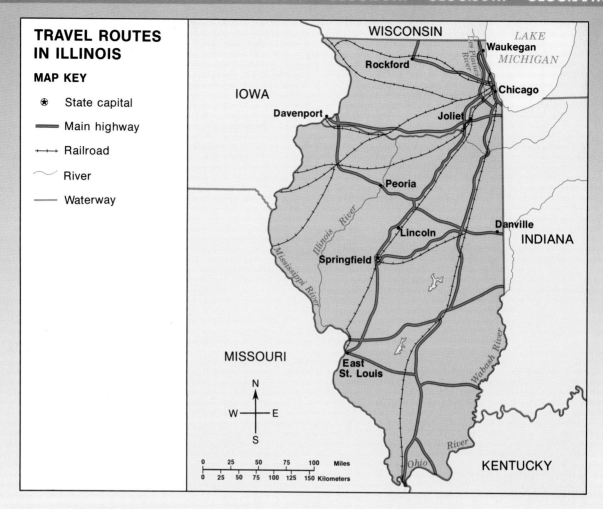

TRAVEL ROUTES IN ILLINOIS

MAP KEY

✸ State capital
━━ Main highway
┼─┼─┼ Railroad
∿ River
── Waterway

Travel Routes in Illinois

The map above shows some travel routes in Illinois. Find Chicago on the map. Railroads, highways, and waterways go to and from Chicago. Waterways are made up of rivers and canals.

Find Joliet on the map. The map shows ways to go from Chicago to Joliet. You could take a train, or you could take a boat on the Des Plaines River. You could also go by car.

CHECKING YOUR SKILLS

Use the route map to help you answer these questions.

1. What kinds of routes run between Chicago and Rockford?

2. What are two ways to get from Chicago to Springfield?

3. If you took the railroad north from Springfield, what city would you reach?

4. How could you ship goods from East Saint Louis to Peoria?

140

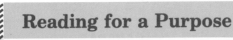
Look for these important words:

Key Words
- coast
- ferryboats

Places
- Seattle, Washington
- Puget Sound
- Olympic Mountains
- Cascade Mountains

Look for answers to these questions:
1. What is a coast?
2. Where are many goods from Seattle shipped?
3. What kinds of jobs can people in Seattle do?

4 SEATTLE, WASHINGTON

Seattle is the largest city in **Washington.** Washington is a state on the west **coast** of our country. A coast is land next to an ocean. Washington is next to the Pacific Ocean.

Seattle and the land around it are beautiful. The mild, wet climate keeps trees and fields green most of the year.

Seattle is a port city. Seattle is located on a natural harbor in **Puget Sound** (PYOO•juht SOWND). Puget Sound is a part of the Pacific Ocean. Seattle also sits between the **Olympic Mountains** and the **Cascade Mountains.**

There are many places to have fun in Seattle. People like to go to the Space Needle. The top of this tall tower turns slowly, like a wheel. People can eat lunch there and watch the changing view. Later they can go to the Pike Place Market. There they find outdoor sidewalk shops. They can buy fresh things like flowers, fish, and fruit.

The Space Needle was built in 1962 to honor astronauts' first trip in space around the Earth.

141

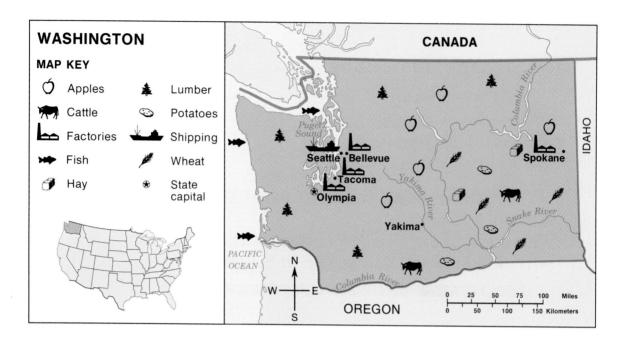

WASHINGTON

MAP KEY

🍎 Apples   🌲 Lumber

🐄 Cattle   🥔 Potatoes

🏭 Factories   🚢 Shipping

🐟 Fish   🌾 Wheat

🌱 Hay   ✳ State capital

CANADA

IDAHO

Puget Sound

Seattle • Bellevue

Columbia River

• Tacoma

Yakima River

✳ Olympia

Spokane

Snake River

Yakima •

PACIFIC OCEAN

Columbia River

N W E S

OREGON

| 0 | 25 | 50 | 75 | 100 | Miles |
| 0 | 50 | 100 | 150 | Kilometers |

Many people who live in Seattle love the water. On a nice weekend thousands of boats are out on Lake Washington, to the east of Seattle. Every August there is a big celebration called Seafair. People come from all over to join in the fun.

On opening day of yachting season, Union Bay is crowded with people on boats.

142

Ships and Boats in Seattle

Many goods shipped in and out of Seattle come from or go to the country of Japan. Goods also come from or go to the state of Alaska. Seattle's location near the Pacific Ocean makes this possible.

Most of the ships that come to Seattle carry cargo in containers. Seattle is one of this country's four busiest container ports.

Passenger ships and huge **ferryboats** dock in Seattle, too. Ferryboats are boats that carry people and cars. Ferryboats from Seattle go to islands in Puget Sound and to ports in British Columbia, Canada.

A ferryboat loaded with passengers from Seattle is on its way to Vancouver, Canada.

Making airplanes is one of the most important businesses in Seattle.
Workers put the airplanes together in huge buildings.

There are many different jobs for people living in Seattle. The biggest company in Seattle makes very large airplanes.

Other people in Seattle work for companies that make railroad cars or ships. Still others work to make fish or wood ready to use.

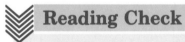

Reading Check

1. What mountains are near Seattle?
2. Why do many goods from Seattle go to Japan?

Think Beyond Why do ferryboats go from Seattle to the islands in Puget Sound?

144

IN FOCUS

LIGHTHOUSES

For almost as long as there have been people sailing on the seas, there have been lighthouses. Lighthouses are used to warn sailors of dangerous rocks and reefs. They also help guide ships into ports.

Early lighthouses were poles placed on top of towers. The poles held metal baskets in which coal or wood was burned. Later, wicks dipped in oil were used to provide light.

Lighthouse keepers kept the lights burning. They climbed the towers each evening to light the oil lamps. They had to climb them again in the morning to put out the burning wicks. Today most lighthouses operate without keepers. They use radio signals to send their warnings. The lights are powered by electricity.

Today the West Point Lighthouse uses radio signals and automatic lights to warn ships.

Seattle's harbor, known as Elliott Bay, has two old lighthouses—West Point and Alki Point. For many years their friendly lights have helped ships move through the island-filled waters of Puget Sound into Elliott Bay.

In 1981 the community of Seattle celebrated the one-hundredth anniversary of the West Point Lighthouse. People recalled the old days and the former lighthouse keepers. They especially remembered one family who lived there with nine children, four dogs, and a cat named Fred. If you visit Seattle, you can go to see the lighthouses.

Think Beyond Lighthouses help protect ships at sea. What things help protect automobile drivers from dangers along the road?

The Alki Point Lighthouse is near the place where Seattle's first European settlers landed.

One of the duties of the lighthouse keeper is to change the lamp when it burns out.

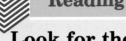
Look for these important words:

Key Words
- industries
- lumber
- sawmill

Look for answers to these questions:

1. How do machines help people in the lumber industry?
2. What happens to lumber in a sawmill?
3. What are some kinds of fish caught near Seattle?

5 LUMBER AND FISHING IN SEATTLE

In the next pages, you will read more about work in Seattle. You will visit a classroom in Seattle. Students in Mr. Drake's class will talk about two **industries** (IN•duhs•treez) in Seattle. Industries are big businesses.

The Lumber Industry in Seattle

"The **lumber** industry is very important in Seattle," said Mr. Drake. "Lumber is wood that is sawed and used to make goods. Sam, can you tell us about Seattle's lumber industry?"

"The first industry in Seattle was cutting and shipping logs," said Sam. "Trees were cut down with handsaws. The logs were rolled or dragged to a river. They were then chained together in a big raft. The raft was floated to the **sawmill.**

Mr. Drake's class talks about important industries in Seattle.

147

Sam talks about lumber.

Wood chips fly as a worker saws a tree. On the right, logs are pushed down the river to the sawmill.

A sawmill is a factory at the edge of the river in a logging area. At the sawmill big saws cut the logs into boards."

"How are trees cut down today?" asked Mr. Drake.

"People use chain saws to cut them. Chain saws have motors. Chain saws cut down trees much faster than handsaws. Tractors pull the logs out of the forest. Then most of the logs are put on trucks. The trucks take them to sawmills near Seattle.

"Trucks and tractors have made a big difference in the lumber industry. Yet some of the logs are still chained together and floated down to the sawmill.

"At the sawmill, very strong sprays of water wash the logs and take off the bark. Huge electric saws cut the logs into lumber. The lumber is used for things like fences, houses, and other buildings.

"Sawdust and wood chips come from sawing the wood. These are used to make things like paper and cloth."

"Where does the lumber go from the sawmill?" asked one student.

"Much of it is shipped in containers to other countries," answered Sam. "Some of it is used for houses and other buildings in the United States."

At the sawmill, huge saws cut through logs. The picture on the right shows the cut lumber.

The Fishing Industry in Seattle

Lynn talks about the fishing industry in Seattle.

Mr. Drake asked Lynn to tell the class what she knew about Seattle's fishing industry.

"There are hundreds of big fishing boats that work from Seattle," Lynn began. "Many of these boats bring back salmon (SAM•uhn). Salmon live most of their lives in the ocean. Then they swim back up rivers to the place they were born.

"Many of the boats from Seattle go all the way to Alaska," Lynn continued. "Some bring back crabs. Others catch halibut, a large fish."

GEOGRAPHY CONNECTION

Salmon are born in freshwater streams. The young fish swim downstream to the ocean to feed and to grow big. Then they return to the place where they were born to lay their eggs.

For many years the salmon had only to fight the strong river currents to swim upstream to where they were born. They could leap over waterfalls as high as ten feet. Now large dams have been built across the rivers. Salmon cannot leap up the steep spillways. They need help.

To help the salmon swim past the dams, people have built special kinds of ladders. The ladders are like a series of pools. Each pool is slightly higher than the next one. On very high dams fish elevators have been built. Now salmon can continue their long journey to lay their eggs.

150

At Seattle's Pike Place Market, shopkeepers offer crab and other seafood fresh from the Pacific Ocean.

"How are fish caught?" a student asked.

"Each kind of fish may be caught in a different way," Lynn replied. "Sometimes huge nets are used. Long lines with bait and hooks are also used."

"What happens to the fish after they are caught?" asked another student.

"Some of the fish are sold fresh in our stores. Many of the salmon are frozen in Seattle. Some are put in cans here, too. The fish are sent to all parts of our country. Many frozen or canned fish are shipped to other countries, like Japan."

 Reading Check

1. Why does Seattle have many sawmills?
2. What happens to fish after they are caught?

Think Beyond Why is it important to use paper wisely?

SKILLS IN ACTION

USING FLOW CHARTS

Suppose you are going to give your dog a bath. You must do some things before you do others.

First, brush the dog to get rid of extra hair. Next, get a tub and fill it with water. Then, put the dog in the tub and get the dog wet. Scrub the dog with soap. Now rinse the dog. Last, take the dog out of the tub and dry the dog off.

These steps need to be done in order. If you dry the dog before rinsing the soap off, you will have a soapy, itchy dog.

Many things have steps that must be done in order. The right order can be shown in a **flow chart.** A flow chart has arrows to show the order of steps. To read this chart, just follow the arrows.

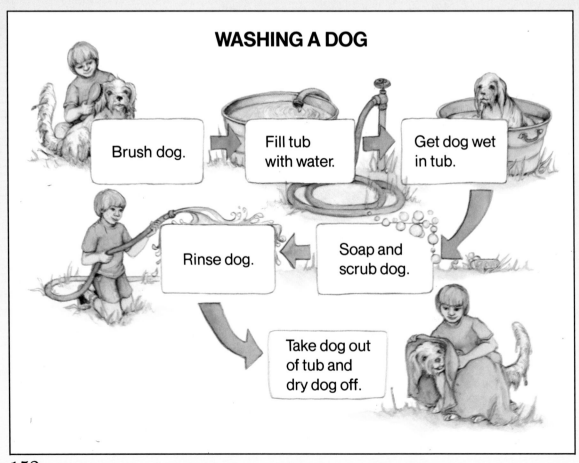

WASHING A DOG

Brush dog.

Fill tub with water.

Get dog wet in tub.

Rinse dog.

Soap and scrub dog.

Take dog out of tub and dry dog off.

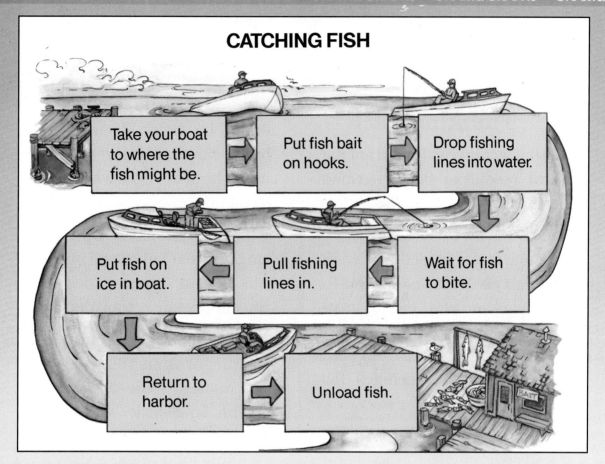

CATCHING FISH

A Flow Chart for Fishing

The second flow chart shows the steps to take to catch fish. In Seattle's fishing industry, many workers take these steps. Follow the arrows and read the chart.

Find the box that says "Drop fishing lines." Follow the arrow from this box to the box below it. What does it say? The arrows in the second row go in the opposite direction from the first line of the chart. Reading this flow chart is a little like following a path that goes back and forth.

CHECKING YOUR SKILLS

Use the flow chart "Catching Fish" to answer these questions.

1. What is the first step in catching fish?

2. What is the second step in catching fish?

3. What must you do before you wait for the fish to bite?

4. Which comes first, putting the fish on ice in the boat or pulling in the fishing lines?

5. What must be done after all the fish have been put on ice?

153

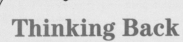
Thinking Back

- Clean water is an important natural resource. People cannot drink the ocean's salt water. People need fresh water.

- People must protect their water resources. Water is needed for drinking and washing, for growing crops, and for making goods. Water power from dams on rivers runs machines that make electricity.

- People build communities near water so they can move goods easily by boat. Factories are built near lakes or rivers so they have the fresh water they need to make goods.

- Chicago, Illinois, is a port city on the Great Lakes and near the Mississippi River. Chicago is an important transportation center.

- Seattle, Washington, is a port city on the Pacific Ocean. Many people in Seattle work in the fishing, lumbering, and aircraft building industries.

Check for Understanding

Using Words

Number your paper from 1 to 5. Match the words with their correct meanings.

1. **industries**

2. **transportation**

3. **canal**

4. **cargo**

5. **port**

a. moving people or things from one place to another

b. a community where ships dock

c. goods carried on ships or planes

d. people-made waterway used by ships and boats

e. big businesses

Reviewing Facts

1. How is water used in people's homes?

2. Name four things that different groups of people can share in a city.

3. What are Chicago's important kinds of transportation?

4. What are three important industries in Seattle?

5. How has the lumber industry in Seattle changed over the years?

Thinking Critically

1. Big loads are moved more easily and cheaply by boats than by trains or trucks. Why do you think all big loads are not moved by boats?

2. How does being near water help Seattle's industries? How does it help the industries in Chicago?

3. Does your community have lakes or an ocean nearby? If so, how do you think they help the community?

Writing About It

Write a description of Chicago or some other port community for the travel section of your newspaper. Make sure your description tells about places that would be interesting to visitors.

 Practicing Chart Skills

Using Flow Charts

Think about something you do every day. Make a flow chart that shows how you do it.

On Your Own

Social Studies at Home

Draw a map that shows your home and a building you know on a nearby street. Show a route for walking from your home to this building. Use the symbol • • • • •. Then show a route for driving from your home to this building. Use the symbol — — — — .

Read More About It

Life on a Fishing Boat: A Sketchbook by Huck Scarry. Prentice-Hall. Drawings by the author, show different types of boats and fish and the jobs to be done on a fishing boat.

Lumberjack by William Kurelek. Houghton Mifflin. Learn about a lumberjack's life some years ago.

Truck Song by Diane Siebert. T. Y. Crowell. Ride with a truck driver on a cross-country trip.

Why People Work

Pretend that you have a huge piggy bank at home. It is filled with wonderful coins. What could you buy with them? Would that shiny penny buy a bicycle? Would that brand-new quarter buy a pair of boots? Of course not! You know that because you know the **value** (VAL•yoo) of the coins. Value is how much something is worth.

Suppose you buy something for ten dollars. You are trading your ten dollars for something having the same value as ten dollars.

Some of the things people buy are **goods.** Goods are things like food, clothing, roller skates, and washing machines. Goods are things that you can see and touch. Sometimes people buy **services.** Services include piano lessons, car repairs, haircuts, or checkups with the doctor. Services are jobs you pay someone else to do for you.

How People Use Money

People work to earn money that they can use to buy goods and services. The money people get is called **income.** We use our income to meet our needs and wants.

Needs are things we must have in order to stay alive. Food, clothing, and shelter are needs. Wants are those things we would like to have but can do without. Pets, bicycles, and vacations are all wants. Can you think of any other wants?

People usually spend a lot of their income on their needs. Then they try to put aside, or save, a little money. People often keep their money in banks.

The money people set aside is called **savings.** Savings are "just in case" money. Sometimes a person needs money because something unexpected happens. Savings can also be used for college or to buy a house.

The money that people do not save or spend on needs is used for wants. People decide what they want to buy with this money.

Tinker, An Auto Mechanic

Tinker is an auto mechanic. An auto mechanic fixes cars and makes sure they run well. Tinker gives the service of fixing cars. She makes an income from this service. Tinker likes her work. It is a way for her to be active and useful. It also makes her feel that she is helping her community. These are good things that she gets from her job in addition to the money.

Tinker is a **producer** (pruh•DOO•suhr) when she is working at the garage. Producers make goods or give services. The service Tinker gives is fixing other people's cars.

Tinker spends much of her income on her needs. She needs to eat, so she buys good food. For clothing, she buys coveralls for work and nice

clothes for parties and other special times. She uses a big part of her income to pay rent for her apartment.

Once Tinker's needs are met, she can buy other things. She might buy flowers for her apartment. She also likes to see movies. When Tinker spends money, she is a **consumer** (kuhn•SOO•muhr). This means she is buying goods or services.

The money Tinker has not spent at the end of the month goes into her savings. It will be there for her to use if she needs it.

The money that consumers pay for goods or services goes to the producers. When producers spend the money they have made, they become consumers. It is all a big circle, with money going from consumer to producer and back again.

PRODUCERS AND CONSUMERS

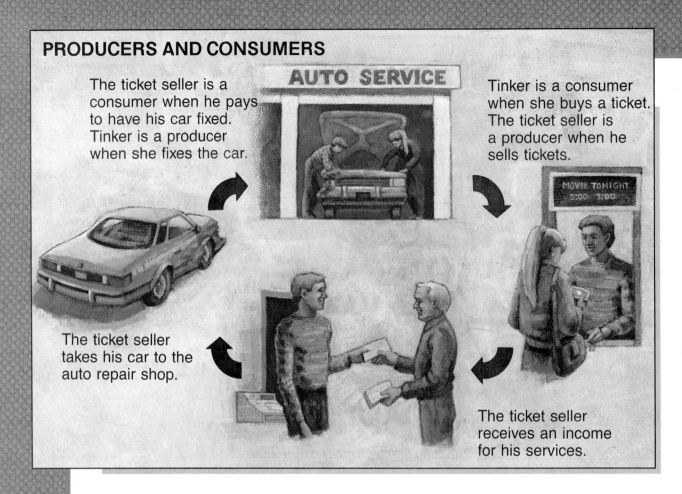

The ticket seller is a consumer when he pays to have his car fixed. Tinker is a producer when she fixes the car.

AUTO SERVICE

Tinker is a consumer when she buys a ticket. The ticket seller is a producer when he sells tickets.

MOVIE TONIGHT 5:00 7:00

The ticket seller takes his car to the auto repair shop.

The ticket seller receives an income for his services.

How Economics Works

We can show this information in a flow chart. The flow chart shows how **economics** (eh•kuh•NAHM•ihks) works in our country. Economics means how our goods, services, and money are traded back and forth.

Look at the flow chart. Tinker is a producer when she fixes the ticket seller's car. When is Tinker a consumer? What is she buying?

The ticket seller is a producer when he sells Tinker a ticket to the movie. When is the ticket seller a consumer?

Unit Review

WORDS TO REMEMBER

Number your paper from 1 to 10. Use the words below to fill in the blanks. Use each word only once.

containers   harbor
dairy farms   industries
energy   natural resources
fuels   refinery
goods   transportation

1. Air, soil, and water are ____ .

2. ____ are people-made things such as paper and glass.

3. Cows are raised for their milk on ____ .

4. ____ give off heat when they are burned.

5. ____ is power that makes things work.

6. Oil goes through pipes or by trucks to a ____ .

7. Shipping and railroads are important kinds of ____ in the city of Chicago.

8. Ships and boats are safe in a ____ .

9. Goods are often packed into large steel boxes called ____ .

10. Fishing and lumber are important ____ in Seattle.

FOCUS ON MAIN IDEAS

1. How do people use natural resources?

2. How are all farms alike?

3. What is a farming community?

4. Name some things that happen to milk at a creamery.

5. How do workers in a mining community depend on one another to meet their needs?

6. How do we use mineral resources?

7. How do we get oil?

8. Why is it important for us to have clean, fresh water?

9. What are some important industries in Chicago? Why are these industries important to other communities in our country?

10. Name two big industries in Seattle. Why are they important both to Seattle and to other parts of our country?

THINK/WRITE

Interdependence describes the way that people depend upon one another. Choose a miner or a farmer and write a paragraph on how you depend upon these workers. How do they depend on other workers?

ACTIVITIES

1. **Art**   What new kind of transportation might be invented someday? Draw a picture of how it might look.

2. **Making a List**   Think of all the ways you use water. Make a list of everything you would not be able to do without water.

3. **Make Up a Quiz**   Make up ten true or false questions about what you have read in this unit. Give your test to another student in your class.

SKILLS REVIEW

1. **Landform Maps**   Look at the landform map in the Atlas in the back of this book. Then answer these questions.

a. Are most of the plateaus in the eastern or in the western part of our country?

b. Name three states on the west coast of our country that have mountains.

c. What mountains stretch across West Virginia?

2. Finding Routes

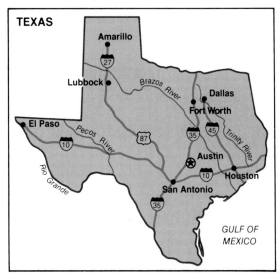

a. If you took I-45 south from Dallas, what city would you reach?

b. Could you travel to Austin from Fort Worth by boat?

c. Which highway connects El Paso with San Antonio?

3. **Flow Charts**   Make a flow chart showing the steps in coal mining or tomato growing.

EXPLORING
YOUR COMMUNITY

In this unit you read about a farming community, an oil-drilling community, and a coal-mining community. You found out communities have different kinds of natural resources. Use the following activities to learn about your community's natural resources.

MAKING A NATURAL RESOURCE MURAL

1. Work with other students to find out about natural resources near your community. Make a class mural showing people working with resources.

TAKING A FIELD TRIP

2. Write to or visit a farm, factory, or other business in your community. Find out how natural resources are used there. Write a report telling what you learned.

MAKING A POSTER

3. Make a poster telling people why they should recycle cans, bottles, and newspapers.

MAKING A TABLE

4. On a separate piece of paper, complete the table below.

	STATE	RESOURCES
Your Community		
Midland		
Seattle	Washington	Lumber

MAKING A RESOURCE MAP

5. Draw a map of your state. Then on your map draw symbols for crops and animals raised near your community.

LEARNING ABOUT WATER

6. Think of ways in which water is used for fun in your community. Draw pictures of people having fun in or near the water.

LEARNING ABOUT TRANSPORTATION

7. Look at a transportation map of your state. Make a list of the railroads, airports, or major highways that connect your community to other places.

UNIT 3

COMMUNITY GOVERNMENTS AND SERVICES

Community Facts and Figures

Location	Santa Rosa, California	Newfane, Vermont	Washington, D. C.
Population (estimated)	109,000	1,500	626,000
Landmark	Fountaingrove Round Barn	The Newfane Commons	Lincoln Memorial
Nickname/Motto	The City Designed for Living		The Capital City

Look at the picture. School buses are just one of the services a community provides for the people who live there. Many people work to see that people in the community have the services they need. Other people help make sure that the rules of a community are obeyed.

In this unit you will see how communities make rules. You will also read about the many services that communities provide. You will see how people work together to make communities run smoothly.

Think Beyond How would not having school buses make life different in your community?

Location	Orlando, Florida	Durham, North Carolina
Population (estimated)	146,000	114,000
Landmark	Lake Eola Fountain	Duke Chapel
Nickname/Motto	The City Beautiful	City of Medicine

CHAPTER 6

Communities Have Rules and Governments

"I therefore believe it is my duty to my country to love it; to support its Constitution; to obey its laws; to respect its flag; and to defend it against all enemies."

—from "The American's Creed"
by William Tyler Page

Look for these important words:

Key Words
- responsible
- detour
- laws
- citizens

Places
- Santa Rosa, California

Look for answers to these questions:
1. How do rules help people?
2. Why are many rules the same around the country?
3. What do we call the rules that communities make?

1 RULES IN COMMUNITIES

Rules help people know what to do. When you are riding a bicycle, you know you should stop at a red light. If you do not stop, you might run into a car or a person. Someone could get hurt. Other people count on you to be **responsible** (rih•SPON•suh•bil). Responsible means following rules.

People in communities everywhere obey rules. Many rules are the same around the country. Because many rules are the same, people know what they should do in different places. If you went to a community in another state, you would know to stop at a red light. You would also know that you should cross the street when the light turns green.

When people obey rules, it helps everyone in the community. Now let's look at how people obey rules in a medium-sized city in California.

Santa Rosa, California

Mary Pang and her mother live in **Santa Rosa, California.** Santa Rosa is a city in northern California. There are many new businesses in Santa Rosa. There are redwood forests nearby. People grow fields of grapes in the area around the city.

Mary and her mother have just been shopping in downtown Santa Rosa. Now they are driving home from the store. Suddenly, Mrs. Pang stops the car. Mary sees that the road is blocked. A sign says that there is a **detour** (DEE•toor).

"What does 'detour' mean?" Mary asks.

"It means we will have to go around," her mother says. "We will have to go a different way."

"Why?"

"Well, maybe there has been an accident. Or maybe the city is repairing the street. For some reason, it is not safe to drive on this road," says Mrs. Pang.

When Mary Pang and her mother saw the detour sign, they knew to go a different way.

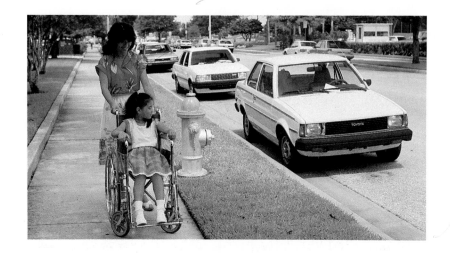

Look at the car on the right. There is a ticket on it because there is a law against parking in front of fire hydrants.

"Do people always do what the sign says?".

"Usually they do," Mrs. Pang answers. "You see, most people understand that rules make our community safer."

Laws in Communities

"The rules that our community makes are called **laws.** Laws are rules for everyone. If people break laws, they may be punished," says Mrs. Pang. "Sometimes they have to pay money. Or, if a very serious law has been broken, they may have to go to jail.

"It is better for everyone to obey laws," says Mrs. Pang. "When we obey laws, we are being good **citizens.** A citizen is a member of a community, state, or country. We are all citizens of the United States."

Reading Check

1. What does "detour" mean?
2. What is a citizen?

Think Beyond   Why might laws be alike in many communities?

LAWS AND RULES OF LONG AGO

On a day more than 300 years ago a man sat in the middle of Boston. His legs were locked between wooden boards called stocks. As people walked by, they made fun of him. He was being punished by the community for breaking one of its laws. His crime was charging too much money for building the first stocks in Boston. Now he was the first person to be punished in them!

The early settlers worked hard and lived simply. Some of their laws were strict. Swearing, laziness, and even too much merry-making were crimes. People who broke laws were punished, often by being embarrassed in front of the community.

Some New England communities even had watchers who made sure citizens obeyed rules and laws. The watchers reported anyone who looked lazy. They

People could be placed in the stocks for hours or days depending on their crime.

also reported anyone who worked on Sunday instead of attending church services.

Some of the laws communities have today come from the old laws. Some states still have laws that do not allow certain businesses to open on Sunday. These laws are called blue laws. They are called that because long ago they were printed on blue paper.

Many of the laws that communities made long ago were good ones. For example, in 1647 the people of Massachusetts passed laws that started the public school system. They required villages with 50 or more people to hire a teacher. They also required

Criminals were often put in a wooden cage and taken to the marketplace, where they were put on display.

every town with 100 or more families to open a school. If it were not for those laws, you might not be reading this page now.

Think Beyond Why do you think communities have passed laws requiring children to attend school?

The ducking stool was used as a form of punishment in the English colonies.

Look for these important words:

Key Words
- government
- lawmakers
- mayor

- judges
- city council
- city manager

- elect
- courts

Look for answers to these questions:
1. Who are the lawmakers in Santa Rosa?
2. Who helps the mayor in Santa Rosa?
3. What do judges in Santa Rosa do?

2 HOW GOVERNMENTS WORK

Every community has a **government.** A government is a group of people who make laws, and make sure laws are obeyed. The government of a community does the things needed to keep the community safe and pleasant.

People in Governments

Governments usually have three parts. In one part, people make laws. These people are called **lawmakers.** In another part, there is a leader who makes sure things get done. In many communities, this leader is called the **mayor.**

The third part of government is made up of **judges.** Judges are people who decide if laws have been broken. If laws have been broken, judges decide what punishments should be given out.

Together, lawmakers, leaders, and judges make up the government.

Lawmakers and leaders work together at a city council meeting in Santa Rosa. People in the community often listen and add ideas.

Government in Santa Rosa

Santa Rosa has a mayor and a **city council.** The people on the city council are the lawmakers. The mayor is the leader. In Santa Rosa, there is a vice mayor to help the mayor. There is also a **city manager** in Santa Rosa. The city manager also helps make sure things get done.

Many people work for the mayor and city manager. Police officers and fire fighters work for Santa Rosa, and so do highway and parks people.

Together, the mayor and the city council make plans for Santa Rosa. They try to do what the people of Santa Rosa want and need.

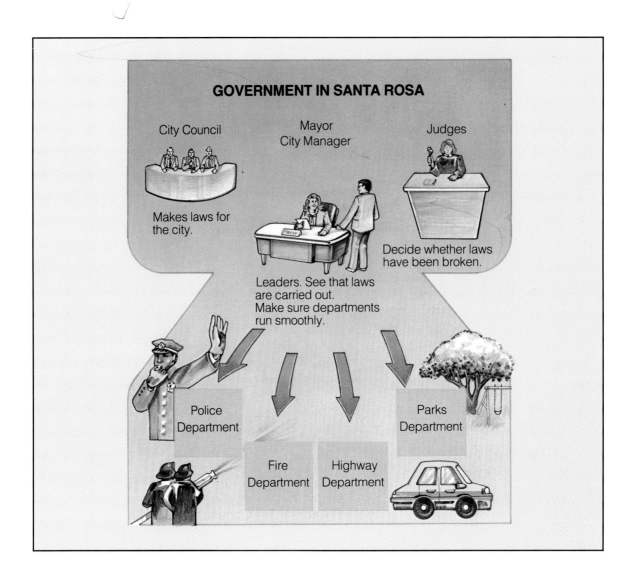

GOVERNMENT IN SANTA ROSA

City Council

Makes laws for the city.

Mayor
City Manager

Leaders. See that laws are carried out. Make sure departments run smoothly.

Judges

Decide whether laws have been broken.

Police Department

Fire Department

Highway Department

Parks Department

The people in Santa Rosa **elect,** or choose, judges. The judges decide whether people are obeying Santa Rosa's laws. The judges also decide how people who break laws should be punished. Judges work in places called **courts.**

Reading Check

1. What is a government?
2. How are the judges chosen in Santa Rosa?

Think Beyond Why are fire and police services not run by private companies?

Look for these important words:

Key Words
- town meeting
- Board of Selectmen

Places
- Newfane, Vermont

Look for answers to these questions:
1. What kind of community is Newfane, Vermont?
2. How do the people in Newfane, Vermont, take part in their community's government?
3. What do people do at a town meeting?

3 NEWFANE, VERMONT

Newfane, Vermont, is a small town. It is located in the rolling hills of southern Vermont. About 1,500 people live in and around Newfane. Many of the people who live near Newfane are farmers. Others have jobs in one of the larger towns many miles away.

Town buildings surround the central green in Newfane, Vermont.

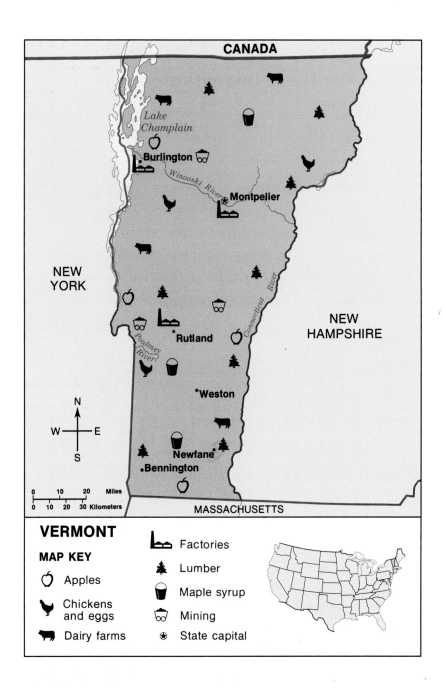

CANADA

Lake Champlain

Burlington

Winooski River

Montpelier

NEW YORK

Connecticut River

NEW HAMPSHIRE

Rutland

Poultney River

Weston

Newfane

•Bennington

MASSACHUSETTS

| 0 | 10 | 20 | Miles |
| 0 | 10 | 20 | 30 Kilometers |

N
W E
S

VERMONT

MAP KEY

🍎 Apples

🐔 Chickens and eggs

🐄 Dairy farms

Factories

🌲 Lumber

🪣 Maple syrup

Mining

✳ State capital

Government in Newfane

On the first Tuesday in March each year, the people of Newfane gather together. They meet in Grange Hall or in a big hall called the Union Hall. There all of the people have a **town meeting.** A town meeting is a way for everyone to take part in Newfane's government.

In Newfane, there is no city council or mayor. Instead, the government is a group of five people. This group is called the **Board of Selectmen.** The Board helps run the town. One of the jobs of the Board of Selectmen is to choose the heads of town departments, like the Police Department.

People on the Board of Selectmen are elected each year at the town meeting. Both men and women can be Selectmen.

The citizens of Newfane help choose what to talk about at the town meeting. If enough people want to talk about something or make a new law, it is put on a special list. The list lets everyone know what will be talked about at the meeting.

Newfane has a lot of snow in the winter. That makes travel difficult. So this problem is talked about at the town meeting. Should the town buy a new snow plow? Should town workers put more salt on the roads to make them less icy? Anyone who wants to has a chance to talk.

The town meeting in Newfane is held every other year in Union Hall.

HISTORY CONNECTION

Early in our country's history, people did not have television, radio, or newspapers. People had to listen to the town crier for up-to-date information. The town crier walked around the town calling out the news at every corner.

When people began printing newspapers, the town crier slowly disappeared from town life. Today modern communication tells us not only about events happening in our community but also about what is happening around the world.

The legal voters of the Town of Newfane, Vermont, are hereby notified and warned to meet at the Union Hall on Tuesday, March 7, 1989, at 9:00 A.M. to act upon the following articles:

Article 1   To elect a Moderator and Town Clerk.

Article 2   To act on the Auditors' Report.

Article 3   To see how the Town will vote to collect taxes for the ensuing year.

Article 4   To see how much the Town will vote to pay its officers for the ensuing year.

Article 5   To see if the Town will authorize the Selectmen to appoint one or two Road Commissioners for the ensuing year, or elect them by ballot.

Above is a list of some articles that were discussed at a town meeting in Newfane.

People often have different views. Sometimes the talk gets very lively. Then a vote is taken. In Newfane the people are the lawmakers.

If more people vote yes, the plan or law "passes." This means that the plan will be carried out, or that the law must be followed. If more people vote no, the plan or law "fails." This means that the government does not do anything about it. After people vote on all the plans and laws, the town meeting is over. The town's business has been settled for another year.

Reading Check

1. What group helps run the government in Newfane?
2. How do people make laws in Newfane?

Think Beyond   Why is it important for the citizens of a town to attend the town meeting?

? SKILLS IN ACTION

MAKING CHOICES

Personal Choices

Making a choice means picking one thing instead of another. If you choose to watch one television show, you are choosing not to watch other shows. You cannot watch two shows at the same time.

You make many choices every day. Did you ever think about the reasons for making the choices you make?

Here are some reasons you might have for making choices.

- **You like one thing more than another.** Maybe some of your friends are going to play baseball after school. Some of your other friends want to go roller skating. You like roller skating better, so you decide to go roller skating.

- **One thing is more important than the other thing.** Maybe you have time to either clean your fish tank or play soccer with your friends. It may be more important to clean the fish tank. The fish could get sick if you do not.

- **Your choice depends on a rule.** Suppose you want to ride your bike on the playground. However, there is a rule against this. You would get into trouble for breaking the rule if you rode on the playground. You might also run into someone on the playground. If you put your bike in the bike rack instead, you will not hurt anyone. You will also be following the rules.

Some choices are harder to make than others. We must always think carefully before choosing.

These children are following a rule by walking their bikes to the bike rack.

179

Community Choices

People in communities also have to make choices. These may be very hard choices to make. Suppose a new highway is being built. It can be built through the town, or it could pass by the town.

Some people in the community want the highway to go through the town. Then people passing through can stop at the town restaurants and stores. The town will get more business that way.

Not everyone agrees. Other people don't want the highway to go through town. They say all the cars going through could cause big traffic problems. People don't want their children having to cross a busy highway to get to school.

In our country, people can meet together to talk about choices. The more information we have about choices, the better choices we can make. People can talk about the good and bad points of each choice. Then they can **vote.**

When people vote, they say what their choices are. People vote for leaders and lawmakers. They also vote for or against things.

In an **election,** people go to special voting places. They write their choices down or use a machine to vote. Then all the votes are counted. The choice with the most votes wins the election. This is called **majority rule.** Majority rule means that more than half of the people voted in the same way.

On voting day, people in the community make important decisions. They put their votes on machines in voting booths.

Government Leaders and Choices

Government leaders make many choices for the community. People who want to be leaders tell what kinds of choices they might make. Voters usually elect someone they agree with.

Here are some things that a government leader might have to make choices about.

- Should a piece of land be used for a new park or for a parking lot?

- Should the city spend money to repair some streets with holes in them? Or should it put up stoplights at a busy corner?

- Should the city build a new city hall or fix up the old one?

- Should the city pay police officers more, or hire more police officers with the money?

These choices may sound simple, but each choice means spending thousands of dollars. Also, each choice might change how people live. Government leaders must think long and hard before they make important choices like these.

The people standing want to be on the city council. They are telling some voters their views about government.

CHECKING YOUR SKILLS

Tell or write the answers to these questions.

1. What does making a choice mean?

2. What are two reasons people choose one thing instead of another?

3. How do communities in the United States make choices?

4. Look at the list on this page of choices that government leaders have to make. Choose one pair of choices. Then think of some reasons that a leader might have for making each choice. Tell these reasons.

181

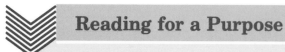

Reading for a Purpose

Look for these important words:

Key Words	Places
• governor	• Washington, D.C.
• Congress	
• Supreme Court	

Look for answers to these questions:
1. Where do state governments meet? Where does the government for our country meet?
2. Who leads state government?
3. What is the Supreme Court?

4 GOVERNMENTS FOR OUR STATES AND COUNTRY

You have read about community governments. We also have state governments. Our country has a government, too, which meets in **Washington, D.C.**

State Governments

A state government makes laws for the whole state. It also takes care of state parks, state forests, and public schools.

Each state government has lawmakers. Each state also has a leader called a **governor.** The lawmakers and the governor are both elected by the people. There are also state judges. Many judges are not elected. They are chosen by the governor. Each state government meets in the state capital.

Our Country's Government

The United States government also has lawmakers, a leader, and judges. The people of each state elect lawmakers from their state. These lawmakers from all the states together meet in Washington, D.C. to form the **Congress.** The Congress makes laws for the whole country.

The leader of our nation is the President of the United States. The President is elected, too. The citizens in our country help elect the President.

The President chooses the judges who are part of our country's government. Nine judges make up the **Supreme Court.** The Supreme Court is our most important court.

This picture shows President George Bush speaking to the Congress.

It is important for leaders to share ideas with the citizens of a community. Here, California lawmaker Gwen Moore tells Brownie troop members about her job.

You have read how lawmakers, leaders, and judges run our government. Citizens help run our government, too. They choose the people to be our leaders. They tell our government how they feel about what the government is doing. The people in our government have to listen if they want to be elected again.

 Reading Check

1. What is the leader of a state called?
2. How is a state capital like Washington, D.C.?

Think Beyond What would you tell your state lawmakers about schools in your state?

People MAKE HISTORY

Wilma Mankiller
1945–

▶▶▶▶▶▶▶▶▶▶▶▶▶▶▶▶

Wilma Mankiller smiles when people ask about her last name. She explains that it is a common name among Cherokee Indians. Why would so many people ask about her name? They ask her because she is the main chief of the Cherokee Nation.

As the first woman leader of a group of American Indians, Mankiller is working to make life better for her people. To do this, Mankiller has started programs to improve education and health care for all group members. She is working to create more jobs and business opportunities for the Cherokees.

Mankiller has also started a program to preserve the Cherokee language and culture. Each summer Cherokee students travel to a special school where they learn how to read and write the Cherokee language. The students then return to their communities. They teach others what they have learned.

Mankiller wants others to see American Indians as she knows them, a people filled with strength, beauty, and creativity. She says, "I want to be remembered as the person who helped us restore faith in ourselves."

Think Beyond Why is it important for you to feel good about yourself?

SKILLS IN ACTION

FINDING THE INFORMATION YOU NEED

How do you find out information about things? There are a number of places you can look to find news and information.

Television and Radio News

News programs on television and radio can tell you what is going on in your community, your country, and the world. They bring you news very quickly. The news they bring you can be important.

For example, imagine that a big storm has hit your community. Your telephone does not work. You want to know whether your school has been closed because of the storm.

You can get a lot of information by watching television news programs.

To find out, you might listen to news on the radio. You may watch news on television. Perhaps the reporter tells you your school is closed for the day. Then you know that you should stay home.

Radio and television give news of our country and the world, too. These news reports are often very short. So when you need to know more about a news story, you must look somewhere else.

News in Newspapers

Newspapers are another place to find information. Newspapers cannot bring you news as fast as the television and radio stations can. However, stories in a newspaper are usually more complete.

A newspaper tells you more about community happenings than a television or a radio program does. A newspaper has news about community and world events. A newspaper also has sports stories. A newspaper tells about movies, television programs, and special radio programs.

Newspapers also have ads, or **advertisements,** in them. Stores and businesses pay to have the newspaper print their ads. Advertisements might give readers information such as where and when a sale is being held.

Information on Signs

Another way people get information about their community is by reading signs. For example, a ROAD CLOSED sign may tell you that a road is not safe to drive on. Signs tell people what the rules of a community are.

Information in Your Telephone Book

A telephone book can give you information. **Emergency** phone numbers are usually on the inside front cover of the phone book. These numbers tell you where to call if you see a fire or need police help quickly.

If you need help quickly, you can dial an emergency number on your phone.

Pages that tell about **first aid** are near the beginning of many telephone books. These pages tell you how to help someone who is hurt in an accident. These pages may also tell what to do in weather emergencies.

CHECKING YOUR SKILLS

Read the sentences below. Tell or write where you could find information in each of the cases.

1. You want to know whether you are allowed to ride your bicycle in the park.

2. It has been raining hard all day. Is the river that runs through your town going to flood?

3. Hurricanes sometimes happen where you live. You want to know what you should do in case of this weather emergency.

187

Thinking Back

- Governments are groups of people who make laws and see that they are obeyed. Governments usually have lawmakers, judges, and a leader. Citizens vote to elect these people.

- In communities such as Santa Rosa, California, the leader is the mayor. The lawmakers are the members of the city council. They plan how the city can provide what the people want and need. Police officers, fire fighters, and highway and parks people work for the city.

- Newfane, Vermont, is a small community. It has a board of selectmen to run the town. Each year the citizens have a town meeting. They choose what to talk about, and they vote on ideas and plans.

- States have governments to make laws for the whole state. State governments take care of state parks and forests and public schools. Each state has a leader called a governor.

- Our whole country has a government, too. The lawmakers are the members of Congress. The judges are the people of the Supreme Court. The leader of our country is the President of the United States.

Check for Understanding

Using Words

Number your paper from 1 to 5. Use the words below to fill in the blanks. Use each word only once.

citizens	**judges**	**elect**
city council	**laws**	

We are all _____ (1) of the United States. People here can _____ (2) people for the government. In many communities, we vote for our _____ (3) and our _____ (4). These special people help make and carry out the _____ (5) of our government.

Reviewing Facts

1. What are laws?

2. What are the three parts of most governments?

3. What are some groups of people that work for the mayor of Santa Rosa?

4. What does the Board of Selectmen do in Newfane, Vermont?

5. How do citizens help run our government?

Thinking Critically

1. What are two important laws you know? Why are these laws important?

2. What would you want to talk about if your community had a town meeting?

3. A mayor is the leader of a community. The President is the leader of our country. How are their jobs alike and different?

Writing About It

Imagine that you are a reporter for a small community newspaper. Write a newspaper story about one problem you think might be discussed at the town meeting.

 Practicing Study Skills

Finding Information

Decide where you could find out about each of these things.

a. whether there are any traffic problems on nearby roads

b. what to do if someone is hurt

c. what is on sale at a store

On Your Own

Social Studies at Home

A group of your friends wants to do something together on Saturday. List some of the things you could choose to do. Tell how the group makes a decision.

Read More About It

Deadline! From News to Newspaper by Gail Gibbons. T. Y. Crowell. This book takes a look at a small daily newspaper.

Local Government by James A. Eichner. Watts. Learn more about state and city governments.

My Mother Is the Smartest Woman in the World by Eleanor Clymer. Atheneum. A young girl wants her mother to be mayor.

CHAPTER 7

Communities Provide Services

❝It looks like any building
When you pass it on the street,
Made of stone and glass and marble,
Made of iron and concrete.

· · · · · · · · · · · · · · · ·

You cannot tell its magic
By the way the building looks,
But there's wonderment within it,
The wonderment of books. ❞

—from the poem "The Library" by Barbara A. Huff

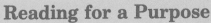

Look for these important words:

Key Words
- property
- crime
- detectives

- public property
- private property

Look for answers to these questions:

1. How did people meet their needs before there were community services?
2. Who chooses people to run community services?
3. How does a police department protect people and property?

1 COMMUNITY SERVICES PROTECT US

Long ago, many people lived on farms or in houses far from one another. They had to do many things for themselves. They made most of their own clothes. They had to build their own houses. Sometimes neighbors would come and help with big jobs. There were no community workers to do things for people.

Today we live together in communities. It does not make sense to do everything by ourselves. That is why communities provide services. Communities can provide more services than people working by themselves could.

Every community has services for its people. The people in community governments make sure these services run smoothly. They choose people to run the services. For example, they choose the heads of the police and fire departments.

Police Protection

The police department protects **property.** Property is land, buildings, and other things people own. One kind of property is **public property.** Public means open to all. Zoos, parks, libraries, and museums are kinds of public property. Anyone may visit them. They belong to everyone.

Another kind of property is **private property.** Homes and businesses are kinds of private property. It is part of the job of the police to see that private property is not entered without permission.

Public property belongs to everyone. You must be careful not to damage it.

You must respect private property. You may not enter private property without permission.

The police department also helps us in many other ways. Police officers direct traffic when the signals are broken. They help people when their cars have trouble on the roads. Sometimes they give us directions when we are lost. They help keep our community a safe place to live and play.

You can find police officers easily. Most communities have police stations. These are places where police officers are on duty 24 hours a day, every day. There they work at many different jobs.

Directing traffic is one important job police officers have. Here, an officer directs people and cars on a busy street.

After this store was robbed, Detective Lewis brushed the cash register for fingerprints. This may help the police find the person who did the crime.

The police do not stay just in the station. Sometimes they walk in the community to make sure everything is safe. They drive around the community in police cars, too. Then they can move quickly if there is a call for help or a **crime.** A crime is something that is against the law.

Sometimes when there is a crime, the police do not know who did it. So, specially trained **detectives** try to find out. They ask questions and look for clues. The tiniest bit of cloth or a fingerprint might lead to the person who did the crime.

 Reading Check

1. Name two important community services.
2. Who owns public property?

Think Beyond Would you enjoy being a police officer? Tell why or why not.

Look for these important words:

Key Words
- hazards
- crew

Places
- Orlando, Florida

Look for answers to these questions:

1. What do fire fighters do when they first get to the fire station?
2. Why do fire fighters study the streets in their part of the city?
3. Why do fire fighters visit different homes and businesses?

2 | A FIRE DEPARTMENT IN ORLANDO, FLORIDA

Orlando is a city in the middle of **Florida.** Plains cover much of Florida. The climate in Florida is warm and rainy.

There are many beautiful lakes and parks in Orlando, Florida. Across this lake, you can see some buildings in the city.

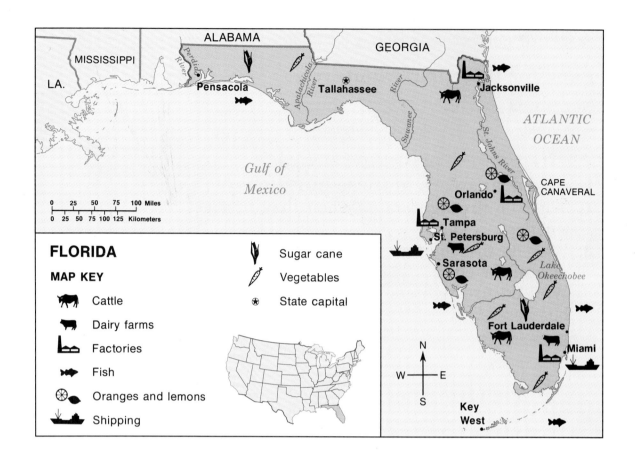

FLORIDA

MAP KEY

Cattle

Dairy farms

Factories

Fish

Oranges and lemons

Shipping

Sugar cane

Vegetables

State capital

Killer whales are the stars in the whale show at Sea World in Orlando.

Visitors are the most important industry in Florida. Orlando is a very important visitor center. There are many places to see, such as Walt Disney World and Sea World. Cape Canaveral, where space ships blast off, is near Orlando.

Orlando has many community services. One of these services is the fire department.

Fire fighters in Orlando go to the fire stations at 8:00 A.M. The first thing they do is put their work things on the trucks. They also check all the equipment on the trucks. They make sure the hoses and ladders are ready to go.

Sometimes the fire fighters go to a special school in the morning. They attend classes to learn new ways to fight fires and save lives.

A Visit to a Fire Station

In the afternoon, a class from the neighborhood school may visit the fire station. The children get to see how the fire fighters live and work. A fire fighter shows them the equipment on the truck. He or she tells them how it works.

The fire fighter also tells the children how to spot fire **hazards** in their homes. A hazard is a danger. A fire hazard is something that could cause a fire. The children are told to make sure plugs and wires are not worn out. They are told not to put things that can catch fire near a flame or heater. The fire fighter tells the children to practice getting out of their homes quickly. That way, they will be ready if a fire happens.

Fire fighters sometimes visit schools. Below, the class listens as a fire fighter explains how to use a fire extinguisher.

Fire fighters in Orlando make sure their fire engines are clean and ready to be used.

The fire fighters may spend part of the afternoon studying the streets in their part of Orlando. They have to know if a street is closed for repairs. They need to know which streets are usually blocked with traffic.

Fire fighters also visit homes and businesses. They look for fire hazards and tell people how to get rid of them. Keeping fires from happening is a big part of a fire fighter's job.

At 8:00 A.M. the next day, a new **crew**, or group, takes over at each fire station. The first crew gets two days off. Still, if there is a big fire and extra help is needed, they will be there to protect the people of Orlando.

 Reading Check

1. Why should we know about fire hazards?
2. Why do fire fighters go to a special school?
Think Beyond What kind of person do you think would make a good fire fighter?

SKILLS IN ACTION

USING MAPS AND GRIDS

A **grid** shows lines that cross one another. Grids use letters and numbers to help you find things. Look at the grid below.

The pictures in this grid are symbols you might find on the map of a community. Put your finger on the number 1. Now move it down until your finger is even with the letter D. Your finger should be on the box with the symbol for "river" in it. This square is called box D-1. Now find the tree on the grid. Look at the top of the column. The number 4 is there. Look across to the letters. The letter C is across from the tree. What box is the tree in? Find box B-3. What is in it?

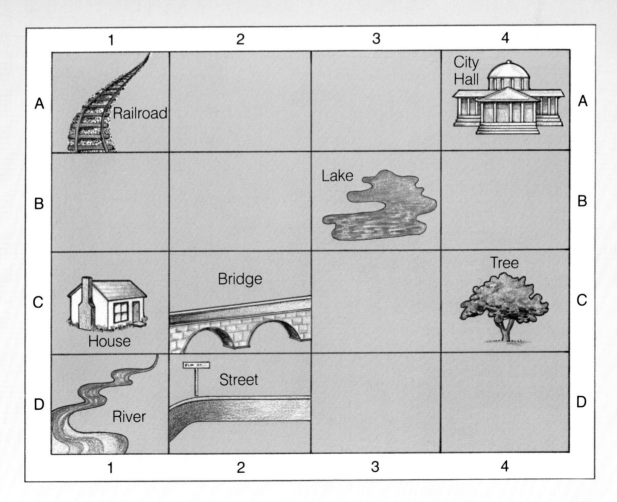

199

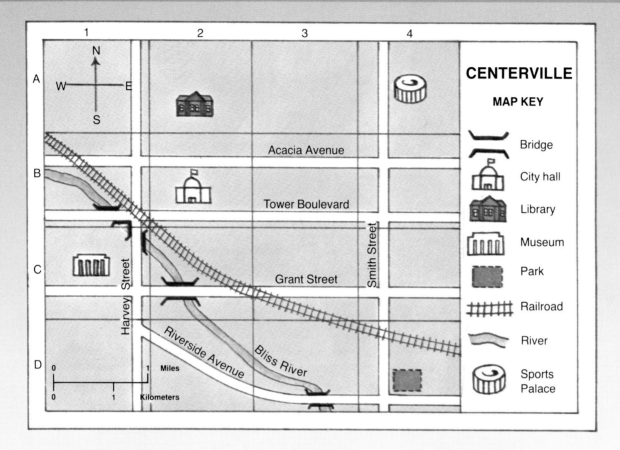

Maps often have grids to help you find places on them.

This map of Centerville has a grid. Find the library and put your finger on it. Move your finger up to the number above the map. It is the number 2. Now move your finger from the library to the letter at the side of the map. It is A. The library is in box A-2 on this map.

Now find box C-1. What building is shown in that box? Find Tower Boulevard. Notice that it runs through four boxes—B-1, B-2, B-3, and B-4. What other road runs through these four boxes?

CHECKING YOUR SKILLS

Use the map to help you answer these questions.

1. What large building is in box A-4?

2. In which box is City Hall?

3. Find the place where the Bliss River goes under the bridge at Grant Street. What box is the bridge in?

4. What things do you see in box D-4?

5. What road runs through boxes D-1, D-2, D-3, and D-4?

200

Look for these important words:

Key Words
- public works
- reservoirs
- sewage
- sewage treatment plants
- public transportation
- clinics
- board of education

Look for answers to these questions:
1. What does the public works department do?
2. What are two kinds of public transportation?
3. What does a board of education do?

3 MORE COMMUNITY SERVICES

The **public works** department provides services to meet our day-to-day needs. We depend on it for many things. Public works crews see that the streets are kept clean and in good repair.

City workers in New York are laying down bricks for a new crosswalk.

201

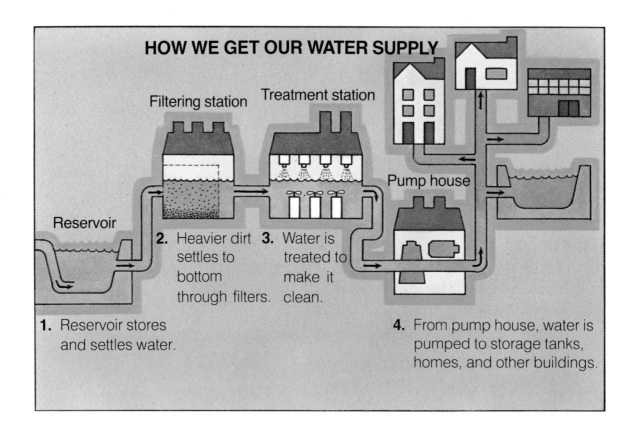

HOW WE GET OUR WATER SUPPLY

Filtering station   Treatment station

Reservoir

Pump house

1. Reservoir stores and settles water.

2. Heavier dirt settles to bottom through filters.

3. Water is treated to make it clean.

4. From pump house, water is pumped to storage tanks, homes, and other buildings.

Water is cleaned at a sewage treatment plant.

Whenever you turn on the faucet in your house, you expect clean, fresh water to come out. Public works crews make sure this happens. They put in pipes to pump water from rivers or **reservoirs** (REZ•urv•wahrz). A reservoir is a lake used for collecting and storing water. The crews treat the water to make it clean.

Public works departments take care of the waste water from homes, businesses, and streets. This waste water is called **sewage.** It is carried in pipes to buildings called **sewage treatment plants.** Sewage treatment plants clean the water before returning it to the rivers. That way, the sewage does not hurt fish, plants, or animals.

In some communities, the public works department collects garbage. If garbage is not removed, it can be a health hazard.

Transportation Services

Do you take a city bus to school? If so, you are using **public transportation.** Buses and trains are two kinds of public transportation. They are another kind of service many communities provide to people. Buses and trains can carry many people. People pay money when they ride public transportation.

Health Services

Many communities have hospitals to care for people who are very hurt or sick. Most hospitals have emergency rooms. People can get help right away at a hospital emergency room.

Community **clinics** are also places that treat people who are hurt or ill. At many clinics there are doctors and dentists who can take care of the whole family.

Public transportation (left) and medical clinics (right) are two services that communities provide.

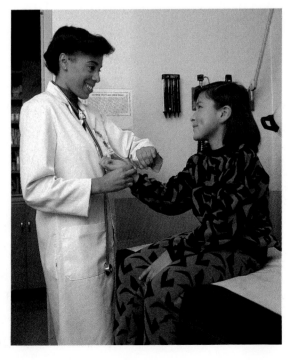

At a board of education meeting, people meet together to make decisions about how the schools should be run.

Public Schools

One community service you know about is the public school system. Most communities have a **board of education.** Its members are elected by the people of the community.

In many communities, it is up to the board of education to help choose teachers. The board decides how the schools should be run. The board does an important job. A good education gives people a good start in life.

 Reading Check

1. Which department is in charge of a community's water supply?
2. Why is the board of education important?

Think Beyond Public transportation makes a community a better place to live. Why?

People MAKE HISTORY

Anne Carroll Moore
1871–1961

▶▶▶▶▶▶▶▶▶▶▶▶▶▶▶▶▶

Even as a young child, Anne Carroll Moore loved to read. Books were very important to her. She became a librarian to share her love of books with others. Moore also believed that library services were important to the community.

The New York Public Library, in New York City, hired Moore as a children's librarian. Moore made sure that children visiting the library had quiet places to read and many books to choose from. Moore often read aloud to the children.

Moore believed that children deserved to read books that were well written. Authors and book publishing companies listened to her ideas. They started to produce better books. In addition, Moore started to write her own books.

People began to notice the good things Moore was doing at the library. Visitors from all over the world came to talk with her and see the library. Because of Moore's work, thousands of children have learned that reading is exciting and that going to the library is fun.

Think Beyond How do you think your school librarian could help you learn more about books?

Look for these important words:

Key Words	Places
• recreation	• Durham, North Carolina

Look for answers to these questions:

1. What can you find out about at a library? What, besides books, do libraries often have?
2. What services are provided by the parks and recreation department?
3. Where, besides libraries, can people go to learn about many things?

4 LIBRARIES, PARKS, AND MUSEUMS

Do frogs have toes? How long would it take to get to Mars? Whatever you want to know, you can usually find out about at your public library.

Librarians are there to help you. They can help you find books on just about anything that interests you. Some libraries also have records, films, and pictures you can borrow.

A librarian can help you answer questions and find information.

Parks and Recreation

Many communities have parks and public gardens. People can go to these places to enjoy nature and open space. This is especially important to city people. They often live in apartments or houses without gardens.

Parks give people a place to play, too. A community's parks and **recreation** (rek•ree•AY•shuhn) department provides many services. Recreation is something you do for enjoyment. Reading, playing games, and listening to music are all kinds of recreation.

Parks and recreation departments take care of community swimming pools. They also take care of baseball diamonds, basketball and tennis courts, and golf courses. In the summer, the parks and recreation department offers special programs for children.

The children below are keeping cool and learning how to swim at their community pool.

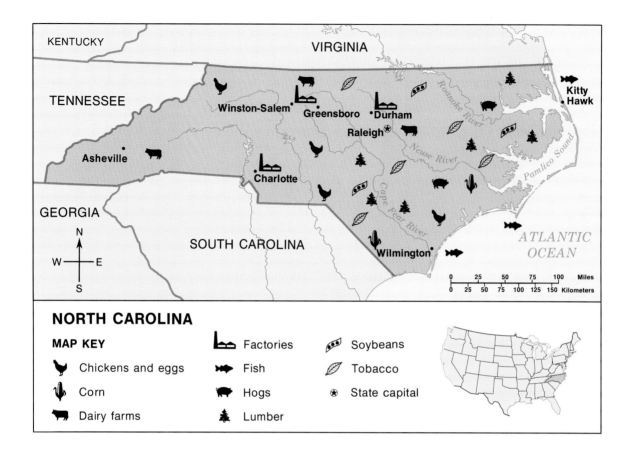

MAP KEY

🐔 Chickens and eggs   🏭 Factories   🫘 Soybeans

🌽 Corn   🐟 Fish   🍃 Tobacco

🐄 Dairy farms   🐖 Hogs   ✪ State capital

     🌲 Lumber

A Museum in North Carolina

Durham, North Carolina, is a medium-sized city. North Carolina is in the eastern part of our country. Durham is famous for its very fine museum. The museum is the North Carolina Museum of Life and Science.

Many school classes come to visit the North Carolina Museum of Life and Science. Let us join one class on its visit.

First, the students are greeted in the main building by a museum guide. The guide tells the visitors about things in the museum.

The students go to a room to hear a talk about the space program. After the talk, the students see many things from our space program. The Durham museum has a large space exhibit.

Children with hearing problems use sign language to discuss airplanes at the Durham museum.

So much is going on at the Durham museum. The students cannot see it all in one day. There is a wildflower trail, a wildlife area, and a small railroad. Computer classes are given. There are classes on protecting animal and plant life—and much, much more.

 Reading Check

1. Why are parks important?
2. What is recreation?

Think Beyond   What recreation do you enjoy in your community? What would you add?

IN FOCUS

GOLDEN GATE PARK

In San Francisco more than 100 years ago, workers were busy leveling sand dunes. They were getting the land ready for a park. The citizens of San Francisco had decided they needed a park. Their city was growing crowded with people and buildings. They wanted more room for walking, picnicking, and enjoying nature. They named the piece of land Golden Gate Park.

To turn sand dunes into a park was a difficult job. Again and again the blowing sand covered up the grass the workers planted.

Barren sand dunes were changed into valleys and low hills covered with more than a million trees and shrubs.

Then a new kind of grass was planted. It grew faster than the sand could cover it. Soon special flowers and other plants from Europe, Asia, and South America were planted. They grew well in their new surroundings. More than a million trees were planted.

The Japanese Tea Garden is one of the most popular areas in the park.

A small herd of buffalo grazes in the park's Buffalo Paddock.

Finally the park looked the way the people of San Francisco wanted it.

Over the years the park has added many attractions. The California Academy of Sciences and the Museum of Natural History are there. The park also has a conservatory, an aquarium, and a planetarium. It has areas where buffalo graze and where people play sports. It also has a big waterfall and a merry-go-round.

The park has kept its natural beauty. Today Golden Gate Park is one of the largest and best-known parks in the world. It is enjoyed by visitors from near and far. Most people would never guess that this beautiful park was once only blowing sand.

Think Beyond How might a community get land on which to build a park?

The glass Conservatory, a greenhouse, is one of the oldest buildings in the park.

211

Look for these important words:

Key Words
- taxes
- property tax
- sales tax
- volunteer

Look for answers to these questions:
1. How is tax money used?
2. Do large communities or small communities usually get more tax money? Why?
3. What is a volunteer? How do volunteers give community services?

5 TAXES PAY FOR COMMUNITY SERVICES

Community services cost money. The people who work to give people these services must be paid. Equipment must be bought, too.

Where does money that pays for community services come from? Most of it comes from the people in a community. People in communities pay **taxes.** A tax is money people pay to support their government and its services.

One kind of tax that brings money to communities is the **property tax.** This is a tax on the land and buildings a person owns.

Another kind of tax is a **sales tax.** Many states have this kind of tax. People in these states pay a sales tax every time they buy something. The amount they pay as sales tax may be something like five cents for every dollar. So, when a person

Look at the sales slip. How much is the tax?

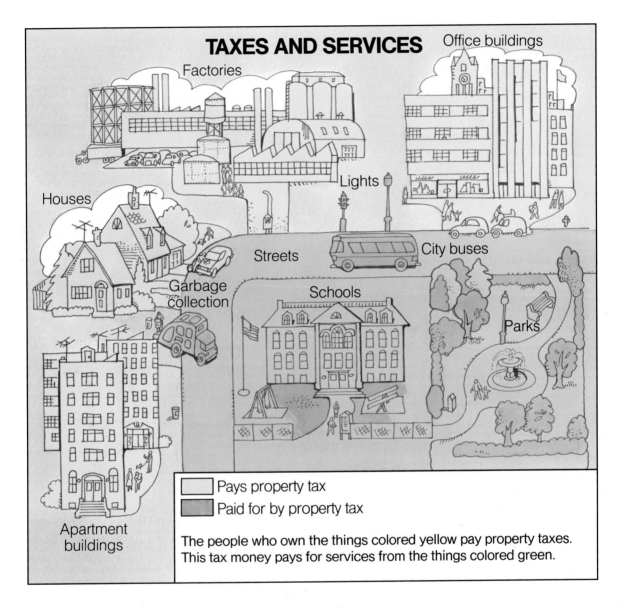

TAXES AND SERVICES

Factories

Office buildings

Houses

Lights

Streets

City buses

Garbage collection

Schools

Parks

Apartment buildings

☐ Pays property tax
▨ Paid for by property tax

The people who own the things colored yellow pay property taxes.
This tax money pays for services from the things colored green.

buys goods for $10.00, the tax would be fifty cents.
The total cost is then $10.50.

Large communities usually get more tax money
because there are more people, stores, and other
property. So large communities can often provide
more services than small communities.

Each community must decide how to spend its
money. Community governments must make
choices based on the needs and interests of the
people.

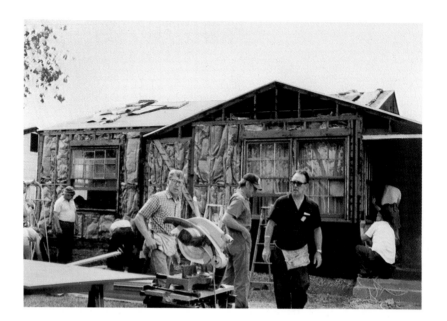

People in Midland, Texas, are helping fix a house during "Christmas in April."

Volunteer Community Services

Most community services are paid for by taxes. However, many communities also have another kind of community service—**volunteer** services. A volunteer is a person who offers to do something for free.

Do you remember the oil-drilling community of Midland, Texas? Every April, people in Midland volunteer their own time and money to a project called "Christmas in April." For one weekend, hundreds of volunteers work together to help people in need. During one "Christmas in April," volunteers repaired more than 120 homes for needy people.

 Reading Check

1. What are taxes?
2. How are community services workers paid?

Think Beyond Tell about volunteers in your community. How might you volunteer?

SKILLS IN ACTION

BEING A RESPONSIBLE CITIZEN

Communities provide many kinds of services. They give people police and fire protection. They build roads and bridges. They run libraries, schools, and hospitals. Communities provide parks.

You have a right to use these services because you are a member of your community. But you also must obey the rules and laws that go along with using community services.

When you follow rules and laws, you are being a responsible, or good, citizen. You are making it easier for people to do their jobs.

Following Rules

Each community has its own set of rules and laws about using its services. Many of the rules are like the ones you will read about here.

Here are some rules that many schools have.

- Take care of school books and other equipment.

- Do not run in the halls.

- Talk only when you are asked to in the classroom.

- Keep the cafeteria or eating area neat.

The students in Mrs. Colbert's class are following a rule. Before they speak in class, they raise their hands and wait to be called upon.

215

Community parks and swimming pools have rules. Read the following ones and think about why each is important.

- Keep the park clean. Put your litter in the special baskets provided.

- Play sports only in places where signs say you can.

- Share tennis courts and playground equipment.

- Do not run in the pool area.

Rules like these are made for reasons. For example, it would be dangerous to play baseball in a place where small children play. Someone could get in the way and be hurt.

Here are some rules for fire safety at home or school. Think about why you should follow each of them.

- Do not put matches on hot stoves or pipes.

- Keep a screen in front of the fireplace.

- Do not let papers or rags pile up anywhere.

- Keep gasoline, paints, and paint thinner away from heat. These liquids catch fire easily.

How are the children in this picture being responsible citizens?

What fire safety rule is being followed in this picture?

A guard is helping these children cross a busy street safely. Drivers follow safety rules by stopping when they see her sign.

Following Laws

There are many rules and laws for safety. Here are a few of them.

- Never play in streets.

- Cross streets only at corners. Look both ways before crossing.

- Never try to cross a street when you hear a police car or fire engine coming.

- Always do what a police officer tells you.

- Always do what a fire fighter tells you.

- Never call an emergency fire or police number unless there is a real emergency.

CHECKING YOUR SKILLS

Tell or write the answers to these questions.

1. What are two rules schools have?

2. Why should you not run at swimming pools?

3. Why should you do what a fire fighter tells you?

4. Why should you look both ways before crossing a street?

217

Thinking Back

- An important job of government is to provide public services. Community governments choose people to run departments that protect citizens and their property.

- Police officers direct traffic and keep the community safe. When there is a crime, detectives work to find out who did it.

- Fire fighters train every day to save lives and property. They teach people about fire safety.

- Public works departments take care of community streets and water supplies. They run sewage treatment plants and collect trash.

- Public transportation is a community service. Health services include hospitals and clinics. In most communities a board of education runs the public schools.

- Parks and recreation departments run sports programs and swimming pools. Most communities have libraries and museums.

- Money from taxes pays for public services. Volunteers help, too, by doing things for free.

Check for Understanding

Using Words

Number your paper from 1 to 5. Match the words with their correct meanings.

1. reservoir   4. recreation

2. hazard   5. property

3. taxes

a. a danger

b. a lake used for collecting and storing water

c. things you do for enjoyment

d. land, buildings, and other things people own

e. money that people pay to support their government and its services

Reviewing Facts

1. Why do communities provide services?

2. What community departments help protect people?

3. What department provides day-to-day services?

4. How are community services paid for?

5. What happens at "Christmas in April" in Midland, Texas?

Thinking Critically

1. What two community services do you think are most important? Explain your answers.

2. Imagine that your community has enough money to build either a public library or a new park. Which do you think should be built? Why?

3. Why do you think museums are important?

Writing About It

Fire fighters follow directions on how to use and care for their equipment. Write directions for the proper use of a piece of equipment or tool in your home.

 Practicing Citizenship Skills

Being a Responsible Citizen

Here are three rules. Tell why you need to obey each rule.

a. Be quiet in a library.

b. Never put your hand or arm out the window of a bus.

c. Do not swim alone.

On Your Own

Social Studies at Home

Plan what your family should do in case of a fire. Draw a map to show how to safely get out of your home. Hold a fire drill to make sure everyone knows what to do.

Read More About It

A Day in the Life of a Fire-fighter by Betsy Smith. Troll. A fire fighter describes his duties.

Pioneer Children of Appalachia by Joan Anderson. Clarion Books. The author tells how people did their daily tasks long ago.

State Patrol by Patrick Nau. Carolrhoda Books. Our state police protect us, too.

The *San Diego* ZOO

▲ **Animals from many parts of the world live at the San Diego Zoo. The elephant in this picture first lived in Africa.**

The big yellow school buses pull into the parking lot and the children jump out. Already they can hear the peacocks and other animals. The children follow the sounds into the world-famous San Diego Zoo.

This zoo is in a park owned by the city of San Diego, California. The zoo is a service that the community provides to everybody. The zoo was started in

1916 with just a few animals. Today it has one of the biggest collections of animals and plants in the world.

Most of the animals in the zoo live in big areas. The zoo makes these areas as much like the animals' natural homes as it can. This gives visitors a chance to learn how the animals behave in nature. The animals are happier and healthier this way, too.

▲
This is one of the orangutans at the zoo.

Animals and Escapes

Keeping animals in their areas is not always easy. The orangutans (uh•RANG•uh•tangz) are a good example. They are very good at getting out of places they are supposed to stay in.

In 1975 a group of five orangutans was moved to a new area of the zoo. Within a few months, they escaped from their area. Swinging on a net from their jungle gym, an orangutan grabbed a bamboo branch. The bamboo branch was growing outside the orangutan area. The orangutans used this branch as a ladder. Two of them climbed up and out. They did not seem interested in going too far—just out.

The giraffes are much easier to keep in their area of the zoo. Giraffes are very heavy on top. Their legs are very long and thin. Giraffes do not like to step down into things. So workers dug a ditch that is only 5 feet (about 1.5 m) deep around the giraffe area. The giraffes do not try to get away.

At about 18 feet tall, giraffes are the tallest animals alive.

The Biggest Birdcage

Birds are a different case. The question is how to keep them inside the zoo and still give them flying room. The zookeeper's answer was to build one of the biggest birdcages in the world.

The cage holds the zoo's collection of South American birds. Walking inside the cage is like entering a jungle. The cage is thick with trees and flowering plants. The cries of the colorful birds fill the air.

Animals in the Nursery

Animals living in zoos do not always act as they would outside the zoo. In the wild, most animal mothers care for their young. In the zoo, though, sometimes they cannot or will not. Then the babies are taken to the zoo nursery. They are raised by people.

"NO VISITORS ARE ALLOWED IN," says a large sign on the nursery door. This sign is very important. Many times the baby animals that are

▲
The pictures above show the huge birdcage at the San Diego Zoo.

Top, a zoo worker feeds a baby aardvark. Bottom, a baby spider monkey peeks out from its blankets.

helpers are trained to care for all the animals in the zoo. They especially like checking the young animals in the nursery.

Visitors can watch what is going on through big windows. At first, the zoo nursery looks almost like a regular nursery. There are cribs with blankets, toys, and bottles. But tucked neatly under a special heat lamp is a tiny aardvark. A baby chimp is getting its last bottle of the day.

The big yellow buses roll out of the parking lot at the end of the day. The last visitors leave. In the nursery the light stays on. A baby spider monkey is being rocked to sleep.

brought to the nursery are sick or weak. Baby animals can catch colds or flu from humans. So only nursery workers are allowed inside.

The zoo has its own animal doctors. The doctors and their

Unit Review

WORDS TO REMEMBER

Number your paper from 1 to 10. Use the words below to fill in the blanks. Use each word only once.

citizens
courts
crime
government
hazards
public transportation

laws
public works
sales tax
town meeting

1. Lawmakers, leaders, and judges are parts of our _____ .

2. Some people in government make our _____ .

3. When we obey laws, we are being good _____ .

4. People in Newfane, Vermont, have a _____ once a year.

5. The places where judges work are called _____ .

6. Police move quickly when they hear about a _____ .

7. Electrical plugs and wires that are worn out are two examples of fire _____ .

8. The _____ department sees that streets are clean and in good repair.

9. You are using _____ when you take a train somewhere.

10. When you buy something at a store, you often pay a _____ .

FOCUS ON MAIN IDEAS

1. Why is it important to obey laws in a community?

2. How is the government of a city different from the government of a small town?

3. How do we choose our country's government?

4. Who makes the laws for our country?

5. What is the most important court in our country?

6. How does the police department help your community?

7. Name two services of the public works department.

8. What kinds of recreation do communities provide?

9. How do the taxes people pay help communities?

10. How and why are community services in a big city different from those in a town?

225

THINK/WRITE

Make a list of the branches of government in your state and in our country. Write a paragraph on how your state's government is like our country's government.

ACTIVITIES

1. **Research**   Find out more about your community's government. Who are its leaders? Who makes the laws?

2. **Art/Bulletin Board**   Cut out or draw pictures of parks, libraries, zoos, houses, and businesses. Under each picture, write whether it is public property or private property.

SKILLS REVIEW

1. **Finding Information**   Suppose your community is having a fair. Name two places where you might find information about the fair.

2. **Using Maps and Grids**   The following grid map shows part of a town called Green Hill. Answer these questions.
   a. In what square is City Hall?
   b. What is in square C-3?

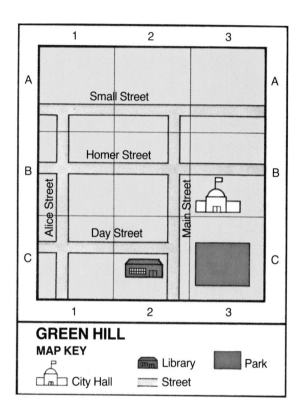

3. **Making a Choice**   Some of your classmates would like to have a classroom fish tank. Others do not think it is a good idea. Make a choice. Tell how and why you made your choice.

4. **Being a Responsible Citizen** Draw a line down the middle of a piece of paper. On one side, make a list of ten rules or laws. Title this side "Being a responsible Citizen." On the other side, write why each rule and law is important. Title this side "Why Being a Responsible Citizen is Important."

226

EXPLORING
YOUR COMMUNITY

In Unit 3 you read about local, state, and our country's government. You also studied about community services. Now find out more about these services in your own community.

LEARNING ABOUT COMMUNITY SERVICES

1. Visit a museum, library, or park in your community. Report to your class about your visit.

LEARNING ABOUT GOVERNMENT

2. You want to be elected mayor. Make a campaign poster for yourself. Tell what you want to do for your community.

3. Find out more about your community's government. Look through your community newspaper to find stories about your local government. Cut out any pictures or stories. With other students in your class, make a scrapbook showing your community government in action.

LEARNING ABOUT MAPS AND GRIDS

4. Find a grid map of your community. Use the map to tell where a fire station, a park, and a school are located.

LEARNING ABOUT VOLUNTEER SERVICES

5. Make a list of three volunteer service groups in your community. Find out what each group does. Choose one group that you would like to join someday. Explain what the group does and why you would like to belong to it.

TAKING A FIELD TRIP

6. With your class or family members, visit a fire station in your community. Ask the fire fighters what you can do to help keep your home and school safe from fire. Ask what you should do in case a fire does start. Draw a map showing the route you take when you have a fire drill in your school.

UNIT

4

COMMUNITIES OF YESTERDAY, TODAY, AND TOMORROW

Community Facts and Figures

Location	Denver, Colorado	Plymouth, Massachusetts	Philadelphia, Pennsylvania
Population (estimated)	505,000	44,275	1,643,000
Landmark	Capitol Building	Plymouth Rock	Independence Hall
Nickname/Motto	Mile High City	Land of the Pilgrims	City of Brotherly Love

Look at the picture. It shows a community with both old and new buildings. Are there any old buildings like these in your community? If the buildings could talk, they might tell some very interesting stories.

Of course, buildings cannot talk. However, we can learn about the past in other ways. We can learn by visiting places. We can talk to people who remember things that happened long ago.

In this unit we will find out about the pasts of communities in the United States. We will see how communities change.

Think Beyond   What changes have happened in your community this past year?

Location	Jamestown (historic Virginia)
Population (estimated)	100 men
Landmark	Old Church Tower
Nickname/Motto	First Permanent English Settlement

CHAPTER 8

Communities Grow and Change

"The buffaloes are gone.
And those who saw the buffaloes are gone.
Those who saw the buffaloes by thousands and how
    they pawed the prairie sod into dust with their
    hoofs, their great heads down pawing on in a
    great pageant of dusk,
Those who saw the buffaloes are gone.
And the buffaloes are gone."

—"Buffalo Dusk" by Carl Sandburg

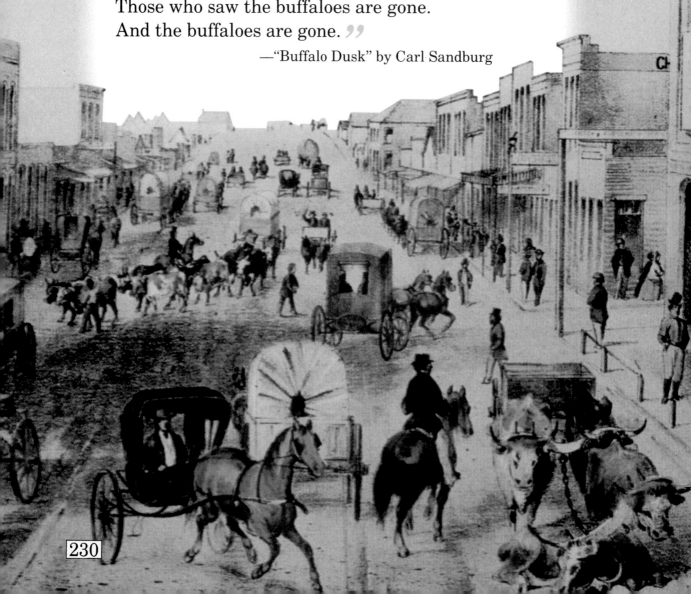

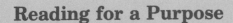
Look for these important words:

Key Words
- history
- trade centers
- crossroads

Look for answers to these questions:
1. What is history?
2. Why did many communities begin near water?
3. Why are communities still starting up now?

1 HOW COMMUNITIES BEGIN

History is the story of the past. Everything that has already happened is history.

All communities have histories. Many communities began long ago. Different communities began for different reasons.

Places Where Communities Began

Many communities began near water. Long ago, one of the main ways to travel was by boat. Goods were shipped by boat, too. A community near water was easy to reach. People could catch food from rivers, lakes, and oceans. They could water their crops with fresh water from rivers and lakes.

Later, railroads were built. Railroads made new places easy to reach. Many new communities started up where the railroads were built. Some became **trade centers**. Trade centers are places where people buy and sell many goods. The railroads carried many of these goods.

Communities also began at **crossroads.** Crossroads are places where main roads meet. Crossroads can also be places where railroads and roads meet. Perhaps a store was built at a crossroad. Soon people stayed at the crossroads instead of going on.

Many communities grew up near natural resources like coal and other minerals. Towns sprang up quickly in places where gold or oil was found. People came to earn money from mining these resources. They built communities.

New Communities Today

This small oil-drilling community in Alaska was built with many underground tunnels. People can travel within the community while being protected from the icy cold.

Today new communities are still starting. They often begin for the same reasons that communities began long ago. In Alaska, new communities are growing where oil has been found. Some new communities start near new businesses or industries. Some start up along new highways.

Other new communities are starting near big cities. This is because some cities have become too crowded or cost too much to live in. So people move outside the cities.

This picture shows an idea for a space station where people could live. The spaceship on the right would travel to and from Earth.

Communities of the Future

Communities will continue to start up. Someday there may be communities in space, high above the Earth. A space station is already planned. There would be places there for people to live, work, and grow food.

Reading Check

1. How did railroads help our country grow?
2. Where might communities begin someday?

Think Beyond   If you could move to a space station, would you go? Tell why or why not.

233

Look for these important words:

Key Words
- ghost town
- tepees
- Arapaho Indians
- Plains Indians
- buffalo

Places
- Denver, Colorado
- Rocky Mountains

Look for answers to these questions:
1. Who first lived where Denver is now?
2. What animal did the Plains Indians use to meet their needs?
3. What important jobs did Arapaho women have?

2 DENVER, COLORADO— THE EARLY YEARS

Communities begin in different ways. They also grow in different ways. Some communities start small and grow into large cities. Others do not grow much at all. Still other communities grow fast but then become **ghost towns.** Ghost towns are places where no one lives anymore.

Many ghost towns began as mining communities. When the mines were empty, people left the towns and moved to new places.

234

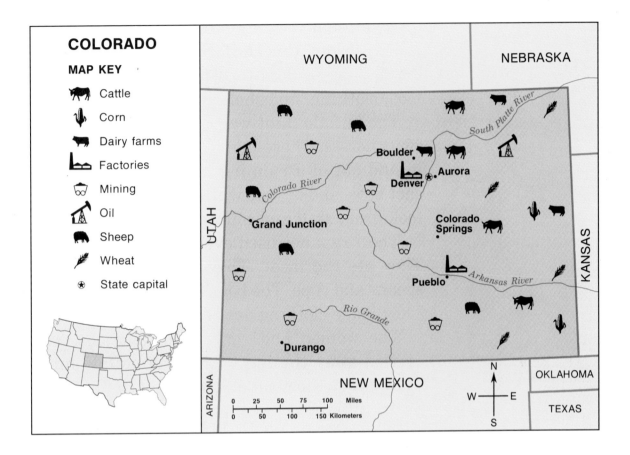

COLORADO

MAP KEY

🐃 Cattle
🌽 Corn
🐄 Dairy farms
🏭 Factories
⛏ Mining
🛢 Oil
🐑 Sheep
🌾 Wheat
✺ State capital

We will now look at how one city has grown and changed. This city is **Denver, Colorado.** Denver is a city near the **Rocky Mountains.**

The Buffalo Hunters

American Indians were the first people to live where Denver is now. They were there long before others came to settle.

The **Arapaho** (uh•RAP•uh•hoh) **Indians** lived in **tepees,** or cone-shaped tents. The Arapahos were **Plains Indians.** Plains Indians lived on the Great Plains east of the Rocky Mountains. The Arapahos moved from place to place and followed the animals they hunted. In the winter, they settled in camps or villages.

The Indians made pottery from clay which they dug from the ground.

235

No animal was more important to the Plains Indians than the **buffalo** (BUHF•uh•loh). This large, shaggy, wild ox gave the Plains Indians food, clothing, and shelter.

The buffalo hunt was exciting. The men rode swift horses. These horses were trained to move in and out of a running buffalo herd. The men shot bows and arrows while riding fast. The hunt took great skill and courage.

The Arapahos used every part of the buffalo. They ate the meat. They made the horns into spoons and cups. The bones were made into tools. They made clothing out of the skins.

The women had very important jobs. They carried away the meat from the buffalo hunts. They cut up the meat and made the buffalo ready for its different uses.

The Plains Indians hunted buffalo for food and for the hides, which they made into shelter and clothing.

This picture shows Indians working on the hide of a buffalo. The tepees in the picture are also made of buffalo skins.

The women used the buffalo skins to make the tepees, too. First, they sewed several skins together. Then they stretched the skins over poles set up in the shape of a cone. The tepees could be moved easily. When the Arapahos moved to where the buffaloes were, they took their tepees along with them.

Reading Check

1. How did the Arapaho depend on buffalo?
2. How did Arapaho women make tepees?

Think Beyond The Arapaho way of life depended on the buffalo. On what do you depend for your way of life?

People MAKE HISTORY

"Buffalo Bill" Cody
1846–1917

▶▶▶▶▶▶▶▶▶▶▶▶▶▶▶▶

William Cody started work when he was 11 years old. He first looked after cows and horses on wagon trains going west. At the age of 14 he became a rider for the pony express. Delivering mail for the pony express was hard, dangerous work. Each rider rode about 75 miles (121 km).

When Will was 17, he joined the army as a **scout**. A scout finds out what is ahead and goes back to tell the group.

In 1867, Will Cody was hired as a buffalo hunter to help feed workers building the railroad. In eight months he killed more than 4,000 buffalo. The workers gave him the nickname Buffalo Bill.

Buffalo Bill loved the West but he knew that many people would never have a chance to see it. He decided to take the West to them. In 1883 he started "Buffalo Bill's Wild West" traveling show. The show included examples of sharp shooting, buffalo hunts,

and pony express rides. Buffalo Bill's show was very popular with people of all ages. He enjoyed sharing his excitement about the West with people all over the world.

Think Beyond Do you think Cody's "Wild West" show gave a true picture of the West? Explain your answer.

238

Look for these important words:

Key Words
- gold pan
- gold dust

Look for answers to these questions:
1. Why was gold important to Denver?
2. Why did Denver become a trading center?
3. How did miners get gold dust from rivers?

3 MINING IN DENVER

"Gold!" That was the cry that started the city of Denver. Gold was found in the sands of Cherry Creek in 1858. Many people came from other states to mine the gold.

A New Community

Soon a community of 25 cabins lined the banks of the creek. The community was not too far from the Arapaho village you just read about.

A store was opened right away. There was not much food, though. There were no farms close by, so food had to be brought from far away in wagons. This made food cost a lot. In fact, food was sometimes harder to find than gold.

The little mining community of Denver began growing fast. A lucky miner found more gold in nearby mountains. Then thousands of people came to the mountains in search of gold. Mining camps sprang up all around.

Children learned to read and write at Denver's first schoolhouse.

Because of its location, Denver became the trading center for all the mining camps. The miners came to buy food and tools. Denver soon had many stores, a hotel, and a bank. Denver's first newspaper was started. The people built a log cabin school for children.

Gold and Silver Mining

Many Mexicans were good at gold mining. They had been finding gold in Mexico for years. From them, gold miners in the West learned ways to mine gold. The Mexicans invented the **gold pan.** It had a wide, flat bottom and sloping sides. Miners used it to get loose grains of gold, called **gold dust,** from the rivers. Water was swished around in the pan. The sand went over the sides of the pan. The heavy grains of gold stayed in the bottom of the pan.

Miners looked for gold in the rivers of the West. Some found gold and became rich, but many found nothing.

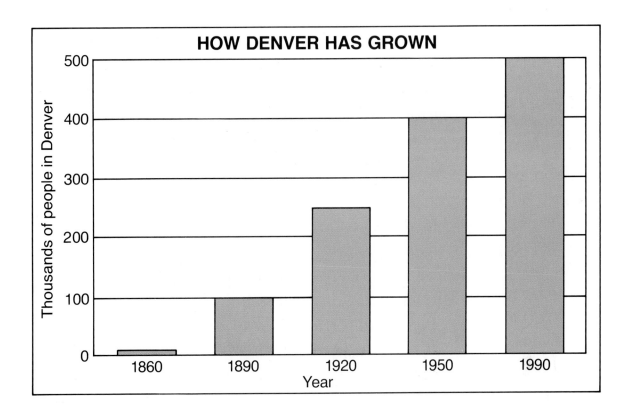

HOW DENVER HAS GROWN

The Mexicans also had special ways to mine gold and silver from rock. They taught the Americans these mining skills, too.

In 1859, when gold and silver mining began, Denver had 5,000 people. Twenty years later, about 35,000 people lived there. Ten years after that, there were about 100,000 people!

By 1889, most of the gold and silver around Denver had been mined. By then, however, the people of Denver had other ways to make a living.

 Reading Check

1. Who taught the miners how to mine?
2. Why did food in early Denver cost so much?
Think Beyond Why would the discovery of new gold mines be important to you as a shopkeeper in early Denver?

241

IN FOCUS

DENVER MINT

The United States Mint in Denver, Colorado, opened for business in 1863. It was first called the United States Assay Office. Miners took their gold and silver there to be measured, weighed, and tested for purity. The Assay Office was one of the most important buildings in Denver.

Several years later, Congress decided that the United States Assay Office should start making coins. The name was changed to the United States Mint at Denver. Today, the Denver and San Francisco mints make most of the coins people use every day.

Until 1965, silver bricks such as these were used to make coins.

242

The assay office was moved to this new building in 1904.

The Denver Mint is a popular tourist attraction. People can take tours to learn how coins are made. First a machine called a press punches out blank coins from wide strips of metal. These blanks are shaken on a metal screen. Blanks that are too small fall through the screen. The blanks that are the right size are put into machines to be cleaned.

The blanks are then taken to a furnace. There they are heated and placed in machines that put a raised, smooth rim around the edge of each blank.

Finally, the blanks are put into a coining press. Here the design is stamped on both sides. This press also adds a rough edge to all coins except pennies and nickels.

The finished coins are counted by machines and put into canvas bags. The bags are sewn shut and stored until they are sent to banks all over the country.

After the tour, visitors can make a coin to take home. They use a special press. The finished coin says "Denver Mint Souvenir Medal." People enjoy having a reminder of their visit to the United States Mint at Denver.

Think Beyond Sometimes the mints stop making a coin because people no longer use it much. Some people feel that pennies should no longer be made. How would not having pennies change the way you use money?

These pennies are just a few of the 32 million coins minted each day.

243

Look for these important words:

Key Words
- spur
- aerospace
- manufactured

Look for answers to these questions:
1. When did the railroad come to Denver?
2. Why has Denver grown in the last thirty years?
3. What problems are people in Denver trying to solve?

4 MODERN DENVER

In 1870, the first train steamed into Denver. The people of Denver were proud. They had raised the money themselves to build the **spur,** or branch of the railroad.

The railroad linked Denver to the rest of the country. Goods could be brought in and out easily. People could travel to Denver more easily, too.

After the railroad was built, people watched for the trains that brought visitors and trade to Denver.

The railroad also made Denver into a market for cattle and farm crops. The ranchers of the Great Plains could now use the railroad. Trains carried their cattle and sheep to Denver. The farmers of the Plains could use the railroad, too. The railroad carried their wheat, corn, and sugar beets to Denver.

Denver Today

For the last 30 years Denver has been growing faster. One reason for Denver's new growth is the **aerospace** (AIR•oh•spays) industry. Aerospace means having to do with air and space. The aerospace industry makes planes and spacecraft.

In Denver today, many different kinds of goods are **manufactured,** or made in factories. These goods include foods, sporting goods, computers, and machines for transportation. There are a lot of different, new jobs for the people of Denver.

Denver, Colorado's capital, is an important transportation and manufacturing center for the whole Rocky Mountain area.

Skiing is a popular sport in the Rocky Mountains near Denver.

Denver is also well known for its location. Thousands of people come every year to ski and hike in the Rocky Mountains.

Much of Denver's new growth happened because oil, coal, and other resources were found in the Rocky Mountain area. Some people in Denver worry that their city might be growing too fast. They worry about the air that people breathe and the water that they drink. They are looking for ways to keep their air and water clean. People in Denver are used to solving problems, though. Several years ago, downtown Denver was full of old, run-down buildings. Today most of these buildings have been fixed up.

Reading Check

1. How did the railroad help Denver's people?
2. What does the aerospace industry make?

Think Beyond How could you help solve the problems caused by rapid growth?

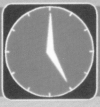

SKILLS IN ACTION

USING PICTURES TO TELL A STORY

The first photograph was made about 150 years ago. Before that time the only way to make a picture was to paint or draw one.

The picture at the bottom of this page was painted before cameras were widely used.

Look at this picture carefully. The picture shows how the Plains Indians lived long ago. You can tell that the picture shows a scene from long ago. There are no modern houses or clothing. There are no television antennas or wires for electricity or telephones.

People still paint pictures today. But you can usually tell whether a painting is very old or new. For example, if a painting shows people in modern clothes, you know the picture cannot be very old.

Photographs

Early photographs did not have color. They could only show things in black, white, and gray. The top picture on the next page is a photograph of Denver, Colorado. It was taken in 1860.

This picture was taken when people used horses and wagons. The streets were made of dirt. The buildings do not look much like the ones we see today.

This picture was painted in 1850. It shows Indian groups on the Great Plains, near where Denver is now.

The photograph at the bottom of this page was taken 40 years later in Denver.

You can tell that this photograph is newer than the top one. You can see cars, street lamps, and wires and tracks for electric streetcars. The buildings in the bottom picture look different from the ones in the 1860 picture, too.

You can tell that the picture at the bottom is not a modern scene, though. The people are wearing old-fashioned clothes. How else can you tell that it is not a modern picture?

This picture of Denver was taken in 1860.

This picture of Denver was taken in 1900.

This picture shows Denver as it looks today. What are some things that tell you it is a new picture?

Now look at this photograph of Denver. The photograph was taken just a few years ago. You can see modern buildings in the background. Modern cars drive down a wide street. The photograph is in color. It shows what Denver looks like today.

CHECKING YOUR SKILLS

Use the pictures to help you answer these questions.

1. Look at the painting on page 247. What clues tell you that it is an old picture?

2. Look at the photograph on this page. What clues tell you that it is a new picture?

3. What are some ways that you can tell whether a photograph is old or new?

4. Has Denver gotten bigger or smaller since 1860? What in the pictures makes you think the way you do?

5. Look at the date of the painting in the first picture. Why didn't the painter use a camera instead of a paintbrush to make this picture?

249

Thinking Back

- Some communities begin near water, railroads, or highways. Other communities start near natural resources.

- Denver, Colorado, began on the Great Plains, where Arapaho Indians hunted buffalo.

- Gold was found near Denver in 1858. Mexicans came and showed Americans how to mine. Denver became a trading center for miners.

- In 1870 the railroad reached Denver. The citizens hoped it would help trade and bring more people.

- Today Denver manufactures many goods. Coal and oil have helped Denver grow large.

Check for Understanding

Using Words

Number a sheet of paper from 1 to 5. Match the words with their meanings.

1. **aerospace**
2. **history**
3. **spur**
4. **tepees**
5. **trade centers**
   a. the story of the past
   b. places where people buy and sell many goods
   c. cone-shaped tents
   d. branch of a railroad
   e. having to do with air and space

Reviewing Facts

1. Where do communities often begin? Name three kinds of places.

2. How did the Arapahos meet their needs for food, clothing, and shelter?

3. Why did people from other parts of the country first come to Denver?

4. How was a gold pan used?

5. Why is Denver a big city today? What do people do there?

Thinking Critically

1. What was life like for the Arapaho Indians? What was important about the way their tepees were made?

2. Why did Denver not become a ghost town? How did Denver change after the gold-mining days?

3. Why was the railroad important to Denver?

4. What might it be like to live in a community that is growing very fast? What would be some good things about having many new people there? What problems might the community's growth cause?

Writing About It

Imagine that you are a hardware store owner in Denver in the 1860s. Write an advertisement for gold-mining supplies.

Practicing Time Skills

Using Pictures to Tell a Story
Choose a picture from this chapter. Do not use one from the skills lesson. Tell whether the picture is from long ago or now. Tell how you know.

On Your Own

Social Studies at Home

Miners sometimes made maps showing where their mines were located. Choose a place in your neighborhood to be your mine. Write directions and draw a map showing your mine's location. See if your family can find your mine.

Read More About It

Anno's U.S.A. by Mitsumasa Anno. This book follows one man's travels across the United States.

Department Store by Gail Gibbons. Harper & Row. You will see a modern trade center as its customers and workers see it.

Frontier Village: A Town is Born by Catherine Chambers. Troll. This book shows the development of a small town.

General Store by Rachel Field. Greenwillow. A poem with pictures takes you to a general store of the early 1900s .

The House on Maple Street by Bonnie Pryor. William Morrow. Two girls find a china cup and an arrowhead from the past.

CHAPTER 9

Our Country Has a History

"Our history sings of centuries
Such varying songs it sings!
It starts with winds, slow moving sails,
It ends with skies and wings."

—"Our History" by Catherine Cate Coblentz

Look for these important words:

Key Words
- Navajo Indians
- Columbus Day
- explorers
- claimed

People
- Christopher Columbus
- Amerigo Vespucci
- John Cabot

Look for answers to these questions:
1. How did American Indians live long ago? Why were there differences in the ways they lived?
2. Why did Christopher Columbus cross the Atlantic Ocean?
3. Why did explorers come to America?
4. What countries claimed land in America?

1 EARLY YEARS IN AMERICA

Long ago, American Indian groups lived in almost every part of our country. The way a group lived depended on where it was and what resources were nearby.

For example, **Navajo** (NA•vuh•hoh) **Indians** lived in Arizona and New Mexico. There it is often warm and sunny. The Navajo Indians raised crops for food. Corn was one important food they grew. The Navajos also hunted for food.

Some Indian groups lived near the ocean in the state of Washington. Their land had thick forests and many rivers. These Indian groups built large houses of wood. They built big wooden boats. They sailed these boats on the rivers and on the ocean. They caught fish for food and they hunted whales.

Navajo shelters are called hogans (HOH•gunz). Hogans are made of earth and wood.

The Indians in this painting lived near the Great Lakes. They are picking wild strawberries for food.

There were many more Indian groups in America. These groups were different from each other in many ways. Their names were different. Their languages were different. Their ways of getting food were different. They built different kinds of shelters. Yet each group was able to meet the needs of its people.

Columbus Sails to America

In 1492, about 500 years ago, **Christopher Columbus** sailed from Spain, in Europe. He wanted to find a new way to get to China from Europe. Christopher Columbus decided to try to cross the Atlantic Ocean.

Columbus and his crew did not reach China. Instead, they found a land that people in Europe did not know about. They found the land that we call America.

After two long months at sea, Columbus was glad to find land. Taking a flag ashore, he said the land belonged to Spain.

The day that Columbus first landed in America was October 12, 1492. Today we have a holiday in October to celebrate the landing. It is called **Columbus Day.** On that day we remember when Columbus landed in America.

Explorers in America

News of Columbus's discovery spread through Europe. Many other sailors from Europe set out across the Atlantic Ocean. They hoped to find gold and other treasures. They were **explorers.** Explorers traveled to new lands. They brought back stories of what they had found.

One of these explorers was an Italian named **Amerigo Vespucci** (ahm•uh•REE•goh veh•SPOO•chee). Later, America was named after him.

This painting shows Amerigo Vespucci as a young man.

255

The picture on the left shows John Cabot, an explorer for England. The picture on the right shows Robert La Salle, who claimed land in America for France.

John Cabot sailed from England five years after Columbus found America. Cabot sailed along the northern coast of America. He told the king of England about the lands he had discovered. The king of England then **claimed** these lands for England. This means that he said that these lands belonged to England.

French explorers also came to America. They sailed up and down the Mississippi, St. Lawrence, and Missouri rivers. They sailed the Great Lakes. They claimed much land for France.

Meanwhile, Spanish explorers were finding gold in the southern parts of America. They claimed much land for Spain.

 Reading Check

1. When did Columbus land in America?
2. How did America get its name?

Think Beyond   Would it have been fun to sail with Columbus? Tell why or why not.

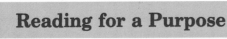
Look for these important words:

Key Words	People	Places
• settlers	• John Smith	• Jamestown
• Mayflower	• Squanto	• Plymouth
• Pilgrims		
• Thanksgiving		
• slaves		

Look for answers to these questions:

1. What are two communities that settlers started in America?
2. How did the Pilgrims meet their needs?
3. What were slaves? How were they not free?

 SETTLERS COME TO AMERICA

In 1607 a group of people sailed to America from England. They were **settlers,** not explorers. Settlers are people who go somewhere to live. These people decided to start a community in what is now the state of Virginia.

Jamestown

The new community was called **Jamestown.** The community did not do well at first. People built shelters that did not keep out the rain or cold. They did not spend enough time planting crops and meeting their needs.

Then a person named **John Smith** became the leader of the community. He made people build better shelters. He sent them to plant crops. Soon the community was doing much better.

The picture below shows John Smith, the leader of Jamestown.

257

The Pilgrims

Another group of settlers came to America in 1620. They sailed from England on a ship called the **Mayflower.** The Mayflower landed at a place called **Plymouth,** in what is now Massachusetts.

These settlers were called **Pilgrims.** Pilgrims wanted to be free to have their own beliefs. They wanted to build their own church.

The Pilgrims worked hard to build their new community. They had chosen a good place for their community. There was clear, fresh water for drinking. They were near a good harbor. They knew how to build good shelters. An American Indian named **Squanto** helped them grow food.

One year after they landed, the Pilgrims picked their first crops. Plymouth was doing well. The Pilgrims had a great celebration that November. They wanted to show how thankful they were for their new way of life. We celebrate this same holiday, **Thanksgiving,** every November.

At the first Thanksgiving, the Pilgrims shared food with the Indians who had helped them. The Indians brought gifts of food to the celebration.

Settlers cleared the land's thick forests and built their houses from wood. To get water, they dug wells.

Soon more and more people came to America. They came from England and France and the Netherlands and Sweden. In America they could own their own land and farm it. Soon people began building towns.

Slaves in America

One group of people in America was not free. People in this group were taken from their homes in Africa. They were brought by ship to America to work for other people. They did not get paid. They were **slaves.** Slaves were people who were owned by other people. Many slaves in America were put to work on large farms. They were often kept apart from their families.

Many Americans believed that slavery was wrong. Years later, a war was fought about this.

 Reading Check

1. Who became the leader of Jamestown?
2. Why did the Pilgrims come to America?

Think Beyond   How might you thank someone who helps you do a difficult task?

IN FOCUS

PLIMOTH PLANTATION

Would you like to talk with a Pilgrim or see a Native American campsite? Would you like to explore a ship like the one in which the Pilgrims sailed to America? You could do these things if you visited Plimoth Plantation in Plymouth, Massachusetts.

Plimoth Plantation is a **living history museum.** A living history museum is a special kind of museum. Here people act out how life used to be at a certain time and place. Visiting Plimoth Plantation is like stepping back to the year 1627.

Plimoth Plantation is made up of three parts. The first part is the Pilgrim village. People who work in the village wear Pilgrim cos-

Daily life in Plymouth, Massachusetts, looked much like this in the 1600s.

Sailors entertained Pilgrim children on the long voyage from England.

This is a ship that has been built to look like the ship in which the Pilgrims sailed to America. The workers on the Mayflower II can tell you about the dangerous ocean crossing the Pilgrims made.

People of all ages enjoy visiting Plimoth Plantation. There is a lot to see and do and the people who work there are glad to answer questions. At Plimoth Plantation, learning about early American communities is fun.

tumes. They do the same kind of work the early settlers did.

The second part of Plimoth Plantation is called the Wampanoag (wahm•puh•NOH•hg) Summer Campsite. Some of the people who work here are relatives of the Wampanoag Indians who helped the Pilgrims.

You have to travel a few miles to visit the third part of Plimoth Plantation. On the waterfront in Plymouth Bay is the Mayflower II.

Think Beyond At what part of Plimoth Plantation would you like to be a worker? What kind of work would you like to do there? Tell why.

Wampanoag Indians traded furs for goods made by the settlers.

Look for these important words:

Key Words
- colonies
- nation
- freedom
- Declaration of Independence
- American Revolution

- Fourth of July
- Constitution

People
- Thomas Jefferson
- George Washington

Look for answers to these questions:

1. In what part of America were the English colonies?
2. Why did Americans want to have freedom from England?
3. What was the Declaration of Independence?

3 A NEW COUNTRY IS BORN

By 1763 there were many communities in America. England now claimed much of the eastern part of North America. That is where most of the communities were. The land in America ruled by England was called the English **colonies.**

Laws in the Colonies

For a long time Americans did not mind being ruled by England. Then lawmakers in England began passing new laws for the colonies. Many of the colonists did not like these new laws. They did not like the taxes that England was making them pay. They also did not like being told what to do by people who lived so far away.

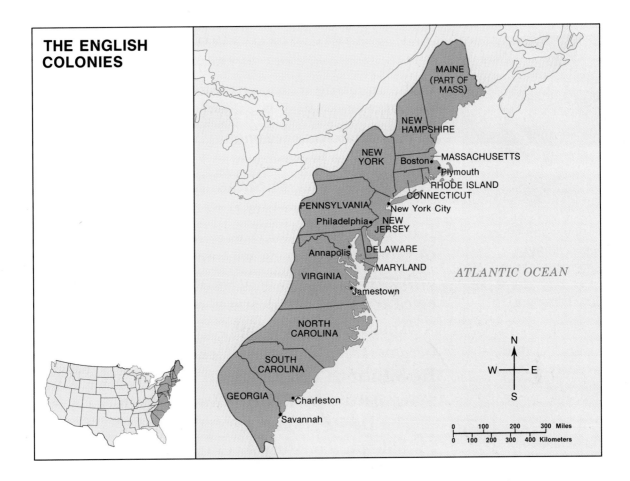

THE ENGLISH COLONIES

MAINE (PART OF MASS.)

NEW HAMPSHIRE

NEW YORK

Boston •— MASSACHUSETTS
• Plymouth
RHODE ISLAND
CONNECTICUT

PENNSYLVANIA
• New York City

Philadelphia • NEW JERSEY

DELAWARE

Annapolis •

MARYLAND

ATLANTIC OCEAN

VIRGINIA

• Jamestown

NORTH CAROLINA

SOUTH CAROLINA

GEORGIA

• Charleston

Savannah

N
W — E
S

0   100   200   300 Miles
0 100 200 300 400 Kilometers

Many Americans felt that they could not obey the new laws or pay the new taxes that England wanted. People began talking about starting a new country, or **nation.** A nation is a land with a government of its own.

The Fighting Begins

In 1775 some American farmers fought against the soldiers from England. The farmers had decided that they needed to be free. They and other Americans decided to fight for **freedom.** Freedom to them meant having their own government in America. Freedom meant that they would be able to make their own laws.

The Declaration of Independence

Leaders from the different parts of America had a meeting in the summer of 1776. They met in Philadelphia, Pennsylvania. The leaders decided that America should become a new nation.

One of the leaders wrote a message to the world. This leader was **Thomas Jefferson.** His message was the **Declaration of Independence.** It told everyone that America no longer belonged to England. America was now a nation with its own government. The new nation would come to be called the United States of America.

Americans had to fight a war with England to become free. This war is called the **American Revolution.** The American soldiers were led in many battles by **George Washington.**

The Declaration of Independence was read in Philadelphia on July 4, 1776. Today the **Fourth of July** is one of our most important holidays. It is the birthday of our country.

Thomas Jefferson was a strong American leader. Later, he became our third President.

Leaders met in Philadelphia to vote for the Declaration of Independence.

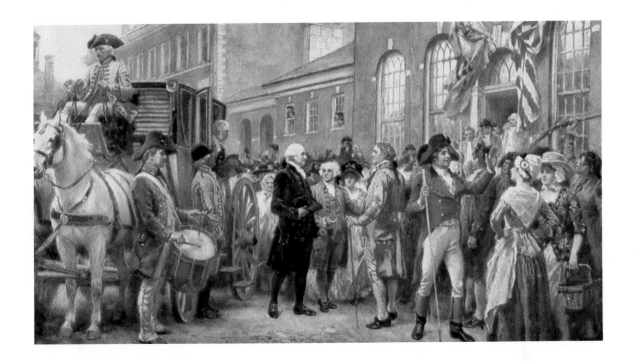

A New Government

Americans wanted a government that would make fair rules. So our country's leaders got together again. They planned how the new government would work.

The leaders wrote laws for the government. These laws were called the **Constitution.** We still use the Constitution today.

Then Americans voted to elect their first President. They chose George Washington. We have a holiday in February to celebrate George Washington's birthday.

The picture above shows George Washington after he was elected President for the second time.

The famous picture below was painted by Gilbert Stuart in 1796.

Reading Check

1. What important statement did Thomas Jefferson write?
2. Why was the Constitution written?

Think Beyond   If England had ruled the colonies well, how might your life be different?

SKILLS IN ACTION

READING CALENDARS AND TIMELINES

Look at this **calendar.** It shows days and months of the year. The months are arranged in three rows. You read each row from left to right.

January, February, March, and April are in the first row. May, the month that follows April, begins the second row. June follows May, July follows June, and August follows July. What month follows August?

Look at the month of January. It ends on Thursday. February starts on Friday. Each month starts on the day after the last day of the month before. March ends on a Sunday. On what day does April begin? On what day does May begin?

JANUARY						
Su	M	Tu	W	Th	F	Sa
	1	2	3	4	5	
6	7	8	9	10	11	12
13	14	15	16	17	18	19
20	21	22	23	24	25	26
27	28	29	30	31		

FEBRUARY						
Su	M	Tu	W	Th	F	Sa
					1	2
3	4	5	6	7	8	9
10	11	12	13	14	15	16
17	18	19	20	21	22	23
24	25	26	27	28		

MARCH						
Su	M	Tu	W	Th	F	Sa
					1	2
3	4	5	6	7	8	9
10	11	12	13	14	15	16
17	18	19	20	21	22	23
24	25	26	27	28	29	30
31						

APRIL						
Su	M	Tu	W	Th	F	Sa
1	2	3	4	5	6	
7	8	9	10	11	12	13
14	15	16	17	18	19	20
21	22	23	24	25	26	27
28	29	30				

MAY						
Su	M	Tu	W	Th	F	Sa
		1	2	3	4	
5	6	7	8	9	10	11
12	13	14	15	16	17	18
19	20	21	22	23	24	25
26	27	28	29	30	31	

JUNE						
Su	M	Tu	W	Th	F	Sa
						1
2	3	4	5	6	7	8
9	10	11	12	13	14	15
16	17	18	19	20	21	22
23	24	25	26	27	28	29
30						

JULY						
Su	M	Tu	W	Th	F	Sa
	1	2	3	4	5	6
7	8	9	10	11	12	13
14	15	16	17	18	19	20
21	22	23	24	25	26	27
28	29	30	31			

AUGUST						
Su	M	Tu	W	Th	F	Sa
				1	2	3
4	5	6	7	8	9	10
11	12	13	14	15	16	17
18	19	20	21	22	23	24
25	26	27	28	29	30	31

SEPTEMBER						
Su	M	Tu	W	Th	F	Sa
1	2	3	4	5	6	7
8	9	10	11	12	13	14
15	16	17	18	19	20	21
22	23	24	25	26	27	28
29	30					

OCTOBER						
Su	M	Tu	W	Th	F	Sa
	1	2	3	4	5	
6	7	8	9	10	11	12
13	14	15	16	17	18	19
20	21	22	23	24	25	26
27	28	29	30	31		

NOVEMBER						
Su	M	Tu	W	Th	F	Sa
					1	2
3	4	5	6	7	8	9
10	11	12	13	14	15	16
17	18	19	20	21	22	23
24	25	26	27	28	29	30

DECEMBER						
Su	M	Tu	W	Th	F	Sa
1	2	3	4	5	6	7
8	9	10	11	12	13	14
15	16	17	18	19	20	21
22	23	24	25	26	27	28
29	30	31				

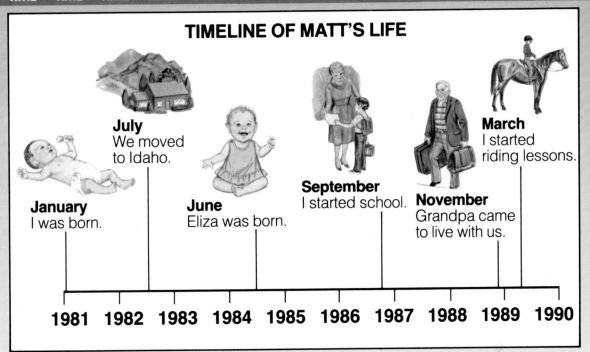

TIMELINE OF MATT'S LIFE

July
We moved
to Idaho.

January
I was born.

June
Eliza was born.

September
I started school.

November
Grandpa came
to live with us.

March
I started
riding lessons.

1981 1982 1983 1984 1985 1986 1987 1988 1989 1990

Reading Timelines

In the study of history, we need to keep track of more than one year. So we use a **timeline.** A timeline can show a number of years at once. It can show when things happened.

The timeline above was made by a boy named Matt. It lists some important things that have happened in his life.

You read a timeline from left to right, just like a sentence. The events on the left happened the earliest. The events on the right happened later. The first thing on this timeline happened in 1981. Matt was born in that year. In 1984, Matt's sister was born. In 1986, Matt started school. The last thing on the timeline was that Matt started his riding lessons. In what year did that happen?

CHECKING YOUR SKILLS

Tell or write the answers to these questions.

1. Look at the calendar in this lesson. On what day of the week is the Fourth of July?

2. On what day of the week does October begin?

3. Look at the timeline on this page. Which happened first for Matt, getting a baby sister or starting school?

4. Did Matt move to Idaho before or after he started riding lessons?

267

Reading for a Purpose

Look for these important words:

Key Words
- reservations
- Civil War
- Memorial Day

People
- Abraham Lincoln

Look for answers to these questions:
1. Why did people move west after the American Revolution?
2. What happened to American Indians when settlers moved to their lands?
3. Why was Abraham Lincoln an important President?

 THE NEW NATION GROWS

The American Revolution took place in the eastern part of our country. Most Americans lived there at the time. However, some people had already moved west. After the American Revolution, more and more Americans moved west.

Many American settlers packed what they owned and headed west in wagons.

268

Colorful, wood-burning steamboats carried passengers and goods along the nation's large rivers.

Moving West

There was plenty of open land for farms in the West. People had to work hard to clear the land and to plant crops. They started new communities.

Some people moved west in wagons pulled by horses or oxen. In time, railroads were built. Railroads made it easier for people to move west. Big steamboats began sailing up and down rivers in the center of the United States. These boats helped move people west.

New settlers often fought terrible battles with the Indians. The settlers were taking land that the Indians had called their own. Many Indians tried to stop the settlers. Finally the Indians lost. There were too many settlers and too few Indians.

Indians were forced to move to reservations. This painting shows one Indian group's move along the "Trail of Tears."

In time, the United States government made most of the American Indians give up their lands. Some were given new lands on which to live. These places were called **reservations** (rez•ur•VAY•shuhnz). Reservations were not always on lands the Indians knew. Indians often could not live in the ways they were used to.

Many people went west to California in 1849. Gold had been found there. New cities were built as more people came west to try to get rich. People were also coming west to farm in Oregon and Washington. Now there were communities in the United States from the Atlantic Ocean to the Pacific Ocean.

The Civil War

In 1861 Americans fought a terrible war. One half of the country fought against the other half. This war between the North and the South is known as the **Civil** (SIV•uhl) **War.**

Many people in the North thought that having slaves was wrong. They wanted a law saying that no one in our country could own slaves.

The problem of slaves was not the only reason for the war. The North and the South did not agree about many other things. People in the South wanted to start their own country. They wanted to have their own government and laws.

Abraham Lincoln was the President of the United States when the Civil War began. He felt very strongly that the country should stay together. He also felt that owning slaves was wrong. In 1863 he said that all slaves in the United States should be set free. We celebrate Abraham Lincoln's birthday on a holiday in February.

Below, Abraham Lincoln meets with soldiers from the North during the Civil War.

271

This picture of Memorial Day was drawn in 1868. It shows people remembering those who died in the Civil War.

The North finally won the war in 1865. It was a sad time for our country, though. Thousands of brave Americans died fighting for the North or for the South. We remember these soldiers on the holiday in May called **Memorial Day.** On this day we also remember other soldiers who have died fighting for our country.

Reading Check

1. Why did American Indians try to keep settlers from moving west?
2. How did President Abraham Lincoln make a difference in our country?

Think Beyond If the South had won the war, might Americans still own slaves? Explain.

People MAKE HISTORY

David Farragut
1801–1870

►►►►►►►►►►►►►►►►►

Captain Porter took his adopted son by the hand. "How would you like to join the Navy?" he asked. "Yes," the boy responded, "I'd like that!"

David Farragut (FAR•uh•guht) was nine years old when he went to sea on his father's ship, the U.S.S. Essex. David's training took place during wartime. The Essex was part of the United States fleet fighting the British in the War of 1812.

When David was 12, the Essex captured a British ship. David was put in charge of delivering the captured ship to port. Captain Porter praised David's performance. He wanted to promote him, but David was too young.

When Farragut was 22, he sailed with his father to the West Indies to fight pirates. The next year he was placed in command of his own ship.

David Farragut became the greatest naval hero of the Civil War. He commanded 17 ships and helped the North capture two important Southern ports. For these victories, President Lincoln made Farragut the first admiral in American history.

Think Beyond David Farragut wanted to become a good sailor and he worked hard to reach that goal. What goal would you like to work towards? What steps can you take to help reach that goal?

Look for these important words:

Key Words
- Labor Day
- labor

Places
- Ellis Island

Look for answers to these questions:

1. In what ways did the United States grow after the Civil War?
2. How did labor make our country strong?
3. How are we trying to make the United States even better today?

5 MODERN AMERICA

After the Civil War, the United States grew faster. Farmers and ranchers settled throughout our country. Mineral resources were discovered. New machines, such as cars, were invented. Big factories were built.

This picture shows automobiles being built in a huge factory in the early 1900s.

More People Come to Our Country

America is a mix of many people. This is because people from many different nations have come to live in America. They have joined together to form one nation.

New Americans came from countries such as Ireland, Germany, England, Italy, Russia, and Mexico. They often chose places to live in America that reminded them of their homeland. For example, many Scotch-Irish people settled in the mountains of Tennessee, Kentucky, and

People who came to America brought different languages. They brought different foods and clothing. They also brought their celebrations and holidays.

For more than 60 years, Ellis Island was used as a reception center for people coming to America. Today it is part of the Statue of Liberty National Monument.

Virginia. The mountains made them think of the land they had left behind. People from Norway and Sweden chose to live in Wisconsin and Minnesota. The weather there was much like the weather in their homeland.

People came to America for different reasons. Some came for land. Some came to find a better way of life. Some came for freedom. However, many were alike in one way. Millions of new Americans took their first step in America at **Ellis Island** in New York Harbor. It was called "The Gateway to the New World."

Most of these people went right to work. They became farmers and fishers. Some went to work in factories. All helped America to grow by working hard.

We have a holiday in September called **Labor Day. Labor** is another word for work. Without hard work nothing would have been built in America. On Labor Day we honor the workers who have made America strong.

Did you know that there are special craft to explore the oceans just as there are special craft to explore space? Underwater craft called submersibles (sub•MUR•suh•buhlz) are carried to the research site by ships. There the submersibles go deep into the ocean. Submersibles help scientists make maps of the ocean floor. They are helping people learn to live in the ocean. Plans are already being made for an undersea city. Maybe one day you will travel in a submersible to your ocean home.

A Land of Freedom

Our country has always stood for freedom. We are proud that so many people have found a better life in the United States. Today, people still come to our country to find a better life. We are working to make tomorrow even better.

We are exploring in space and under the ocean. We are working to solve problems in our growing cities. We are trying to keep our country beautiful while we get the resources we need.

You are part of our country's future. You will help America stay strong, busy, and free.

 Reading Check

1. What is labor?
2. What places are we exploring today?

Think Beyond How would living in an undersea community be different from living in your community? How would it be the same?

SKILLS IN ACTION

USING TIMELINES TO SHOW HISTORY

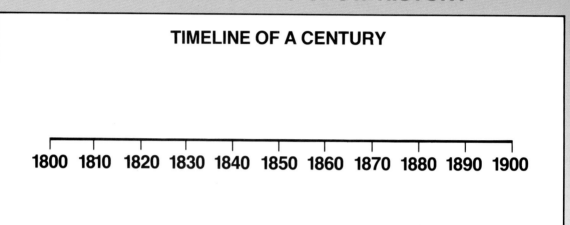

TIMELINE OF A CENTURY

1800 1810 1820 1830 1840 1850 1860 1870 1880 1890 1900

You know that you can put dates on a timeline. A timeline of your life might tell the year you were born and the year you started school. It would show other important dates in your life.

A timeline can also show a much longer amount of time. Reading timelines can help you understand the order of things in history.

The timeline above covers a **century.** A century is 100 years. The year 1900 is 100 years, or one century, later than the year 1800.

On the timeline above, each line stands for ten years. The year 1810 is ten years later than the year 1800. The year 1830 is 30 years later than the year 1800.

Remember that you read a timeline from left to right. The earliest date is on the left. The later dates are on the right.

A Timeline of American Firsts

A timeline shows important events. The timeline on page 279 shows when some important events took place in America's history. The timeline covers the two centuries between 1800 and 2000.

Look at the space between 1800 and 1850 on the timeline. Find the 1830 entry. It says "**1830** Railroad." In 1830, a train made its first run on a railroad track in the United States.

278

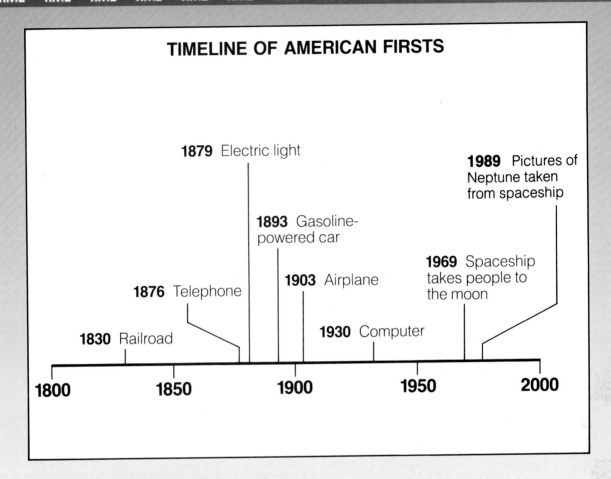

TIMELINE OF AMERICAN FIRSTS

1879 Electric light

1989 Pictures of Neptune taken from spaceship

1893 Gasoline-powered car

1969 Spaceship takes people to the moon

1876 Telephone

1903 Airplane

1830 Railroad

1930 Computer

1800   1850   1900   1950   2000

Now look at the space between 1850 and 1900. Find the first entry in that space. It tells you that the first telephone in our country was used in 1876.

The second entry between 1850 and 1900 says "**1879** Electric light." There is one more entry in the space between 1850 and 1900. What does it say?

CHECKING YOUR SKILLS

Use the timeline on this page to answer these questions.

1. Which came first—the first gasoline-powered car or the first electric light?

2. Did the first airplane flight happen before or after the first telephone was used?

3. Could a person have used a computer in 1970?

4. Did the person who invented the computer use electric lights when he worked?

5. Were pictures of Neptune taken from a spaceship before or after people landed on the moon?

Thinking Back

- Long ago, only American Indians lived in our country. In 1492 Columbus came. More explorers followed.

- In 1607 a group of settlers started a community called Jamestown. Then the Pilgrims settled at Plymouth. Later, slaves were brought to America from Africa.

- The American colonies were ruled by England. After England passed new laws, the colonists declared independence. George Washington became America's first President.

- People began moving west because there was land for farms.

- In 1861 the North and South fought each other in the Civil War. In 1863 President Abraham Lincoln freed the slaves.

- The United States grew. People came from many countries to work in the new factories. They helped make America strong.

Check for Understanding

Using Words

Use one of the words in parentheses to complete each sentence.

1. Amerigo Vespucci was an _____ . (explorer, Indian)

2. _____ were not freed until the Civil War. (Pilgrims, Slaves)

3. The land in America ruled by England was called the English _____ . (reservations, colonies)

4. People in America wanted to start a new _____ . (nation, town)

5. American Indians often had to live on _____ . (reservations, labor)

Reviewing Facts

1. On what holiday do we remember the person who found America in 1492?

2. When and where was the first Thanksgiving?

3. What happened on July 4, 1776?

4. Why did the Civil War happen?

5. Why do we have Labor Day?

Thinking Critically

1. How are settlers different from explorers?

2. Why was being able to make their own laws important to the English colonists?

3. How have people from other countries made America special? How might America be different if they had not come?

Writing About It

Fold a sheet of paper to form eight boxes. Number the boxes from 1 to 8. In each box, write a sentence about an event in America's history. The events should be in order.

Practicing Time Skills

Using Calendars

Look at a calendar for this year. Find the dates of these holidays.

1. Flag Day

2. Columbus Day

3. Thanksgiving

On Your Own

Social Studies at Home

Settlers in America took with them only what they could not find or make in the new land. How would this be different for space settlers? Draw a space station and ask your family to help you list all the things you would need to take with you to live there.

Read More About It

Buttons for General Washington by Peter and Connie Roop. Carolrhoda Books. In this true story, a young boy takes coded messages hidden in his buttons to General Washington.

Follow the Drinking Gourd by Jeanette Winter. Alfred A. Knopf. A family travels to freedom on the Underground Railroad.

Wagon Wheels by Barbara Brenner. Harper & Row. An African-American family settles in Kansas in the 1870s.

We the People: The Constitution of the United States of America by Peter Spier. Doubleday. Beautiful pictures provide a then-and-now look at the Constitution of the United States.

The House on Maple Street

by Bonnie Pryor

Several hundred years have brought many changes to the land that is now Maple Street. Its history tells the story of how our country grew and how the past is with us still today.

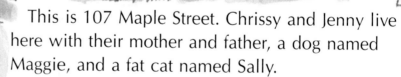

This is 107 Maple Street. Chrissy and Jenny live here with their mother and father, a dog named Maggie, and a fat cat named Sally.

Three hundred years ago there was no house here or even a street. There was only a forest and a bubbling spring where the animals came to drink.

One day a fierce storm roared across the forest. The sky rolled with thunder, and lightning crashed into a tree. A deer sniffed the air in alarm. Soon the woods were ablaze.

The next spring a few sturdy flowers poked through the ashes, and by the year after that the land was covered with grass. Some wildflowers grew at the edge of the stream where the deer had returned to drink.

One day the earth trembled, and a cloud of dust rose to the sky. A mighty herd of buffalo had come to eat the sweet grass and drink from the stream.

People came, following the buffalo herd. They set up their tepees near the stream, and because they liked it so much, they stayed for the whole summer.

One boy longed to be a great hunter like his father, but for now he could only pretend with his friends. In their games, one boy was chosen to be the buffalo.

His father taught the boy how to make an arrowhead and smooth it just so, the way his father had taught him. But the boy was young, and the day was hot.

He ran off to play with his friends and left the arrowhead on a rock. When he came back later to get it, he could not find it.

The buffalo moved on, searching for new grass, and the people packed up their tepees and followed.

For a long time the land was quiet. Some rabbits made their home in the stump of a burned tree, and a fox made a den in some rocks.

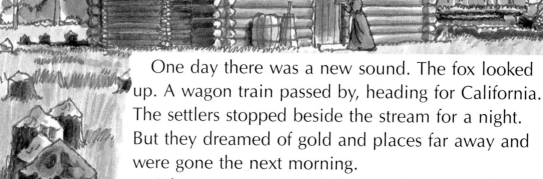

One day there was a new sound. The fox looked
up. A wagon train passed by, heading for California.
The settlers stopped beside the stream for a night.
But they dreamed of gold and places far away and
were gone the next morning.

Other wagons came, following the tracks of the
first. The fox family moved into the woods, but the
rabbits stayed snug in their burrows until the people
had gone.

Soon after, a man and a woman camped along the
stream. They were heading west, but the woman
would soon have a child. They looked around them
and knew it was a good place to stay. The man cut
down trees and made a house.

He pulled up the tree stumps left from the fire and
planted his crops. The child was a girl, and they
named her Ruby and called her their little jewel.

Ruby had a set of china dishes that she played
with every day. One day when she was making a
mudpie on the banks of the stream, she found an
arrowhead buried deep in the ground. She put it in a
cup to show her father when he came in from the
fields.

Ruby's mother called her to watch the new baby.
While she was gone, a rabbit sniffed at the cup and
knocked it off the rock. It fell into the tunnel to his
burrow, and the rabbit moved away to a new home
under the roots of a tree.

Ruby grew up and moved away, but her brother stayed on the farm. By now there were other people nearby, and he married a girl from another farm. They had six children, and he built a larger house so they would all fit.

Now the old wagon trail was used as a road, and the dust got into the house. When his wife complained, Ruby's brother planted a row of maple trees along the road to keep out the dust and shade the house. After the children were grown, he and his wife moved away, but one of their daughters stayed on the farm with her husband and children.

One day the children's great-aunt Ruby came for a visit. She was an old lady with snow-white hair. The children loved to hear her stories of long ago. She told them about the cup and arrowhead she had lost when she was a girl.

After she left, the children looked and looked. But they never found them, though they searched for days.

The town had grown nearly to the edge of the farm, and another man up the road filled in the stream and changed its course. For a while there was a trickle of water in the spring when the snow melted, but weeds and dirt filled in the bed, until hardly anyone remembered a stream had ever been there.

New people lived on the farm. It was the schoolteacher and his family and they sold much of the land to others. The road was paved with bricks, so there was no longer any dust, but the maple trees remained. The branches hung down over the road,

making it shady and cool. People called it Maple Street. Automobiles drove on the road, along with carts and wagons, and there were many new houses.

The house was crumbling and old, and one day some men tore it down. For a while again, the land was bare. The rabbits lived comfortably, with only an occasional owl or fox to chase them. But one day a young couple came walking along and stopped to admire the trees.

"What a wonderful place for a home," said the young woman. So they hired carpenters and masons to build a cozy house of red bricks with white trim.

The young couple lived happily in the house for several years. The young man got a job in another town, and they had to move.

The house was sold to a man and a woman who had two girls named Chrissy and Jenny and a dog named Maggie, and a fat cat named Sally.

The girls helped their father dig up a spot of ground for a garden, but it was Maggie the dog who dug up something white in the soft spring earth.

"Stop," cried Chrissy, and she picked up the tiny cup made of china. Inside was the arrowhead found and lost so long ago.

"Who lost these?" the girls wondered. Chrissy and Jenny put the cup and arrowhead on a shelf for others to see. Someday perhaps their children will play with the tiny treasures and wonder about them, too. But the cup and arrowhead will forever keep their secrets, and the children can only dream.

Unit Review

WORDS TO REMEMBER

Number your paper from 1 to 10. Use the words below to fill in the blanks. Use each word only once.

buffalo	gold pan
colonies	history
crossroads	labor
explorers	manufactured
freedom	settlers

1. Our country has a long and proud ____ .

2. Communities often began at ____ .

3. The Plains Indians used the ____ for food, clothing, and shelter.

4. The Mexicans invented the ____ .

5. Machines, cars, and computers are ____ goods.

6. Christopher Columbus and Amerigo Vespucci were ____ .

7. People in both Jamestown and Plymouth were ____ .

8. People in the English ____ wanted to have their own government.

9. Americans decided to fight for ____ from England.

10. The work that has made our country strong is ____ .

FOCUS ON MAIN IDEAS

1. Where and why did communities begin in the past? Where and why do they begin now? What kinds of communities are we planning for the future?

2. Who started the community of Denver? How was their way of life different from that of the Arapaho Indians? What is the community of Denver, Colorado like today?

3. Why did the community of Jamestown do so poorly at first? How did the Pilgrims begin their community differently? How did these two groups of people meet their needs?

4. What did the Declaration of Independence tell people? What is the Constitution?

5. Why are people still coming to live in our country today? What do they hope to find?

THINK/WRITE

Imagine that you are an American Indian in the time before the settlers. One day you see some boats coming to the shore. Strange-looking people dressed differently from you get off the boats. Write a story telling how you might feel about these newcomers arriving in your land.

ACTIVITIES

1. **Drama**   Choose something that happened in Denver's history. Work with other students to act this out. For example, you might act out making a tepee or panning for gold.

2. **Research/Oral Report**   A penny has a picture of Abraham Lincoln on it. Look at some other coins and bills. Tell a little about the people whose pictures are on them.

3. **Art**   Think of what freedom in America means to you. Draw a picture that shows how you feel about being free. At the bottom of the picture, write a sentence that tells why you feel this way.

SKILLS REVIEW

1. **Using Pictures**   Look at the picture. Is it old or new? Name two ways that you can tell.

2. **Using Calendars**   Look at the calendar on page 266 and answer the following questions.
   a. What month follows May?
   b. Christmas is December 25. Looking at this calendar, tell on what day of the week Christmas is.
   c. In which month is your birthday? Find the month on the calendar.
   d. How many months come between this month and your birthday?

3. **Using Timelines**   Make a timeline of your life. Show five important things that have happened to you or that you have done since you were born.

EXPLORING
YOUR COMMUNITY

In this unit you have seen how communities begin and how they grow. You have also seen how our country began. Use the following activities to see how your own community started.

LEARNING ABOUT PEOPLE

1. Find out from what countries people in your community came. Maybe a street or lake in your community has a Spanish or French name. Maybe your town is named after a town in another country. Name one thing that shows how early settlers from other countries have made a difference in your community.

YOUR COMMUNITY'S HISTORY

2. Find the following information in the library.
   a. when your community was started
   b. why people settled there
   c. three important events in your community's history
   Use this information to make a timeline showing the history of your community.

3. Find out if there are any places of history near your community. Maybe your community is near the site of a Civil War battle. Perhaps a President's home is nearby. Write a paragraph about any place of history near your community. Tell why it is important.

4. Find out what your community looked like long ago. Go to the library or talk to people who have lived in your community a long time. Find some old pictures of your community. Make a class scrapbook or bulletin board showing how your community has changed.

LEARNING ABOUT SETTLERS

5. Find out about the first settlers in your community. When did they come to your community? What businesses were first started? What crops did they grow? Draw a picture showing how they lived and worked.

UNIT 5
AROUND THE WORLD

Community Facts and Figures

City	Jun Tan	Caracas	Haifa
Country	China	Venezuela	Israel
Continent	Asia	South America	Asia
Population (estimated)	Unknown	1,044,851	596,100
Interesting Fact	More people live along the Chang Jiang (River) than in the whole United States.	Caracas was founded in 1567 by Spaniards looking for gold.	People have lived in the area near Haifa for 3,000 years.

Long ago, people dreamed of sailing the seas and discovering new, exciting lands. Today, you can visit many parts of the world in only hours or days.

Look at the picture of market day in the country of Mali. This community probably looks very different from your community. Yet in many ways, people in Mali and everywhere else are the same. People everywhere work to meet their needs. People everywhere live in communities and have fun together. In this unit you will see how people live around the world.

Think Beyond   How is the way you shop in your community different from shopping in Mali?

Dar es Salaam Tanzania Africa 1,394,000 Dar es Salaam's name means "haven of peace".	London England Europe 6,765,000 London has almost been destroyed twice.	Paris France Europe 2,188,918 Paris has one of the oldest universities in the world.	Mexico City Mexico North America 10,061,000 Mexico City is the largest city in the world.	Amsterdam The Netherlands Europe 691,738 Amsterdam has more than 100 canals.

CHAPTER 10

Meeting Needs Around the World

" I'd like to go around the world
And get a chance to see
The boys and girls of other lands
And let them all see me.

• • • • • • • • • • • • •

I'd like to get to know them well
Before my journey's end;
For only when you know someone
Can he become your friend. "

—from the poem "Face to Face"
by Anita E. Posey

Look for these important words:

Key Words	• pasta	• Greece
• grain	• shish kebab	• Finland
• sashimi	**Places**	• Italy
• feta cheese	• Japan	• Turkey
• rice	• Uruguay	

Look for answers to these questions:
1. What foods do we get from animals?
2. What foods do we get from plants?
3. What kinds of foods do people in hot, rainy climates often eat?
4. How do we get foods from other countries?

1 FOODS AROUND THE WORLD

We all need food to live. Food is a need that everyone in the world must meet. Not everyone eats the same kinds of food, though. People in different parts of the world often eat different kinds of food. They prepare and make food in different ways, too.

Where We Get Our Food

We get all our food from plants and animals. We get meat, eggs, and dairy products from animals. We get fruits, vegetables, nuts, and **grain** from plants. Grain is small, hard seeds from certain plants, such as wheat. People around the world use grain. They use grain to make bread, pastries, and cereal.

293

Foods From Animals

What people eat often depends on where they live. People who live near water often eat a lot of fresh fish.

Japan is a country of islands in Asia. Fish is an important food in Japan. The Japanese like to eat raw fish, called **sashimi** (SAHSH•uh•mee). They dip sashimi in different sauces. People in Japan eat a lot of cooked fish, too.

In places where there are rich grasslands, people often raise cattle for food. **Uruguay** (YUR•uh•gway) is in South America. In Uruguay, the grass grows to be as high as you are. There is enough grass for many cattle.

In **Greece,** many people raise goats and sheep. They use milk from these animals for cheese. This cheese is called **feta** (FET•uh) **cheese.**

Sashimi is a favorite food in Japan.

Raising cattle is important in Uruguay. The weather is mild, and cattle graze year round on the rich grassland.

Rice grows well in warm, wet Bali. Young rice is bright green. When it ripens, rice turns yellow and can be picked.

Foods From Plants

In some parts of the world, the climate is hot and rainy. Fruits and vegetables can grow all year long. So it is not surprising that people who live there eat many fruits and vegetables.

In countries where the weather is often cold, the growing season is short. In these countries, people often grow crops such as potatoes and beets. These crops grow well in cold weather. The main part of the plant grows under the ground, where it is not so cold. **Finland** is a country that grows a lot of potatoes. Potatoes are one of the main vegetables there.

Rice grows well in many parts of the world. Rice is a grasslike plant with seeds. It is a grain. Rice needs lots of water to grow. About half the people in the world eat rice as their main food.

People buy and sell potatoes at an outdoor market in Finland.

Together, meat and vegetables make up a shish kebab.

Pasta comes in many different shapes and sizes.

Special Foods Around the World

Every country has special kinds of food. **Italy** is known for **pasta** (PAHS•tuh). Pasta is noodles made from flour, water, salt, and eggs.

Shish kebab (SHISH kuh•BAHB) is a special food in countries such as **Turkey.** Shish kebab is made by roasting cubes of lamb, tomatoes, peppers, and onions on a long, metal rod.

Many years ago, some foods were only known in certain parts of the world. Yet many people now eat foods from all over the world. One reason is that people now travel more. Sometimes they move to other countries. When they move, people bring the foods of their countries with them.

There is another reason why different foods are eaten in more places now. Today, planes and ships can carry foods quickly around the world.

 Reading Check

1. What do people use grain for?
2. How did airplanes change the foods we eat?

Think Beyond What might happen if everyone in the world ate the same food?

SEAWEED

Do you eat seaweed? You might and not know it! Seaweed helps make some soups thick and some ice creams creamy. You may have eaten seaweed the last time you had Chinese food.

People around the world eat seaweed. The Chinese use a lot of seaweed in their cooking. People in Korea and Japan serve seaweed at fancy parties. People in Denmark also eat seaweed. For hundreds of years, Native Americans ate seaweed—and some still do. Some Native Americans used seaweed seeds to make bread. People in Hawaii eat more than 70 kinds of seaweed. Some Scots feed seaweed to their sheep.

Seaweed can be made into a powder and used as a seasoning or for tea. Some seaweed is eaten fresh from the ocean. Some is made into a crunchy snack like potato chips. Unlike potato chips, however, seaweed is high in protein and filled with vitamins and minerals.

Giant kelp can grow up to two feet (60 cm) a day.

In some parts of the world seaweed is farmed along the shore and underwater. The Hawaiians may have had the first seaweed farms. The Japanese use long poles and heavy nets to farm seaweed underwater. Because there is so much of it, because it grows so fast, and because it is so healthful, seaweed could become a very important crop. Someday seaweed farming could help solve the problem of hunger around the world.

Think Beyond   Why should you eat healthful foods like seaweed?

A Japanese woman gathers seaweed along the rocky shore of Tokyo Bay.

Japanese seaweed farmers proudly show their harvest.

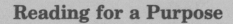
Look for these important words:

Key Words
- sarongs
- reflects
- cotton

Places
- Tibet
- Samoa
- Saudi Arabia

Look for answers to these questions:

1. How do clothes protect people from cold weather? Give examples.
2. How do clothes protect people from hot weather? Give examples.
3. In what ways are clothes around the world different? In what ways are they often alike?

2 CLOTHING AROUND THE WORLD

You have read about some different kinds of food around the world. There are many different kinds of clothing around the world, too. Now you will look at some clothing around the world.

Cold Weather Clothing

The man in the picture on the right lives in the Himalayan Mountains of **Tibet.** Tibet is in Asia and is now part of China. It gets very cold in Tibet. The man must wear a warm cap.

The cap is lined with fur. Even the earflaps are lined with fur. A warm cap is very important in the cold mountains of Tibet.

People must wear very warm clothing in cold climates. They wear heavy sweaters, coats, and furs. They often wear mittens and boots.

The ear flaps on this Tibetan cap can be turned down in very cold weather.

Warm Weather Clothing

In other parts of the world, people dress to stay cool in the heat.

The boys in the picture on the left live in **Samoa.** Samoa is an island in the Pacific Ocean. The weather in Samoa is very hot. The boys do not need shirts. They wear **sarongs.** A sarong is a piece of cloth wrapped around the waist.

It is even hotter in **Saudi Arabia** than in Samoa. Yet people in Saudi Arabia cover themselves with clothes. The sun is so hot there that people must wear headdresses and long white robes to stay cool. The color white **reflects,** or throws back, the sun's rays. This kind of clothing also protects people from the sting of desert sands.

The people in both Samoa and Saudi Arabia are dressed to stay cool in hot weather.

The picture on the left shows a silk-printing factory in England. Some of the colorful cotton that is made in India is shown on the right.

Using Different Materials for Clothing

The kind of clothing people wear sometimes depends on where they live. People often make clothing from materials they can get nearby.

People in many countries of the world grow **cotton.** Cotton comes from a plant. People use soft white cotton to make clothing.

People in China have made the cloth called silk for many thousands of years. Silk is spun by silkworms, which feed on the leaves of the mulberry tree.

Special Clothing Around the World

People around the world wear clothing for the same reasons. They wear clothing to protect them from the weather. They wear special clothing to do certain jobs. They wear clothes because they look nice or are fun to wear.

People wear very special clothes sometimes. In the pictures on this page, people are wearing clothing for special events.

Transportation makes it a lot easier to send clothing materials around the world. That is one reason clothing is becoming more alike around the world.

People in Japan wear kimonos (kuh•MOH•nuhz) for holidays and festivals. On the right, people in Scotland wear skirts called "kilts" for a special dancing event.

How are these people in Japan and Scotland dressed alike?
How are their clothes different from those on page 302?

Clothing is also becoming more alike because people know more about clothing in other countries. Newspapers and magazines show us the kinds of clothing people everywhere are wearing.

Look at the pictures on this page. Do the clothes in these countries look like the clothes you see people wearing in the United States?

 Reading Check

1. How is the clothing of Samoa different from the clothing of Saudi Arabia?
2. Why is clothing becoming more alike around the world?

Think Beyond What type of clothing do people in your community wear on special days?

People MAKE HISTORY

Levi Strauss
1829–1902

▶▶▶▶▶▶▶▶▶▶▶▶▶▶▶▶

Levi Strauss was born in Europe. He moved to the United States to live with his brothers. They gave him a job selling **dry goods**. Dry goods are fabrics, clothing, and household odds and ends.

In 1853 Strauss moved to California to sell dry goods to the miners. He took along canvas fabric because he thought the miners would need it for tents. The miners quickly bought all of his supplies except for the canvas.

One day a miner came by. "Shoulda brought pants," the miner said. "Pants don't wear worth a hoot in the diggin's. Can't get a pair strong enough to last." These words were all Strauss needed to hear. He used the strong canvas fabric to make pants. His pants became so popular that he could not make them fast enough.

Strauss ordered more canvas from his brothers. Instead of canvas, they sent a new fabric. Strauss used the new cloth to make more pants. These pants became even more popular than the canvas pants.

During the California Gold Rush, Levi Strauss found his "gold mine" not in the ground but in clothing. Today Levi Strauss & Company is the world's largest clothing manufacturer.

Think Beyond   Miners need sturdy clothing. What other jobs require special clothing?

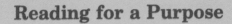
Look for these important words:

Key Words
- salt box house
- shingles
- thatched roofs

Places
- Sweden
- Nova Scotia
- Egypt

- Ireland
- Thailand
- Nairobi, Kenya

Look for answers to these questions:

1. How do people decide what material to use in their shelters?
2. Why do shelters in Nova Scotia have very steep roofs?
3. Why are many Thailand houses built on poles?

3 SHELTERS AROUND THE WORLD

People all around the world live in shelters. Shelters keep out wind, rain, heat, and cold.

People often build shelters or homes from materials found near where they live. Shelters can be made from wood, brick, concrete, or stone. They can also be made from animal skins and other materials.

Using Wood for Shelters

There are lots of trees for lumber in **Sweden,** in northern Europe. People in Sweden use the lumber to build homes. People carve the wood trim into pretty shapes. Sometimes they paint colorful designs inside and out. The picture on page 306 shows a house in Sweden.

Many houses in Sweden (left) and Nova Scotia (right) are built from wood.

Nova Scotia (NOH•vuh SKO•shuh) is in Canada. Look at the picture above of the house in Nova Scotia. Like the houses in Sweden, it is made of wood. It is called a **salt box house.** Long ago, salt came in little boxes that looked like this house.

The house is covered with **shingles.** Shingles are thin pieces of wood laid over each other in rows. Look at how steep the roof is. It is steep for a reason. Large amounts of snow fall in Nova Scotia. The wooden shingles and the steep slant of the roof let snow slide off easily.

People around the world often use the same materials for building shelters. Yet you have just seen that a wooden home in Sweden is different from one in Nova Scotia. People around the world have different ideas of what they like. They have different ways of building shelters.

306

Using Other Materials for Shelter

Egypt, in northern Africa, is a country of deserts. In Egypt, people often build shelters from bricks made by mixing mud and straw. The bricks are dried in the sun. They make thick walls that keep the desert heat out.

Ireland, in Europe, is famous for its fields of emerald-green grass. Rocks and stones dot the fields. Farm families in Ireland sometimes live in stone houses with **thatched roofs.** A thatched roof is made from bundles of straw.

Another picture on this page shows a house in **Thailand** (TY·land), in Asia. This house is standing on poles above the water. Thailand has many rivers and a lot of heavy rain. When it floods, the houses on poles stay above the water.

The top left picture shows brick shelters in Egypt. On the bottom left is an Irish house with a thatched roof. On the right is a house built on poles in Thailand.

307

How do these business centers in Toronto, Canada (left) and Nairobi, Kenya (right) look alike?

Some Shelters Are the Same

The shelters you have just read about are very different from one another. Some shelters around the world, though, look very much alike.

Shelters in very big cities often look alike. A business center in Toronto, Canada, might look much like a business center in **Nairobi, Kenya.** Yet these two cities are halfway across the world from each other.

 Reading Check

1. Why are many homes in Sweden made from wood?
2. Why are shelters built in Ireland different from shelters built in Thailand?

Think Beyond How might a country make sure forests are not destroyed for housing needs?

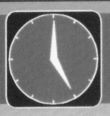

SKILLS IN ACTION

TIME, THE EARTH, AND THE SUN

We use many words to say when we do things. In the "morning" we get up and eat breakfast. Around "noon" we eat lunch. In the "evening" we eat dinner. At "night" we go to sleep.

To tell the time more exactly, we use clocks. Each day is divided into 24 hours.

Morning is the time between sunrise and noon. The afternoon goes from noon until the sun starts to set. Then the evening begins. After a few hours, night comes. Night lasts until the sun rises again.

We call the hours between midnight and noon **A.M.** For example, 9 A.M. means nine o'clock in the morning. The letters stand for words that mean "before noon." We call the hours between noon and midnight **P.M.** These letters stand for words that mean "after noon."

Why We Have Day and Night

To explain day and night, we usually say it is light during the day and dark at night. From Earth, it looks as if the sun rises in the east. The sun seems to travel across the sky during the day. In the evening it seems to set in the west.

The sun does not really move at all. If you were on a spaceship far from Earth, you would be able to see what really causes day and night. You would see that the Earth slowly **rotates,** or turns around.

The Earth is always rotating. It takes the Earth 24 hours to spin completely around. We call those 24 hours one day.

As the Earth rotates, places on the Earth turn toward the sun and then away from it. When your community is turned away from the sun, it is night.

309

The picture on this page shows how the Earth rotates.

The Earth is a sphere, or ball. Light can shine on only part of it at a time. It is daytime on the part of the Earth facing the sun. It is nighttime on the part facing away from the sun.

Day and Night in Different Places

Look at the Earth in the picture below. The Earth is rotating in the direction shown by the arrows. Kansas City is moving toward the sun. That means the sun is about to rise in Kansas City, Missouri. It is already morning in Belém, a city in South America. It is still night in Anchorage, Alaska.

Kansas City will move all the way around as the Earth spins. When it returns to the same spot, 24 hours will have passed.

Anchorage and Belém are far apart from each other. You can see that they do not face the sun at the same time. When two places are that far apart, they have day and night at very different times.

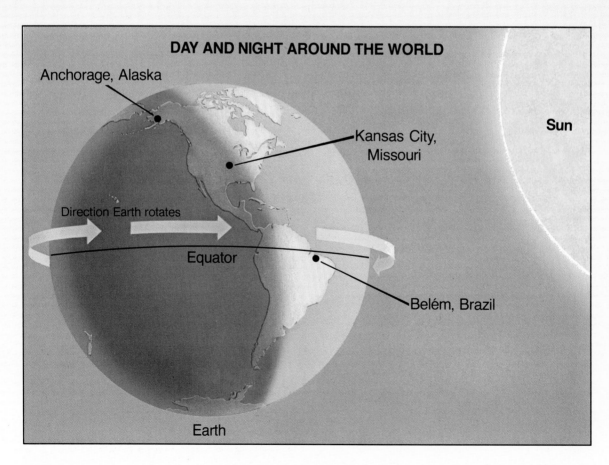

DAY AND NIGHT AROUND THE WORLD

Anchorage, Alaska

Sun

Kansas City, Missouri

Direction Earth rotates

Equator

Belém, Brazil

Earth

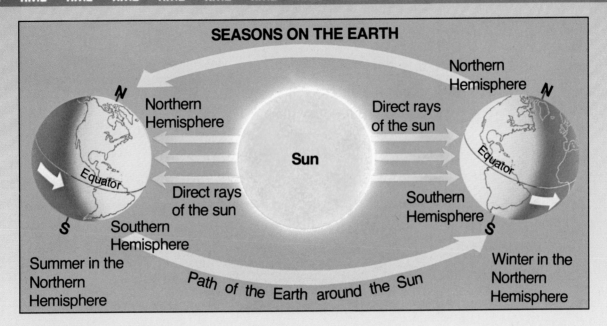

SEASONS ON THE EARTH

Northern Hemisphere

N

Northern Hemisphere

Direct rays of the sun

Sun

Equator

Direct rays of the sun

Southern Hemisphere

N

Equator

Southern Hemisphere

S

Summer in the Northern Hemisphere

S

Winter in the Northern Hemisphere

Path of the Earth around the Sun

The Earth Revolves

You have seen that the Earth rotates once every 24 hours. The Earth also moves in another way. It **revolves** (ree•VAHLVZ) around the sun. That means it slowly travels all the way around the sun. It takes 365 days for the Earth to revolve all the way around the sun. That is how we measure a year.

Weather and Seasons

Because of the Earth's shape, some parts of the world have more sun. Places near the equator get more sun. They are hot or warm most of the year. Places near the North Pole and the South Pole have less sun. They are quite cold all year long.

Many places on Earth are warm in summer and cold in winter. The Earth has different seasons.

Seasons happen because the Earth is tilted. We have summer when northern parts of the Earth are tilted toward the sun. We have winter when northern parts are tilted away from the sun.

CHECKING YOUR SKILLS

Tell or write the answers to these questions.

1. What do "A.M." and "P.M." mean?

2. Why do we have day and night?

3. How long does it take for the Earth to revolve around the sun?

4. Is it usually colder near the equator or at the North Pole?

5. Why do we have seasons?

311

Thinking Back

- People around the world need food, clothing, and shelter. They meet these needs in different ways, depending on the land and climate where they live.

- People who live near water eat a lot of fish. Those who live on grasslands raise cattle. People in wet countries can grow rice. Farmers in cold countries often grow potatoes.

- People get meat, eggs, and dairy foods from animals. Fruits, vegetables, nuts, and grains come from plants.

- Clothing must suit the climate. In cold countries people wear heavy clothes. In warm, damp lands they wear lightweight clothing. In hot, dry lands they wear white robes to reflect the sun.

- People use fur from animals. Cotton comes from a plant. Silk comes from silkworms.

- People build shelters from the materials they can get nearby. Homes in snowy areas have steep roofs. In places that flood, houses are sometimes built on poles.

Check for Understanding

Using Words
Use one of the words in parentheses to complete each sentence.

1. People around the world use ____ to make bread and cereal. (cotton, grain)

2. A common meal in Italy is ____ . (pasta, sashimi)

3. ____ is used to make clothing. (Cotton, Sarong)

4. Houses in Nova Scotia have ____ . (flat roofs, steep roofs)

5. Houses in Thailand are often built on ____ . (rocks, poles)

Reviewing Facts

1. Why does what people eat often depend on where they live?

2. Why can people around the world eat many of the same foods?

3. Why does what people wear sometimes depend on where they live? Give two examples.

4. What are some clothes people wear in cold weather?

5. What are three materials people use to build shelters?

Thinking Critically

1. Many years ago, some foods were known only in certain parts of the world. Explain why this has changed.

2. What kinds of clothes do people in your community wear in hot weather?

Writing About It

Pick an area of the world. Fold a sheet of paper to form three columns. Use the three columns to describe the foods, clothing, and shelters of the area.

Practicing Time Skills

Time, the Earth, and the Sun
It is now daytime where you live. Look at a globe or a world map. Name a place where it is nighttime.

On Your Own

Social Studies at Home

On poster board, draw each member of your family very large. Decide what type of climate you want your family to be dressed for. Cut clothes from fabric or paper and dress each person. Show your picture to your family.

Read More About It

A Family in Kenya by Michael Griffin. Lerner. You can meet one family living in Kenya today.

How My Parents Learned to Eat by Ina R. Friedman. Houghton Mifflin. An American sailor and his Japanese bride must come to terms with their different ways of eating.

Our House on the Hill by Philippe Dupasquier. Viking. Over the course of a year, a family needs different clothing as the weather changes.

People by Peter Spier. Doubleday. This book tells about the foods, shelters, and clothing of people all over the world.

What Makes Day and Night by Franklyn M. Branley. T. Y. Crowell. Learn how day turns into night.

CHAPTER 11

Living in Communities Around the World

"Ring around the world
Taking hands together
All across the temperate
And the torrid weather.
Past the royal palm-trees
By the ocean sand
Make a ring around the world
Taking each other's hand;
In the valleys, on the hill,
Over the prairie spaces,
There's a ring around the world
Made of children's friendly faces."

—"Ring Around the World" by Annette Wynne

Look for these important words:

Key Words
- plot
- beisbol
- subway

Places
- Jun Tan, China
- Caracas, Venezuela
- Haifa, Israel
- Mount Carmel

Look for answers to these questions:

1. What natural resources are important to Jun Tan, China?
2. How did the discovery of oil help Caracas, Venezuela, to grow?
3. Why is Haifa, Israel, a big transportation center?

1 COMMUNITIES USE NATURAL RESOURCES

In Unit 2 you read how natural resources are important to communities. You read about farmers using natural resources to raise crops in Merced, California. You saw how coal mining is important in Pikeville, Kentucky. You saw how important shipping is in Chicago, Illinois.

People in communities around the world use natural resources to make a living. There are farming, mining, and port communities around the world.

In the next pages, you will look at communities in the countries of China, Venezuela, and Israel. You will read about how important natural resources are to the people who live in these communities.

Food for millions of people is grown in many farming communities like Jun Tan, China. Here, workers care for the crops with hoes and other simple tools.

Jun Tan, China

Jun Tan is a farming community in eastern **China.** Jun Tan has the natural resources needed for farming. It has rich soil, plenty of water, and a good climate for farming.

The land in Jun Tan is owned by the government. Until recently, many families shared the land to be farmed. Now, however, individual families may rent the farmland from the government. Rent is paid by giving the government a certain amount of the crop grown.

In the past, the farmers were told by the state which crops to grow on their **plot.** A plot is a piece of land. Farmers had to give all their crops to the government. Now the farmers are allowed to grow any crop they choose. After the rent is paid they may sell what is left. They use the money to buy tractors and tools to help them grow food.

In parts of China, farming is still done with hand tools like hoes. Water buffaloes and other animals pull the plows. In other parts of China, machines like tractors are used. Some people even own their own machines. Others share.

Besides farming, the people in Jun Tan often do other jobs. One farmer might also be a carpenter. Another farmer might be a teacher or a bricklayer. Workers in the community make many of the goods they need.

Do you remember the community of Merced, California? Look back at pages 76–81 to remember. Jun Tan and Merced are both farming communities. Yet the ways people live and work in each place are very different.

The man below is a carpenter. He works at a workshop in Jun Tan, China.

Caracas, Venezuela

Caracas (kah•RAH•kuhs) is the capital city of **Venezuela** (ven•uhz•WAY•luh). Venezuela is on the north coast of South America.

Caracas began many hundreds of years ago. You can find buildings that are 400 years old in Caracas.

Caracas was not always as big as it is now. One important thing that helped it grow was the discovery of oil.

In 1922 oil was found in Venezuela. More and more people came to drill for oil. Many of them came to Caracas. Caracas grew very quickly. It is still growing.

Caracas is an old city, but finding oil made many new jobs for people. Money from oil was used to build new buildings.

This picture shows oil drilling in Lake Maracaibo, Venezuela's largest lake. Much of Venezuela's oil is found under this lake.

Money from oil has been used to build many new skyscrapers and freeways. Now Caracas is almost a brand new city. Yet because Caracas has grown so fast, it has had to face new problems. The city needed homes for the many people who moved there. The government of Venezuela built many apartment houses in the city. Today, however, the city still needs more homes.

A favorite sport in Caracas is **beisbol** (BAYZ•bahl). This word is a mix of Spanish and English. Can you guess what it means?

Do you remember the oil-drilling community of Midland, Texas? Look back at pages 113–119 to remember. Caracas is a lot older than Midland. That is one way in which the two communities are different from each other.

Haifa, Israel

The port city of **Haifa** (HY·fuh), **Israel,** is on a bay with mountains all around. The bay empties into the Mediterranean Sea.

The bay is deep enough for ocean-going ships. This makes Haifa a very important transportation center. Crops and goods are brought on trucks to Haifa from farms and factories. Then they are shipped from the harbor in Haifa to other places. Goods are shipped into Haifa, too. They are taken by trucks to other parts of Israel.

Haifa is a city of three parts. It is near a mountain called **Mount Carmel.** The lower part of Haifa, by the bay, is where all the shipping goes on. There cargo is loaded and unloaded, and goods

From high on Mount Carmel in Israel, you can view the city of Haifa and part of Israel's coast.

Many people in Haifa use the subway to go from one part of the city to another.

are stored in big buildings. The middle part of Haifa, covering the sides of Mt. Carmel, is where most of the businesses and stores are. The highest part of the city, near the mountaintop, is where most people live.

A long **subway** connects the three parts of Haifa. A subway is a train that is mostly underground. The people in Haifa say the subway links "upstairs" Haifa with "downstairs" Haifa.

Do you remember the American port city of Chicago, Illinois? Look at pages 130–138 to remember. Both Haifa and Chicago are important transportation centers. Crops and goods move into and out of these two communities.

Reading Check

1. Why did Caracas grow so quickly?
2. How are the three parts of Haifa different?

Think Beyond   Why might a farmer in Jun Tan grow more crops now than in the past?

IN FOCUS

WORLD'S FAIRS

Have you ever stepped inside an atom, toured a crystal palace, or stood at the top of a space needle? You could have done all these things if you had visited the world's fairs held in Brussels, London, and Seattle.

World's fairs have more than unusual buildings. Many inventions have been shown for the first time at world's fairs. If you had been at the world's fair held in Philadelphia in 1876, you might have seen Alexander Graham Bell using the telephone for the first time. The ice cream cone

50,000 pieces of colored glass made the Tower of Jewels sparkle at the San Francisco Fair of 1915.

The Trylon and Perisphere were built for the New York World's Fair of 1939.

The Atomium, nicknamed the Brussels Sprout, was built for the Brussels, Belgium, World's Fair of 1958.

Alexander Graham Bell shows his telephone to the Emperor of Brazil at the Philadelphia Fair of 1876.

People rode the first Ferris wheel at the Chicago World's Fair of 1893.

was first served at the St. Louis World's Fair in 1904. Many people saw motion pictures for the first time at the San Francisco World's Fair of 1915.

Do you like baseball? The first all-star baseball game was held during the Chicago World's Fair of 1933. Babe Ruth, one of our most famous baseball players, was there.

World's fairs often celebrate special events. In 1915 San Francisco celebrated the opening of the Panama Canal with a world's fair. In 1992 two fairs will be held—a large one in Seville, Spain, and a smaller one in Genoa, Italy—to celebrate Christopher Columbus's voyage to the New World in 1492.

World's fairs are filled with amazing and wonderful sights. They show how people everywhere work together and depend on one another.

Think Beyond How do world's fairs help people learn more about each other?

SKILLS IN ACTION

READING POPULATION MAPS

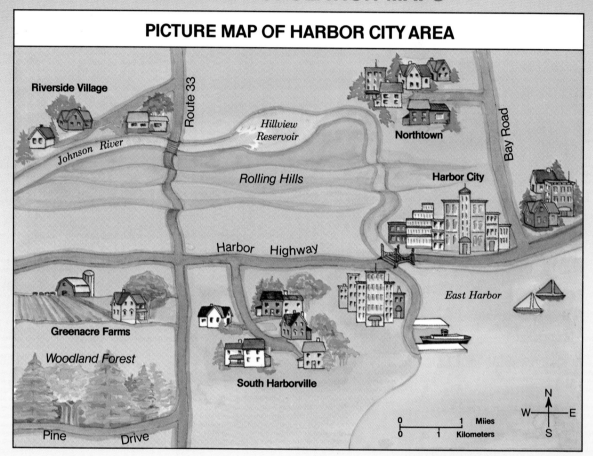

PICTURE MAP OF HARBOR CITY AREA

Maps can show where people live. They can show how many people live in different places.

Look at the picture map on this page. It shows Harbor City and the places around it. Many people live in Harbor City. Near the city are two suburbs.

On the left side of the map are farms and a small town, called Riverside Village. Few people live in this area. The farms are far apart from each other.

Using a Population Map

The same places can be shown on a **population map.** Population means how many people live in a place. Look at the population map on the next page.

324

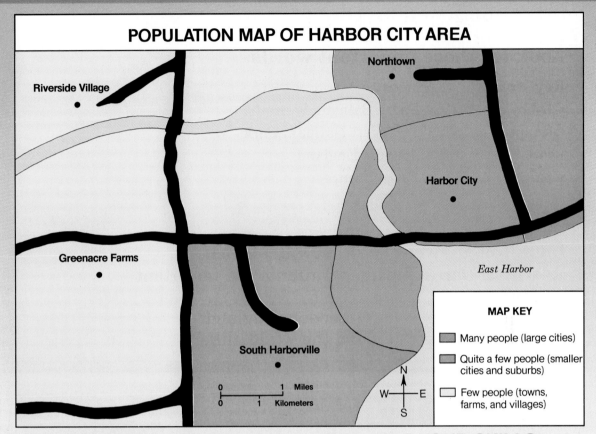

POPULATION MAP OF HARBOR CITY AREA

Northtown

Riverside Village

Harbor City

Greenacre Farms

East Harbor

South Harborville

0   1   Miles
0   1   Kilometers

N
W — E
S

MAP KEY

Many people (large cities)

Quite a few people (smaller cities and suburbs)

Few people (towns, farms, and villages)

Find the blue area on the map. Now look for blue in the map key. The map key tells you that blue areas are where many people live close together.

Find the same area in the first map. The picture map shows many large buildings here. Both the picture map and the population map of Harbor City show that this area is crowded.

Look at the map key again. What does the color yellow stand for? Find the yellow area on the map. Then find the same area in the picture. Is the yellow area farmland or the city?

CHECKING YOUR SKILLS

Use the maps to help you answer these questions.

1. Which city or town has the most people?

2. Which towns or cities have the smallest number of people?

3. Do more people live in Northtown or in Riverside Village? What other place has about the same number of people as Northtown?

4. Find the area that is south of Harbor Highway and west of Route 33. How many people live there?

Look for these important words:

Key Words	Places
• bobby	• Dar es Salaam, Tanzania
• sculptures	• Serengeti National Park
• fort	• London, England
• palace	• Paris, France
	• Louvre

Look for answers to these questions:

1. Why is Dar es Salaam, Tanzania, an important city?
2. What do bobbies do in London, England?
3. How are services around the world alike?

2 GOVERNMENTS AND SERVICES AROUND THE WORLD

Communities around the world have rules and laws. This is true of countries, too. Every country has a government. Every country has a capital. Every country provides services to its people, too.

This picture shows a government building in the capital of Tanzania.

Dar es Salaam, Tanzania

Dar es Salaam (DAHR ES suh•LAHM) is in **Tanzania** (tan•zuh•NEE•yuh). Tanzania is a large country in eastern Africa.

There are many factories in and near Dar es Salaam. People make cement, glass, cloth, and footwear in the factories.

Dar es Salaam is the capital of Tanzania. Laws for the whole country are made there.

Some important laws in Tanzania have to do with the way land is used. There are many animals and much beautiful scenery in Tanzania. Farmers use some of the land to grow crops.

Some years ago, more food was needed in Tanzania. Lawmakers passed a law. They took some land from the **Serengeti** (ser•uhn•GET•ee) **National Park** and made it into farmland.

Lions, elephants, and zebras roamed freely on this land. The law let farmers fence off this land and use it for farming. The wild animals could not live on the land anymore.

At the same time, the lawmakers set aside some nearby land for the wild animals. They said that this land would be only for the animals, not for farms or factories. It is against the law to kill or trap any of the animals there.

By making these laws, the lawmakers tried to meet the people's need for food. They also tried to meet the animals' need for a place to live.

Gnu, (NOO) graze on Tanzania's grassland. They can run very quickly.

327

Services Around the World

Communities all over the world provide services for people. There are police and fire departments, parks, schools, libraries, and museums in cities all over the world.

In **London,** the capital of **England,** a police officer is called a **bobby.** The bobbies of London do many of the same things police everywhere do. They direct traffic. They help people who are lost or who have problems. They make sure the laws are obeyed.

Paris, France, is one of the most beautiful cities in the world. Many people come to visit this city's gardens, parks, and buildings. Paris also has some of the best-known museums in the world.

A bobby stands guard near a government building in London, England.

The Louvre, left, is one of the largest art museums in the world. Many sculptures, such as the one on the right, are kept in the Louvre.

The **Louvre** (LOO•vr) is an art museum in Paris. Many thousands of paintings can be seen here. Other works of art, such as **sculptures,** are also at the Louvre. A sculpture is a figure made from stone, clay, or metal.

The Louvre began as a **fort** long, long ago. A fort is a place for protecting soldiers. Soldiers lived inside the safe walls of the fort. Later the Louvre was used as a **palace,** a place for kings to live. Each king added more and more buildings to the Louvre. Today, if all the rooms of the Louvre were placed end to end, they would make a building 8 miles (about 13 km) long!

Reading Check

1. What is the capital of Tanzania?
2. Why is the Louvre so big?

Think Beyond   London bobbies do not carry guns. How might a bobby's job be different from that of an American police officer?

People MAKE HISTORY

Mother Teresa
1910–

▶▶▶▶▶▶▶▶▶▶▶▶▶▶▶▶▶▶

When Agnes was a little girl, she had everything she needed. Her father owned a business in Yugoslavia. As Agnes was growing up, she decided she wanted to become a Roman Catholic **nun**. A nun is a woman who devotes her life to God.

When Agnes was 18 years old, she went to Calcutta, a city in India. She became a nun known as Sister Teresa. For 19 years, she stayed inside her **convent**, the place where the nuns lived, teaching school.

One day Sister Teresa went outside the convent. She saw hundreds of hungry and sick people. Sister Teresa wanted to help them.

Soon afterward, she left the convent to care for sick and homeless people. Other nuns came to live and work with Sister Teresa. They called themselves the Missionaries of Charity. As their leader, Sister Teresa was now called Mother Teresa.

Today the Missionaries of Charity work in 70 countries. Mother Teresa has received many awards for her work. Yet she says her greatest reward is seeing the smile on the face of a child who is no longer hungry.

Think Beyond   What do you think your community should do to help the sick or homeless? What can your family do to help?

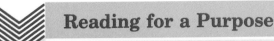
Look for these important words:

Key Words	Places
• pyramid	• Mexico City, Mexico
• Aztec Indians	• Amsterdam, The
• sea level	Netherlands
• dikes	

Look for answers to these questions:
1. Why is Mexico City both old and new?
2. Why isn't The Netherlands covered with water?
3. What are canals in Amsterdam used for?

3 THE HISTORIES OF TWO CITIES

Mexico City is the capital of **Mexico.** It lies in a mountain valley. It is on very high land.

Amsterdam is a city in western Europe. It is the capital of **The Netherlands.** Amsterdam is on low land near the sea.

Both of these cities have long, interesting histories. Over the years they have changed and grown.

Mexico City, Mexico

Mexico City is more than 600 years old. You can see Mexico City's past in the buildings in the picture on page 332. Do you see the stone steps? They are the steps of a **pyramid** (PIHR•uh•mihd) that once stood in this place. A pyramid is a building with flat sides that come to a point on

This picture shows the famous Plaza of Three Cultures in Mexico City. There, you can find the steps of an Aztec pyramid, an old Spanish church, and modern buildings.

top. The **Aztec Indians** lived in Mexico City about 600 years ago. They built the pyramids.

Do you see the church behind the pyramid steps? That church is more than 400 years old. It was built by the Spanish. They came to Mexico City when the Aztecs already had a busy city.

In 1521, Spanish explorers fought against the Aztecs and won. Much of the beautiful Aztec city was destroyed. The Spanish took over the city and built a new city in its place.

Look again at the picture. Do you see the tall, modern buildings behind the church? Each year, many more are built in Mexico City.

Today Mexico City is a mix of the old and new. Its old buildings show its past. Its new buildings show its present and future.

Amsterdam, The Netherlands

The Netherlands is a country in Europe. Much of The Netherlands is below **sea level.** Sea level is the level of the ocean.

You may wonder why lands below sea level are not covered with water. The answer is that huge **dikes,** or dams, hold back the sea. There are 1,500 miles (2,400 km) of dikes in The Netherlands. The dikes protect the land from flooding.

Workers build dikes around water-covered lands. Then they pump out the water and drain the lands. They pump the water into canals. The dry land that is left can be used for farming and to build communities.

Cars travel along a dike in The Netherlands.

HISTORY CONNECTION

Long ago people used wind power to pump water, grind grain, and run machinery. In the 1800s as many as 9,000 windmills were in use in The Netherlands alone. Today, very few are used. They have been replaced by electric or gasoline-powered pumps and motors.

Now scientists are working on new designs for windmills. They want to use wind power to make electricity. Wind power does not pollute our environment. Windmills also need very little upkeep or care. Large projects using as many as 15,000 windmills may one day supply some of the electricity for our communities.

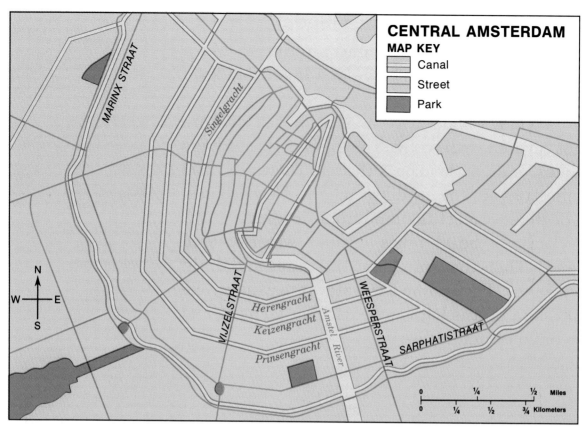

Amsterdam is a city of canals. Amsterdam was built on land that had once been under water. Dikes and canals were built so that people could use the land. Canals became important waterways. They were used to move goods to lakes and seas. Then the goods could go to other countries.

Amsterdam is still growing. The people of Amsterdam go on building canals. Amsterdam keeps growing and changing.

Reading Check

1. How do you think the Plaza of Three Cultures, in Mexico City, got its name?
2. Why are canals important in Amsterdam?

Think Beyond Why do you think the people of The Netherlands take especially good care of their land?

SKILLS IN ACTION

USING INTERMEDIATE DIRECTIONS

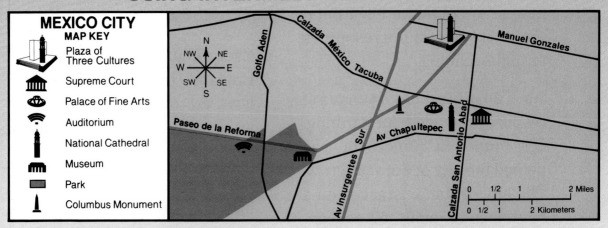

Look at the map above. You can tell by looking at the compass rose that the auditorium is west of the museum. Yet if someone told you that the park is southwest of Columbus Monument, how would you find that direction?

You know which way is west because you have learned the four cardinal directions, north, south, east, and west. There are also four "in-between" directions, southeast, southwest, northeast and northwest. These are called **intermediate directions.** The intermediate directions lie between the four main directions.

To better understand intermediate directions, look at the compass rose. Find the line that passes halfway between south and west. The letters **SW** stand for southwest. The park is southwest of Columbus Monument.

CHECKING YOUR SKILLS

Use the map above to help you answer these questions.

1. What do **NE, NW,** and **SE** stand for?

2. What direction is the Plaza of Three Cultures from Columbus Monument?

3. If you went from the court to the Palace of Fine Arts, in which direction did you go?

335

Thinking Back

- People in communities around the world use natural resources to make a living.

- Jun Tan, China, has the natural resources needed for farming. Oil found in Venezuela has helped the city of Caracas grow. The city of Haifa, Israel, is on a bay deep enough for ocean-going ships to use.

- Every country has its own laws, rules, and government. The country of Tanzania has passed laws that set aside part of that country's land for wild animals to use.

- Every country has services. In England bobbies make sure laws are obeyed. In France an art museum was made from a palace.

- Old cities can have interesting histories. In Mexico City parts of pyramids built by the Aztecs can still be seen. Amsterdam is built on land that was under the sea. After dikes were built the water was pumped into canals.

Check for Understanding

Using Words

Number a sheet of paper from 1 to 5. Write **true** beside the number of each sentence that is true. Write **false** beside the number of each sentence that is not true.

1. Families in Jun Tan, China, may rent a plot to farm.

2. A police officer in Paris, France, is called a bobby.

3. The Louvre is a museum in Paris, France.

4. The people of Amsterdam built pyramids.

5. There are many dikes near Amsterdam.

Reviewing Facts

1. What are two different ways of farming in China?

2. Why is Haifa, Israel, an important city?

3. What choice did lawmakers in Dar es Salaam, Tanzania, have to make about the land?

4. What can a person see at the Louvre in Paris, France?

5. Why are there many dikes in The Netherlands?

Thinking Critically

1. Why are natural resources important to the cities of Jun Tan, Caracas, and Haifa?

2. Compare Pikeville and Amsterdam. How are they alike? How are they different?

Writing About It

Imagine that you are an animal in the Serengeti National Park. Describe your life at the park.

Practicing Map Skills

Reading a Population Map

Look at the population map on page 325. Answer these questions.

1. What do population maps show?

2. What kinds of areas have the fewest people?

3. What kinds of areas have the most people?

On Your Own

Social Studies at Home

Make a game to play with your family and friends. Write the name of a city on an index card. On another card, write a fact about that city. Make nine pairs of cards. To play the game, each player turns up a card from the city pile and one from the fact pile. If the cards match the player keeps the pair. Make up additional rules for your game.

Read More About It

A Family in China by Peter Jacobsen. Franklin Watts. In this book learn about a Chinese family's everyday life.

A Family in Holland by Peter Otto Jacobsen. Franklin Watts. You can see how a family lives in The Netherlands.

Tracking Wild Chimpanzees by Joyce Powzyk. Lothrop, Lee & Shepard. On a visit to Kibira National Park you will learn more about chimpanzees.

Where Children Live by Thomas B. Allen. Prentice-Hall. Paintings and words show how children in different countries live.

CELEBRATIONS
Around the World

Masks and costumes are part of Chinese New Year's celebrations. On the top, costumed people walk on stilts. On the bottom is a nighttime parade.

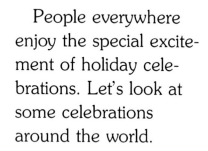

People everywhere enjoy the special excitement of holiday celebrations. Let's look at some celebrations around the world.

New Year's in China

New Year's in China lasts two weeks at some time before the end of February. It is the biggest, brightest celebration of the year.

New Year's is a time to visit family and friends. People hang good luck flags beside their doors. They wear new clothes to start the new year. All over China, there are dances, plays, parades, operas, and acrobats.

Easter in Poland

On the other side of the world, in **Poland,** the biggest celebration of the year is Easter. Families spend days getting ready for the holiday. On Easter, the table is covered with food. There are beautiful Easter eggs, too.

Making Easter eggs is an art in Poland. The eggs are given as presents.

Pesach in Israel

In Israel, one of the happiest times of the year is called **Pesach** (PAY•sahk), or "Passover."

Long ago, the people of Israel were kept as slaves in Egypt. They were treated badly. After many years these people were finally able to leave Egypt. They became free people again.

The people of Israel celebrate Passover for eight days. They retell the story of how the slaves became free. Families gather for special meals called **Seders** (SAY•duhrz).

In Poland, people decorate Easter eggs in many patterns and colors. ▼

During the Seder, special foods are eaten. One important Passover food is a kind of bread called matzo (MAHT•zuh).

339

Brightly colored decorations and piñatas fill the puestos at Christmas time in Mexico.

People in San Francisco celebrate Chinese New Year's with the "dragon dance."

Christmas in Mexico

The Christmas celebration in Mexico continues for more than a week. Nine days before Christmas, the **posadas** (poh•SAH•duhz) begin. Families and neighbors gather to act out a Christmas story. Sometimes families have the posada on only one night. But usually it is acted out every night until Christmas.

Meanwhile, the streets are filled with colorful Christmas stalls called **puestos** (PWAYS•tohz). There, people sell toys, rag dolls, and special foods and candies. Many of the things in the puestos are homemade. There are **piñatas** (peen•YAH•tuhz) in all different shapes and colors, too. These piñatas will be filled with candies and broken open on Christmas Eve.

Celebrations Travel Around the World

Some of the celebrations from around the world also take place in the United States. One of the largest Chinese New Year's celebrations in the world takes place in San Francisco, California. Many Americans celebrate Passover in the same way people do in Israel. In different parts of our country, children break open piñatas at Christmas time.

The holidays you just read about are only a few of the many celebrations held around the world. Which celebration do you like best? Does your community hold any of these celebrations?

Unit Review

WORDS TO REMEMBER

Number your paper from 1 to 10. Use the words below to fill in the blanks. Use each word only once.

Aztec Indians   plot
bobby   reflects
dikes   rice
grain   sea level
palace   subway

1. The bread we eat is made from ＿＿＿ .

2. Many people in the world eat ＿＿＿ as their main food.

3. The color white ＿＿＿ the sun's rays.

4. A ＿＿＿ is a piece of land.

5. A long ＿＿＿ connects the three parts of Haifa.

6. A police officer in London, England, is called a ＿＿＿ .

7. The Louvre, in Paris, France, was once a ＿＿＿ .

8. The ＿＿＿ built tall pyramids where Mexico City stands.

9. The community of Amsterdam is below ＿＿＿ .

10. The ＿＿＿ in Amsterdam hold back the sea.

FOCUS ON MAIN IDEAS

1. Sometimes what people eat depends on where they live. Give examples of this in three countries.

2. Where is cotton grown? How is silk made? Why are cotton and silk important?

3. Why do shelters that are made from the same material often look different when they are built in other countries?

4. Who owns the land in the farming community of Jun Tan? How has life changed for farmers in Jun Tan? What other jobs are in Jun Tan?

5. What happened to Mexico City when the Spanish explorers came? How can you tell that Mexico City is both old and new?

THINK/WRITE

Think of a country you would like to visit. Find out more about that country in an encyclopedia. Write a report telling how that country is different from America.

ACTIVITIES

1. **Art** Make a class travel poster of people, places, and celebrations around the world. Cut out pictures from old magazines, or draw pictures. Paste the pictures onto a large piece of construction paper.

2. **Visiting a Store** Visit a grocery store or clothing store with a parent or other grownup. Find three pieces of clothing or three kinds of food that come from other countries. Tell what country each thing came from.

3. **Making a Bulletin Board** Cut out or draw pictures of different types of shelters around the world. Include shelters from your own community. Display the pictures on the bulletin board. Under each picture, tell in which country it is found.

SKILLS REVIEW

1. **The Earth and the Sun** Look at pages 309–311 and answer the following questions.

   a. What is the difference between "A.M." and "P.M."?

   b. How long does it take the Earth to spin completely around?

   c. Explain why it cannot be dawn in Anchorage and Belém at the same time.

   d. How do we measure a year?

   e. Why is it warmer in Belém than it is in Anchorage?

   f. Why does the Earth have different seasons?

2. **Using Intermediate Directions** Use the map below to answer the following questions.

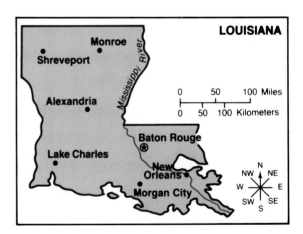

   a. If you went from Shreveport to Alexandria, in which direction would you travel?

   b. Is Morgan City southeast or southwest of New Orleans?

342

EXPLORING
YOUR COMMUNITY

You saw in Unit 5 how people in communities around the world live. You read about different kinds of food, shelter, and clothing. Now find out how these communities are like your own community.

LEARNING ABOUT YOUR COMMUNITY

1. Imagine you have a pen pal in one of the communities you read about in this unit. Write a letter to this pen pal. Tell your pen pal how your communities are alike and different. Ask your pen pal questions.

LEARNING ABOUT FOODS AROUND THE WORLD

2. Find out if any restaurants in your community serve food from other countries. Name two restaurants and tell one thing they make. Tell how it is different from American food.

LEARNING ABOUT HOLIDAYS AROUND THE WORLD

3. The Reading told about celebrations around the world. Do people in your community have any of the same celebrations? Select one celebration you would like to know more about. Use the library to find information about how that holiday might be celebrated in another country.

4. You have read how New Year's is celebrated in China. Write a report telling how New Year's in China is like New Year's in your community. Tell how it is different. Are there any celebrations in your community like New Year's in China? If so, include them in your report.

LEARNING ABOUT CUSTOMS

5. People all over the world have customs. Customs are things that people do at the same time year after year. Fireworks on the Fourth of July is a custom people in our country have. Name one local custom that people in your community have.

FOR YOUR
REFERENCE

Symbols of America — **R2**

Facts About the States — **R6**

Geographic Dictionary — **R19**

Atlas — **R22**

Glossary — **R28**

Index — **R40**

SYMBOLS OF AMERICA

The American Flag

For more than 200 years, the American flag has been a symbol of the people, government, and ideas of our country. Often called the *Stars and Stripes,* the American flag at first had 13 red and white stripes, each standing for one state. There were also 13 white stars on a blue background. Since then a star has been added for every new state to join the country.

Our country's flag should be treated with great respect. There are many rules for making, showing, caring for, and honoring this symbol of freedom. One way we honor our flag and show love for our country is by saying the Pledge of Allegiance.

> I pledge allegiance to the flag of the United States of America and to the republic for which it stands, one nation under God, indivisible, with liberty and justice for all.

The National Anthem

Another symbol of our respect for our country is "The Star-Spangled Banner." During the War of 1812 Francis Scott Key, a prisoner of the British, wrote the words to this poem on the back of an envelope.

Key stood on the deck of a ship, watching the English fire rockets and bombs at Fort McHenry near Baltimore, Maryland. At dawn he saw the American flag still waving over the undefeated fort. When Key was set free the next day, he finished the poem. It was printed in a newspaper. Soon people began to sing the poem to a popular English tune.

In 1931 Congress made "The Star-Spangled Banner" our national anthem. It speaks of the fear we feel when our country is in danger. It reminds us of our pride when America's strength carries the nation through.

This flag inspired Francis Scott Key (above) to write our national anthem. The flag may now be seen at the Museum of History and Technology in Washington, D.C.

The Star-Spangled Banner

Oh, say, can you see, by the dawn's
   early light,
What so proudly we hailed at the
   twilight's last gleaming?
Whose broad stripes and bright stars,
   thro' the perilous fight,
O'er the ramparts we watched were so
   gallantly streaming?
And the rockets' red glare,
   the bombs bursting in air
Gave proof through the night that our
   flag was still there.
Oh, say, does that star-spangled
   banner yet wave
O'er the land of the free and the home
   of the brave?

The Liberty Bell

In 1776 a bell was rung in Philadelphia to call people to listen to the Declaration of Independence. America became a free country, and the bell became known as the Liberty Bell. For 60 years the bell was rung from Independence Hall on important days, such as the Fourth of July. Then, the Liberty Bell cracked. Yet the words upon the Liberty Bell still ring out: "PROCLAIM LIBERTY THROUGHOUT ALL THE LAND UNTO ALL THE INHABITANTS THEREOF."

The Statue of Liberty

The beautiful copper Statue of Liberty was given to America by the people of France. It was a gift to honor 100 years of independence. The Statue of Liberty has been and always will be a symbol of freedom to millions of immigrants entering America. They are welcomed by her torch held high and by the words of an American poet, Emma Lazarus, on the base of the statue: . . .Give me your tired, your poor,
    Your huddled masses yearning to
       breathe free. . .

The Bald Eagle

The majestic bald eagle is America's national bird. It is the eagle's white-feathered head that makes it appear bald. Found only in North America, most bald eagles live in Alaska. Because they are few in number, our national birds are protected from hunters by federal law.

The Capitol

In 1793 President George Washington laid the cornerstone for our national Capitol in Washington, D.C. Congress has met in this building since 1800. Millions of people visit the Capitol each year. Standing in the Great Rotunda under the dome, Americans feel proud of their great history.

National Holidays

Each state in our country decides what holidays to observe. Some special days, such as Arbor Day and Valentine's Day, are popular holidays often observed in school. Our national government has also set aside certain legal holidays for the entire United States.

Martin Luther King, Jr.

New Year's Day (January 1)
Martin Luther King, Jr. Day (3rd Monday in January)
Presidents' Day (3rd Monday in February)
Memorial Day (last Monday in May)
Independence Day (July 4)
Labor Day (1st Monday in September)
Columbus Day (2nd Monday in October)
Veterans Day (November 11)
Thanksgiving (4th Thursday in November)
Christmas Day (December 25)

FACTS ABOUT THE STATES

On the following pages you will find interesting facts about each of the 50 states. Included are the states' abbreviations, nicknames, capitals, and populations. The population figures give the most recent estimates. The outline maps show the states' major rivers and the locations of their capitals. State flags and birds are shown on postage stamps issued by the U.S. Postal Service.

Alabama (Ala., AL)

Yellowhammer State;
   Heart of Dixie; Camellia
   State; Cotton State
Capital: Montgomery
Population: 4,127,000
State Bird: Yellowhammer
State Flower: Camellia

Alaska (Alaska, AK)

Last Frontier; Land of the
   Midnight Sun
Capital: Juneau
Population: 513,000
State Bird: Willow
   Ptarmigan
State Flower: Forget-Me-
   Not

Arizona (Ariz., AZ)

Grand Canyon State;
   Sunset State; Apache
   State
Capital: Phoenix
Population: 3,466,000
State Bird: Cactus Wren
State Flower: Saguaro
   Cactus Blossom

Arkansas (Ark., AR)

Land of Opportunity;
    Natural State
Capital: Little Rock
Population: 2,422,000
State Bird: Mockingbird
State Flower: Apple
    Blossom

California (Calif., CA)

Golden State
Capital: Sacramento
Population: 28,168,000
State Bird: California
    Valley Quail
State Flower: Golden
    (California) Poppy

Colorado (Colo., CO)

Centennial State
Capital: Denver
Population: 3,290,000
State Bird: Lark Bunting
State Flower: Rocky
    Mountain Columbine

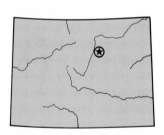

Connecticut (Conn., CT)

Constitution State; Nutmeg
    State
Capital: Hartford
Population: 3,241,000
State Bird: Robin
State Flower: Mountain
    Laurel

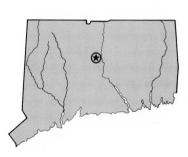

Delaware (Del., DE)

First State; Diamond State
Capital: Dover
Population: 660,000
State Bird: Blue Hen
   Chicken
State Flower: Peach
   Blossom

Florida (Fla., FL)

Sunshine State
Capital: Tallahassee
Population: 12,377,000
State Bird: Mockingbird
State Flower: Orange
   Blossom

Georgia (Ga., GA)

Empire State of the South;
   Peach State
Capital: Atlanta
Population: 6,401,000
State Bird: Brown Thrasher
State Flower: Cherokee
   Rose

Hawaii (Hawaii, HI)

Aloha State
Capital: Honolulu
Population: 1,093,000
State Bird: Nene (Hawaiian
   Goose)
State Flower: Hibiscus

Idaho (Idaho, ID)

Gem State; Spud State

Capital: Boise
Population: 999,000
State Bird: Mountain
  Bluebird
State Flower: Syringa
  (Mock Orange)

Illinois (Ill., IL)

Land of Lincoln; Prairie
  State; Inland Empire

Capital: Springfield
Population: 11,544,000
State Bird: Cardinal
State Flower: Native Violet

Indiana (Ind., IN)

Hoosier State

Capital: Indianapolis
Population: 5,575,000
State Bird: Cardinal
State Flower: Peony

Iowa (Iowa, IA)

Hawkeye State

Capital: Des Moines
Population: 2,834,000
State Bird: Eastern
  Goldfinch
State Flower: Wild Rose

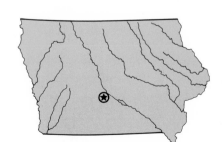

Kansas (Kans., KS)

Sunflower State;
  Jayhawker State
Capital: Topeka
Population: 2,487,000
State Bird: Western
  Meadowlark
State Flower: Sunflower

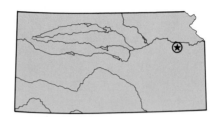

Kentucky (Ky., KY)

Bluegrass State
Capital: Frankfort
Population: 3,721,000
State Bird: Kentucky
  Cardinal
State Flower: Goldenrod

Louisiana (La., LA)

Pelican State; Bayou State
Capital: Baton Rouge
Population: 4,420,000
State Bird: Brown Pelican
State Flower: Magnolia

Maine (Maine, ME)

Pine Tree State
Capital: Augusta
Population: 1,206,000
State Bird: Chickadee
State Flower: White Pine
  Cone and Tassel

Maryland (Md., MD)

Old Line State; Free State
Capital: Annapolis
Population: 4,644,000
State Bird: Baltimore
  Oriole
State Flower: Black-Eyed
  Susan

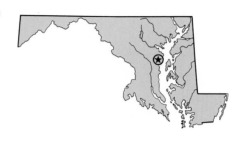

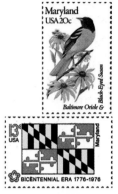

Massachusetts (Mass., MA)

Bay State; Old Colony
Capital: Boston
Population: 5,871,000
State Bird: (Black-Capped)
  Chickadee
State Flower: Mayflower

Michigan (Mich., MI)

Wolverine State; Great
  Lake State; Water
  Wonderland
Capital: Lansing
Population: 9,300,000
State Bird: Robin
State Flower: Apple
  Blossom

Minnesota (Minn., MN)

Land of 10,000 Lakes;
  Gopher State
Capital: St. Paul
Population: 4,306,000
State Bird: Common Loon
State Flower: Pink and
  White (Showy) Lady's
  Slipper

Mississippi (Miss., MS)

Magnolia State
Capital: Jackson
Population: 2,627,000
State Bird: Mockingbird
State Flower: Magnolia

Missouri (Mo., MO)

Show Me State; Gateway to
the West
Capital: Jefferson City
Population: 5,139,000
State Bird: (Eastern)
Bluebird
State Flower: (Red)
Hawthorn

Montana (Mont., MT)

Treasure State
Capital: Helena
Population: 804,000
State Bird: Western
Meadowlark
State Flower: Bitterroot

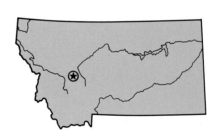

Nebraska (Nebr., NE)

Cornhusker State
Capital: Lincoln
Population: 1,601,000
State Bird: Western
Meadowlark
State Flower: Goldenrod

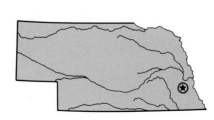

Nevada (Nev., NV)

Silver State; Battle Born
  State; Sagebrush State
Capital: Carson City
Population: 1,060,000
State Bird: Mountain
  Bluebird
State Flower: Sagebrush

New Hampshire (N.H., NH)

Granite State
Capital: Concord
Population: 1,097,000
State Bird: Purple Finch
State Flower: Purple Lilac

New Jersey (N.J., NJ)

Garden State
Capital: Trenton
Population: 7,720,000
State Bird: Eastern
  (American) Goldfinch
State Flower: Purple Violet

New Mexico (N. Mex., NM)

Land of Enchantment;
  Sunshine State
Capital: Santa Fe
Population: 1,510,000
State Bird: Roadrunner
State Flower: Yucca Flower

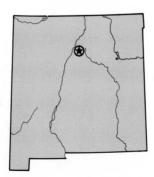

New York (N.Y., NY)
Empire State
Capital: Albany
Population: 17,898,000
State Bird: (Eastern)
  Bluebird
State Flower: Rose

North Carolina (N.C., NC)
Tar Heel State; Old North
  State
Capital: Raleigh
Population: 6,526,000
State Bird: Cardinal
State Flower: Flowering
  Dogwood

North Dakota (N. Dak., ND)
Peace Garden State; Sioux
  State; Flickertail State
Capital: Bismarck
Population: 663,000
State Bird: Western
  Meadowlark
State Flower: Wild Prairie Rose

Ohio (Ohio, OH)
Buckeye State
Capital: Columbus
Population: 10,872,000
State Bird: Cardinal
State Flower: Scarlet
  (Red) Carnation

Oklahoma (Okla., OK)

Sooner State
Capital: Oklahoma City
Population: 3,263,000
State Bird: Scissor-Tailed
　Flycatcher
State Flower: Mistletoe

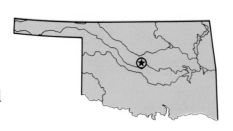

Oregon (Oreg., OR)

Beaver State
Capital: Salem
Population: 2,741,000
State Bird: Western
　Meadowlark
State Flower: Oregon
　Grape

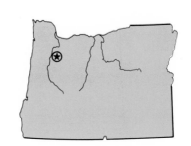

Pennsylvania (Pa., PA)

Keystone State
Capital: Harrisburg
Population: 12,027,000
State Bird: Ruffed Grouse
State Flower: Mountain
　Laurel

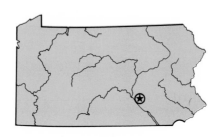

Rhode Island (R.I., RI)

Little Rhody; Ocean State
Capital: Providence
Population: 995,000
State Bird: Rhode Island
　Red
State Flower: Violet

South Carolina (S.C., SC)

Palmetto State
Capital: Columbia
Population: 3,493,000
State Bird: Carolina Wren
State Flower: Carolina
    Jessamine

South Dakota (S. Dak., SD)

Coyote State; Sunshine State
Capital: Pierre
Population: 715,000
State Bird: Ring-Necked
    Pheasant
State Flower: American
    Pasqueflower

Tennessee (Tenn., TN)

Volunteer State; Big
    Bend State
Capital: Nashville
Population: 4,919,000
State Bird: Mockingbird
State Flower: Iris

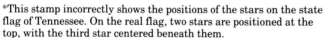
*This stamp incorrectly shows the positions of the stars on the state flag of Tennessee. On the real flag, two stars are positioned at the top, with the third star centered beneath them.

Texas (Tex., TX)

Lone Star State
Capital: Austin
Population: 16,780,000
State Bird: Mockingbird
State Flower: Bluebonnet

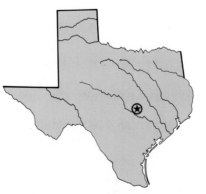

Utah (Utah, UT)

Beehive State
Capital: Salt Lake City
Population: 1,691,000
State Bird: Sea (California)
  Gull
State Flower: Sego Lily

Vermont (Vt., VT)

Green Mountain State
Capital: Montpelier
Population: 556,000
State Bird: Hermit Thrush
State Flower: Red Clover

Virginia (Va., VA)

Old Dominion; Mother of
  Presidents
Capital: Richmond
Population: 5,996,000
State Bird: Cardinal
State Flower: Flowering
  Dogwood

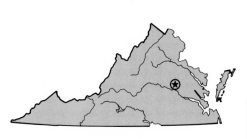

Washington (Wash., WA)

Evergreen State; Chinook
  State
Capital: Olympia
Population: 4,619,000
State Bird: Willow
  (American) Goldfinch
State Flower: Coast
  Rhododendron

West Virginia (W. Va., WV)

Mountain State
Capital: Charleston
Population: 1,884,000
State Bird: Cardinal
State Flower:
   Rhododendron
   (Maximum)

Wisconsin (Wis., WI)

Badger State; America's
   Dairyland
Capital: Madison
Population: 4,858,000
State Bird: Robin
State Flower: Wood Violet

Wyoming (Wyo., WY)

Equality State; Cowboy
   State
Capital: Cheyenne
Population: 471,000
State Bird: Western
   Meadowlark
State Flower: Indian
   Paintbrush

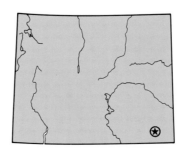

GEOGRAPHIC DICTIONARY

On the following pages are descriptions of some important natural features. Study these pages. Refer to them often as you read.

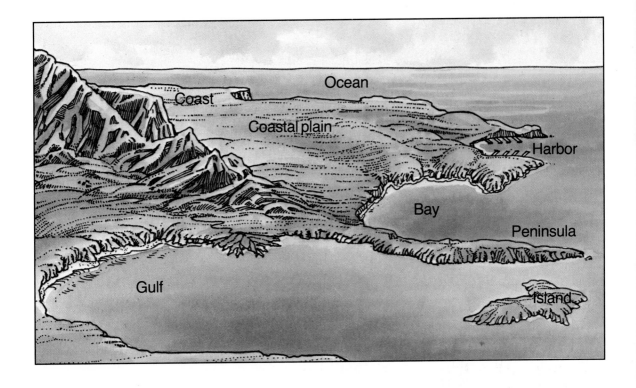

bay a small area of ocean partly surrounded by land

coast the land next to an ocean

coastal plain low, flat land near an ocean

continent one of the Earth's main areas of land

gulf a large area of ocean partly surrounded by land

harbor a place on a coast where ships can dock safely

island land completely surrounded by water

ocean a large body of salt water

peninsula a piece of land with water on three sides of it

sea a large body of salt water surrounded by land

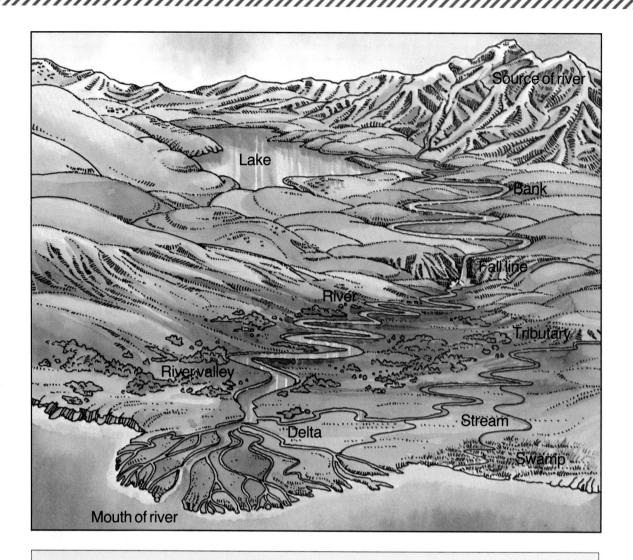

Source of river
Lake
Bank
Fall line
River
Tributary
River valley
Delta
Stream
Swamp
Mouth of river

bank the land on either side of a river

branch a stream or river that flows into a larger one

delta the land formed at the mouth of a river

fall line a place where the height of the land drops suddenly and waterfalls form

lake a body of fresh water or salt water surrounded by land

mouth of river the place where a river empties into a larger body of water

river a large stream of water

river basin all the land drained by a river and its branches

river valley the low land through which a river flows

source of river the place where a river begins

stream a small body of running water

swamp low, wet land

tributary a stream or river that flows into a larger one

waterway a body of water that ships can use

basin a low, bowl-shaped area

canyon a narrow valley with high, steep sides

cliff a high, steep wall of rock

desert dry land where few plants grow

foothill a low hill at the base of a mountain

hill a small, raised part of the land, lower than a mountain

mesa a flat-topped hill with steep sides, common in dry areas

mountain a large, high part of the land with steep sides

mountain range a group or chain of mountains

peak the pointed top of a mountain

plain a large area of flat or gently rolling land

plateau an area of high, flat land

sand dune a hill of sand piled up by the wind

slope the side of a mountain or hill

valley low land between mountains or hills

volcano an opening in the Earth that throws out melted rock and gases

ATLAS

CANADA

• Seattle

Olympia ✪

**WASHINGTON
(WA)**

Portland •

✪ Salem

Columbia River

**OREGON
(OR)**

**IDAHO
(ID)**

✪ Boise

Missouri River

Helena ✪

**MONTANA
(MT)**

Billings •

**NORTH DAKOTA
(ND)**

✪ Bismarck

Snake River

Pocatello •

**WYOMING
(WY)**

Casper •

Pierre ✪

**SOUTH DAKOTA
(SD)**

Sacramento River

Sacramento ✪

✪ Carson City

**NEVADA
(NV)**

Great Salt Lake

Salt Lake City ✪

Provo •

**UTAH
(UT)**

Cheyenne ✪

**NEBRASKA
(NE)**

Platte River

**CALIFORNIA
(CA)**

Denver •

**COLORADO
(CO)**

Colorado Springs •

**KANSAS
(KS)**

Wich

River

**PACIFIC
OCEAN**

Las Vegas •

Los Angeles •

Colorado River

**ARIZONA
(AZ)**

Santa Fe ✪

• Albuquerque

**OKLAHO
(OK)**

Oklahom
C

Phoenix ✪

**NEW MEXICO
(NM)**

Tucson •

**TEXAS
(TX)**

ARCTIC OCEAN

MEXICO

Rio Grande

Austin •

PACIFIC OCEAN

Yukon River

**ALASKA
(AK)**

CANADA

Anchorage •

Juneau ✪

R22

0	250	500 **Miles**
0 250	500	750 **Kilometers**

PACIFIC OCEAN

PACIFIC OCEAN

Kauai

Oahu

Honolulu •

HAWAII (HI)

Maui

Hawaii

0	100	200 **Miles**
0 100	200	300 **Kilometers**

UNITED STATES OF AMERICA

CANADA

MINNESOTA (MN)
Minneapolis • St. Paul

Falls

WISCONSIN (WI)
Milwaukee •
Madison •

IOWA (IA)
Cedar Rapids •
Des Moines •
maha

MICHIGAN (MI)
Lansing •

Lake Superior

Lake Michigan

Lake Huron

Detroit •
Chicago •

ILLINOIS (IL)
Springfield •

Fort Wayne •
INDIANA (IN)
Indianapolis •

OHIO (OH)
Columbus •

Cleveland •

Lake Ontario

Lake Erie

St. Lawrence River

MAINE (ME)
Augusta ✪
• Portland

Burlington •
Montpelier ✪
VERMONT (VT)

NEW HAMPSHIRE (NH)
Concord ✪
Manchester •
• Boston

Albany ✪
NEW YORK (NY)
Springfield •
Hartford •

MASSACHUSETTS (MA)
Providence ✪
RHODE ISLAND (RI)
CONNECTICUT (CT)

Bridgeport •
Newark •
New York City •

PENNSYLVANIA (PA)
Harrisburg ✪
Philadelphia •

Trenton ✪
NEW JERSEY (NJ)

Dover ✪
DELAWARE (DE)

MARYLAND (MD)

Baltimore •
Washington, D.C. ✪
Annapolis ✪

MISSOURI (MO)
Missouri River
Jefferson City ✪
St. Louis •
opeka
Jefferson City

Wabash River

Ohio River

KENTUCKY (KY)
Frankfort ✪
Louisville •

Huntington •

WEST VIRGINIA (WV)
Charleston •

VIRGINIA (VA)
Richmond ✪

Norfolk •

ARKANSAS (AR)
Little Rock ✪
Fort Smith •
sa
River

Memphis •

TENNESSEE (TN)
Nashville ✪

Tennessee River

NORTH CAROLINA (NC)
Raleigh ✪
Charlotte •

• Columbia
SOUTH CAROLINA (SC)
Charleston •

MISSISSIPPI (MS)
Jackson ✪

Mississippi River

ALABAMA (AL)
Montgomery ✪
Birmingham •

Atlanta ✪
GEORGIA (GA)
Columbus •

LOUISIANA (LA)
Baton Rouge ✪
Biloxi •
New Orleans •

Houston •

Tallahassee ✪
• Jacksonville

FLORIDA (FL)

ATLANTIC OCEAN

Gulf of Mexico

BAHAMAS

CUBA

MAP KEY

—— National boundary

— State boundary

( ) Postal abbreviation

✪ National capital

✪ State capital

• Large city

N
NW   NE
W   E
SW   SE
S

| 0 | 100 | 200 | 300 Miles |
| 0 | 100 | 200 | 300 | 400 Kilometers |

R23

LANDFORMS OF THE UNITED STATES

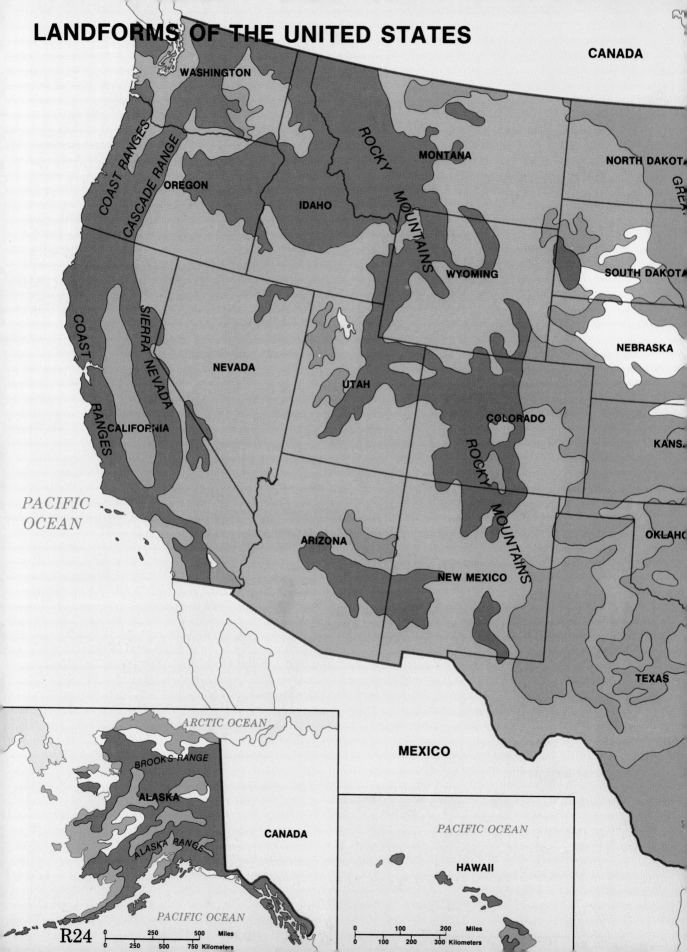

CANADA

WASHINGTON

COAST RANGES

CASCADE RANGE

OREGON

IDAHO

ROCKY MOUNTAINS

MONTANA

NORTH DAKOTA

GREA

WYOMING

SOUTH DAKOTA

COAST RANGES

SIERRA NEVADA

NEVADA

UTAH

COLORADO

NEBRASKA

CALIFORNIA

KANS.

PACIFIC OCEAN

ROCKY MOUNTAINS

ARIZONA

NEW MEXICO

OKLAHO

TEXAS

MEXICO

ARCTIC OCEAN

BROOKS RANGE

ALASKA

CANADA

ALASKA RANGE

PACIFIC OCEAN

HAWAII

PACIFIC OCEAN

R24

	Miles
250	500
250	500	750	Kilometers

	100	200	Miles
100	200	300	Kilometers

CANADA

Great Lakes

MINNESOTA

MICHIGAN

WISCONSIN

MAINE

VERMONT

NEW HAMPSHIRE

NEW YORK

MASSACHUSETTS

RHODE ISLAND

CONNECTICUT

IOWA

PENNSYLVANIA

NEW JERSEY

ILLINOIS

INDIANA

OHIO

MARYLAND

DELAWARE

GREAT PLAINS

WEST VIRGINIA

VIRGINIA

APPALACHIAN MOUNTAINS

MISSOURI

KENTUCKY

NORTH CAROLINA

ATLANTIC OCEAN

TENNESSEE

ARKANSAS

SOUTH CAROLINA

MISSISSIPPI

ALABAMA

GEORGIA

LOUISIANA

N
NW NE
W E
SW SE
S

FLORIDA

Gulf of Mexico

BAHAMAS

MAP KEY

Mountains

Plateaus

Hills

Plains

National boundary

State boundary

R25

| 0 | 100 | 200 | 300 Miles |

| 0 | 100 | 200 | 300 | 400 Kilometers |

CUBA

THE WORLD

—— National boundary

ARCTIC OCEAN

ALASKA

CANADA

North America

UNITED STATES

PACIFIC OCEAN

ATLANTIC OCEAN

BAHAMAS

MEXICO

CUBA

DOMINICAN REPUBLIC

JAMAICA HAITI

BELIZE

HONDURAS

GUATEMALA

EL SALVADOR NICARAGUA

COSTA RICA

PANAMA

PUERTO RICO

TRINIDAD AND TOBAGO

VENEZUELA GUYANA

SURINAME

FRENCH GUIANA

COLOMBIA

HAWAII

Equator

ECUADOR

PERU

South America

BRAZIL

WESTERN SAMOA

BOLIVIA

TONGA

PARAGUAY

PACIFIC OCEAN

CHILE

URUGUAY

ARGENTINA

Antarctica

ALB. Albania
AUST. Austria
C. AF. REP. Central African Republic
CZECH. Czechoslovakia
E. GER. East Germany
HUNG. Hungary
NETH. Netherlands
SWITZ. Switzerland
U. ARAB EMIR. United Arab Emirates
W. GER. West Germany
YEMEN (P.D.R.) People's Democratic
    Republic of Yemen
YUGO. Yugoslavia

ARCTIC OCEAN

GREENLAND

ICELAND

NORWAY
SWEDEN
FINLAND

UNITED
KINGDOM
England
IRELAND
DENMARK
NETH.
E.
GER.
POLAND
W.
GER.
CZECH.
Europe
SOVIET UNION (USSR)

FRANCE
SWITZ.
AUST.
HUNG.
ROMANIA
ITALY
YUGO.
BULGARIA
ALB.
GREECE
TURKEY

MONGOLIA

Asia

N. KOREA
S. KOREA
JAPAN

SPAIN

PORTUGAL

MOROCCO
TUNISIA
LEBANON
ISRAEL
SYRIA
IRAQ
JORDAN
IRAN
AFGHANISTAN
PAKISTAN
CHINA
NEPAL
BHUTAN

WESTERN
SAHARA
ALGERIA
LIBYA
EGYPT
SAUDI
ARABIA
U. ARAB EMIR.
OMAN
INDIA
TAIWAN

MAURITANIA
MALI
NIGER
Africa
CHAD
SUDAN
YEMEN
YEMEN
(P.D.R.)
BANGLADESH
BURMA
(Myanmar)
LAOS
VIETNAM
PHILIPPINES

SENEGAL
GAMBIA
JINEA-BISSAU
GUINEA
BURKINA
FASO
NIGERIA
ETHIOPIA
THAILAND
CAMBODIA

SIERRA LEONE
IVORY
COAST
BENIN
C. AF. REP.
SRI LANKA
BRUNEI

LIBERIA
GHANA
TOGO
CAMEROON
UGANDA
SOMALIA
MALDIVES
MALAYSIA
SINGAPORE

**PACIFIC
OCEAN**

GABON
CONGO
RWANDA
BURUNDI
KENYA
Equator
INDONESIA
PAPUA
NEW
GUINEA
SOLOMON
ISLANDS

ZAIRE
TANZANIA

**INDIAN
OCEAN**

FIJI

ANGOLA
MALAWI
ZAMBIA
ZIMBABWE
MOZAMBIQUE
MADAGASCAR

NAMIBIA
BOTSWANA

**ATLANTIC
OCEAN**

SOUTH
AFRICA

Australia

NEW
ZEALAND

Antarctica

0   500   1,000 1,500 2,000 Miles

0   1,000   2,000   Kilometers

R27

This glossary contains important social studies words and their definitions. Each word is respelled as it would be in a dictionary. When you see this mark ′ after a syllable, pronounce that syllable with more force than the other syllables. The page number at the end of the definition tells where to find the word in your book.

add, **ā**ce, c**â**re, p**ä**lm; **e**nd, **ē**qual; **i**t, **ī**ce; **ŏ**dd, **ō**pen, **ô**rder; t**ŏŏ**k, p**ōō**l; **u**p, b**û**rn; y**ōō** as u in *fuse;* **oi**l; p**ou**t; ə as a in *above,* e in *sicken,* i in *possible;* o in *melon,* u in *circus;*

check; ri**ng**; **th**in; **th**is; **zh** as in *vision.*

address (ə·dres′)   The location of something, usually the street number, community, state, and ZIP code of a building. (p. 49)

advertisements (ad·vər·tīz′mənts)   Information about things that are for sale. (p. 187)

aerospace (âr′ō·spās)   Having to do with air and space. (p. 245)

A.M. (ā·em′)   The hours between midnight and noon. (p. 309)

American Indians (ə·mer′ə·kən in′dē·ənz)   The people who have been living in North and South America for thousands of years. (p.72)

American Revolution (ə·mer′ə·kən rev·ə·lōō′shən)   The war America fought with England to become free (1775–1783). (p. 264)

Anasazi Indians (än·ə·säz′ē in′dē·ənz)   A group of American Indians that used irrigation methods to farm land in the Southwest. (p. 72)

Arapaho Indians (ə·rap′ə·hō in′dē·ənz)   A group of Plains Indians that lived where the community of Denver, Colorado, was built. (p. 235)

architect (är′kə·tekt)   A person who designs and draws plans for buildings. (p. 48)

atlas (at′ləs)   A book or section of a book that has maps. (p. 3)

authors (ô′thərz)   People who write books. (p. 31)

Aztec Indians (az′tek in′dē·ənz)   People who lived in Mexico City more than 600 years ago. (p. 332)

banks (bangks)   Places where people keep money. (p. 20)

bar graph (bär graf)   A graph that uses bars of different heights to show amounts of things. (p. 120)

beisbol (bayz′·bōl)   A game played with a wooden bat and a hard ball in Venezuela. (p. 319)

board of education (bôrd uv ej·ŏŏ·kā′shən)   A group elected by the members of a community to decide how the schools are to be run. (p. 204)

Board of Selectmen (bôrd uv si·lekt′mən)   A group of New England town officials elected to run community government. (p. 177)

bobby (bob′ē)   A police officer in England. (p. 328)

borders (bôr′dərz)   Lines drawn on a map to show where one place ends and another begins. (p. 51)

boundaries (boun′də·rēz)   Another word for *borders*. (p. 51)

buffalo (buf′ə·lō)   A large, shaggy, wild ox used by Plains Indians for food, clothing, and shelter. (p. 236)

business center (biz′nəs sen′tər)   Downtown, where most of the people in a community work. (p. 20)

butterfat (but′ər·fat)   The cream that rises when milk is left standing. (p. 91)

by-products (bī′prod·əkts)   Parts of a resource or product used to make other goods. (p. 105)

calendar (kal′ən·dər)   A table showing the days, weeks, and months of the year. (p. 266)

canal (kə·nal′)   A waterway made by people. (p. 134)

cannery (kan′ə·rē)   A factory where foods are canned. (p. 84)

capital (kap′ə·təl)   A place where rules for a state or country are made. (p. 44)

capitol (kap′ə·təl)   A building where people meet to make rules for a state or country. (p. 50)

cargo (kär′gō)   Goods carried on ships, trains, or planes. (p. 133)

cattle (kat′ əl)   Cows, bulls, and steers raised for milk or meat. (p. 75)

century (sen′chə rē)   One hundred years. (p. 278)

citizen (sit′ə·zən)   A member of a large community. (p. 1)

city council (sit′ē koun′səl)   The lawmakers in a city. (p. 173)

city manager (sit′ē man′ij·ər)   A city leader who helps make sure things get done. (p. 173)

Civil War (siv′əl wôr)   A war fought in America between the North and the South (1861–1865). (p. 271)

claim (klām)   To say that someplace is owned by a country. (p. 256)

climate (clī'mət)   The usual weather in a place, year after year. (p. 67)

clinics (klin'iks)   Places that give medical treatment. (p. 203)

coal (kōl)   A dark brown or black mineral which gives off heat when burned. (p. 97)

coast (kōst)   Land next to an ocean. (p. 141)

colonies (kol'ə·nēz)   Places that are settled and ruled by other countries. (p. 262)

Columbus Day (kə·ləm'bəs dā)   The October 12 holiday honoring the landing of Columbus in America in 1492. (p. 255)

community (kə·myōo'nə·tē)   A town, city, suburb, or other place where people live and work together. (p. 1)

compass rose (kum'pəs rōz)   A guide to directions on a map. (p. 10)

Congress (kong'grəs)   The elected lawmakers from each state who make laws for the whole country. (p. 183)

Constitution (kon·stə·tōo'shən)   The written laws for our country's government. (p. 265)

consumer (kən·sōo'mər)   Someone who buys goods and services. (p. 159)

containers (kən·tā'nərz)   Large steel boxes in which goods are packed for shipping. (p. 133)

continent (kon'tə·nənt)   One of the main land areas of the world. (p. 15)

convent (kon'vent)   A special place where nuns live. (p. 330)

cotton (kot'ən)   The white, fluffy part of the cotton plant used to make cloth. (p. 301)

courts (kôrts)   Places where judges decide how people who break laws should be punished. (p. 174)

creamery (krē'mər·ē)   A factory that makes milk ready for people to buy, and makes other dairy products from milk. (p. 91)

crew (krōo)   A group of people who work together. (p. 198)

crime (krīm)   Something that is against the law. (p. 194)

crop (krop)   Any plant raised by a farmer. (p. 68)

crossroads (krôs'rōdz)   Places where main roads meet. (p. 232)

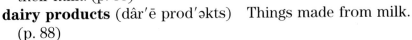
dairy farm (dâr′ē färm)   A farm where cows are raised for their milk. (p. 88)

dairy products (dâr′ē prod′əkts)   Things made from milk. (p. 88)

dam (dam)   A wall built across a river or lake that controls water flow. (p. 127)

Declaration of Independence (dek·lə·rā′shən uv in·di·pen′dəns)   A message written in 1776 that said the colonies no longer belonged to England. (p. 264)

derrick (der′ik)   A tall tower that fits over an oil well. It holds machines for drilling, lifting, and pumping oil. (p. 117)

desert (dez′ərt)   An area of dry land where few plants can grow. (p. 37)

detectives (di·tek′tivz)   People trained to solve crimes. (p. 194)

detour (dē′toor)   A temporary way around a blockage in the road. (p. 168)

dictionaries (dik′shən·âr·ēz)   Books that list words in alphabetical order and tell their meanings. (p. 32)

dikes (dīks)   Dams, or walls, that hold back water. (p. 333)

direction (də·rek′shən)   The way something is going or facing. The main directions are north, south, east, and west. (p. 10)

distance scale (dis′təns skāl)   Something on a map that helps you find out how far one place really is from another. (p. 7)

downtown (doun′toun′)   The main business area of a city or town. (p. 20)

drill (dril)   Pieces of pipe used to make holes deep into the earth. (p. 117)

dry goods (drī goodz)   Items such as fabrics, clothing, and household odds and ends. (p. 304)

D

economics (ek·ə·nom′iks)   How goods, services, and money are traded back and forth. (p. 160)

elect (i·lekt′)   To choose by vote. (p. 174)

election (i·lek′shən)   A time when people make choices by voting. (p. 180)

electricity (i·lek·tris′ə·tē)   Power used for lights, heating, and machines. (p. 105)

E

emergency (i·mûr′jən·sē) A sudden and unexpected event needing immediate attention. (p. 187)

encyclopedias (ən·sī·klə·pē′dē·əz) Books that give facts in alphabetical order about many subjects. (p. 32)

energy (en′ər·jē) Power that makes things work. (p. 99)

equator (i·kwā′tər) A make-believe line around the Earth halfway between the North and South poles. (p. 13)

Eskimos (es′kə·mōz) Groups of people who have been living in the cold parts of Russia, Alaska, Canada, and Greenland for many hundreds of years. (p. 56)

explorer (iks·plôr′ər) A person who travels to new lands to discover things. (p. 255)

factories (fak′tər·ēz) Big buildings where goods are made. (p. 74)

family (fam′ə·lē) The people you live with, especially your parents, brothers, sisters, and other relatives. (p. xiv)

farming community (färm′ing kə·myoō′nə·tē) A community where most of the people work on farms or with the resources from farms. (p. 79)

ferryboats (fer′ē·bōts) Boats that carry people and cars. (p. 143)

fertilizer (fûr′təl·ī·zər) Something added to the soil to feed plants and make them grow better. (p. 70)

feta cheese (fet′ə chēz) A cheese from Greece made from sheep's or goat's milk. (p. 294)

fiction (fik′shən) Something that is make-believe or not true. (p. 31)

first aid (fûrst ād) The emergency help given someone who has been hurt. (p. 187)

flow chart (flō chärt) A chart that shows the order in which something is done. (p. 152)

fort (fôrt) A place for protecting soldiers. (p. 329)

Fourth of July (fôrth uv joō·lī′) The birthday of the United States of America. (p. 264)

freedom (frē′dəm) Not being under someone else's rule. Being able to make many choices about your life and government. (p. 263)

fresh water (fresh wô′tər) Water that does not have salt in it. The water in most lakes and rivers is fresh. (p. 125)

fuel (fyoōl) Something that gives off heat when it is burned. (p. 107)

ghost towns (gōst tounz)   Place where no one lives any-more. (p. 234)

globe (glōb)   A model of the Earth. (p. 12)

gold dust (gōld dust)   Very fine flakes of gold. (p.240)

gold pan (gōld pan)   A wide, shallow pan used by miners to get gold from rivers. (p.240)

goods (go͝odz)   Things made by people. (p. 67)

governor (guv′ ər·nər)   The leader in a state government. (p. 182)

government (guv′ ərn·mənt)   A group of people that makes laws and sees that they are followed. (p. 172)

grain (grān)   Small, hard seeds from certain plants, such as wheat. (p. 293)

grid (grid)   Lines that cross one another. On a grid map, letters and numbers help you find things. (p. 199)

group (groop)   People who get together because they share the same needs and interests. (p. xiv)

growing season (grō′ing sē′zən)   The months in which crops can grow. (p. 71)

guide words (gīd wûrdz)   Words at the top of a dictionary or an encyclopedia page that tell you the first and last words on that page. (p. 32)

harbor (här′ bər)   A protected place where ships or boats can stay. (p. 129)

harvest (här′vəst)   To pick crops. (p. 70)

hazard (haz′ ərd)   A danger. (p. 197)

hemisphere (hem′ ə·sfir)   One of the halves of the Earth. (p. 53)

history (his′tə·rē)   The story of the past. (p. 231)

homogenized (hō·mäj′ə·nīzd)   Mixed in such a way that the butterfat in milk does not seperate from the milk. (p. 81)

hospital (hos′pi·təl)   A place where hurt or sick people can go for medical care. (p. 27)

income (in′kəm)   The money a person earns. (p. 157)

industries (in′dəs·trēz)   Big businesses. (p. 147)

intermediate directions (in·tər·mē′dē·it di·rek′shənz)   The four directions midway between the cardinal directions. (p. 335)

irrigation (ir·ə·gā′shən)   Bringing water from another place to help crops grow. (p. 71)

judge (juj)   A person who decides if laws have been broken and decides punishment if they have been broken. (p. 172)

Juvenile Court (ju·və·nīl kôrt)   A law court that deals with cases involving children. (p. 110)

labor (lā′bər)   Work. (p. 276)

Labor Day (lā′bər dā)   A holiday in September that honors workers. (p. 276)

lake (lāk)   A body of water with land all around. (p. 37)

landform map (lānd′fôrm map)   A map that tells you about the shape of the land. (p. 111)

law (lô)   A written rule that must be obeyed by all the people of a community, state, or country. (p. 169)

lawmakers (lô′mā·kərz)   The people in government who make laws. (p. 172)

librarian (lī·brâr′ē·ən)   A person who takes care of books and helps people find information in the library. (p. 30)

library (lī′brer·ē)   A place where people can find books, magazines, and newspapers. (p. 30)

list (list)   A way to order things by writing them down. (p. 86)

living history museum (liv′ing his′tə·rə myoo·zē′əm)   A special place where people act out how life used to be at a certain time and place. (p. 260)

location (lō·kā′shən)   Where something is. (p. 136)

lumber (lum′bər)   Wood that is sawed and used to make goods. (p. 147)

majority rule (mə·jôr′ə·tē rool)   The idea that if more than half of a group votes for something, the rest of the group has to go along with the choice. (p. 180)

manufactured (man·yə·fak′chərd)   Made by people or machines in factories. (p. 245)

map (map)   A drawing of a place. (p. 6)

map key (map kē)   Something that tells you what the symbols in a map stand for. (p. 6)

Mayflower (mā′flou·ər)   The ship that carried the Pilgrims to America in 1620. (p. 258)

mayor (mā′ər)   The leader in a city or community government. (p. 172)

Memorial Day (mə·môr′ē·əl dā)   A holiday in May honoring those who have died fighting in American wars. (p. 272)

mine (mīn)   A large hole or deep tunnel used to remove minerals from the earth. (p. 97)

mineral (min′ər·əl)   A natural resource found in the earth. (p. 97)

model (mod′əl)   A small copy of something. (p. 4)

mountain (moun′tən)   A large, raised part of the land. (p. 37)

nation (nā′shən)   A country with a government of its own. (p. 263)

national anthem (nash′ən·əl an′thəm)   A song of praise about a country. Our national anthem is "The Star-Spangled Banner." (p. R3)

Native Americans (nā′tiv ə·mer′ə·kənz)   Groups of people who were living in America before the European explorers came. American Indians, Eskimos, and Hawaiians are Native Americans. (p. 260)

natural resources (nach′ər·əl rē′sôr·səz)   Things found in nature that people can use. (p. 67)

Navajo Indians (näv′ə·hō in′dē·ənz)   Indians who lived in Arizona and New Mexico and grew corn long ago. Today the largest group of North American Indians. (p. 253)

needs (nēdz)   Things we must have in order to live. (p. 23)

neighborhood (nā′bər·ho͝od)   A smaller part of a community, made up of the people who live or work near one another. (p. 1)

nonfiction (non·fik′shən)   Something that is true. A book that is not a make-believe story. (p. 31)

nun (nun)   A woman who gives her life to serving God. (p. 330)

ocean (ō′shən)   A huge body of salt water. (p. 13)

oil (oil)   A mineral that is a dark, thick liquid, found deep in the ground. (p. 97)

palace (pal′is)   A grand house built for a king or queen. (p. 329)

pasta (päs′tə)   Noodles made from flour, water, salt, and eggs. (p. 296)

pasteurized (pas´chə·rīzd)   Quickly heated and then cooled in such a way that harmful germs are killed. (p. 91)

pasture (pas´chər)   A field of grass and other kinds of plants that animals eat. (p. 47)

petroleum (pə·trō´lē·əm)   Oil. (p. 114)

Pilgrims (pil´grimz)   People from England who settled in Plymouth, Massachusetts, in 1620. They came to America to be free to have their own beliefs. (p. 258)

plains (plānz)   Low, flat lands. (p. 111)

Plains Indians (plānz in´dē·ənz)   Indians who lived on the Great Plains east of the Rocky Mountains. (p. 235)

plateaus (pla·tōz´)   Lands that are usually high and flat. (p. 111)

plot (plot)   A piece of land. (p. 316)

P.M. (pē·em´)   The hours between noon and midnight. (p. 309)

population map (pop·yə·lā´shən map)   A map that shows how many people live in a place. (p. 324)

port (pôrt)   A community where ships can dock. (p. 129)

President (prez´ə·dənt)   The leader of our country. (p. 44)

private property (prī´vit prop´ər·tē)   Homes, businesses, and other things that belong to individuals. (p. 192)

producer (prə·doo´sər)   Someone who makes goods or gives services. (p. 158)

property (prop´ər·tē)   Land, buildings, and other things people own. (p. 192)

property tax (prop´ər·tē taks)   A certain amount of money paid as a tax on the land and buildings a person owns. (p. 212)

public property (pub´iik prop´ər·tē)   Zoos, parks, and other things that are open to everyone. (p. 192)

public transportation (pub´lik trans·pər·tā´shən)   Services that people pay to use to get from place to place. Buses and trains are two kinds of public transportation. (p. 203)

public works (pub´lik wûrks)   A city department that provides such services as repairing roads, supplying clean water, and so on. (p. 201)

pulp (pulp)   The part of the tomato that is left after the seeds and peels are removed. (p. 85)

pyramid (pir´ə·mid)   A building with flat sides that come to a point on top. (p. 331)

recreation (rek·rē·ā′shən)   Things people do for enjoyment. (p. 207)

recycling center (rē·sī′kling sen′tər)   Place where people bring old newspapers, cans, and bottles so they can be used again. (p. 103)

refinery (ri·fī′nər·ē)   A factory where oil is made ready for different uses. (p. 119)

reflects (ri·flekts′)   Throws or casts back the sun's rays. (p. 300)

reservations (rez·ər·vā′shənz)   Lands the government gave Indians to live on. (p. 270)

reservoir (rez′ər·vwär)   A lake used for collecting and storing water. (p. 202)

resource map (rē′sôrs map)   A map that shows where resources are located. (p. 74)

responsible (ri·spon′sə·bəl)   Obeying rules and laws that go along with using community services. (p. 167)

revolves (ri·volvz′)   The way the Earth moves slowly around the sun. (p. 311)

rice (rīs)   A grasslike plant having seeds that are used for food. (p. 295)

ripe (rīp)   Ready to be eaten. (p. 81)

river (riv′ər)   A long, flowing body of water. (p. 37)

rotates (rō′tāts)   Turns around. The Earth rotates once every 24 hours. (p. 309)

route (rōot)   A way to get from one place to another. (p. 139)

rural (rŏor′əl)   Near forests or farms. (p. 41)

sales tax (sālz taks)   A tax people pay when they buy something. (p. 212)

salt box house (sôlt′boks hous)   A type of house built to look like the boxes that salt used to come in. (p. 306)

salt water (sôlt wô′tər)   Water that contains salt, as the water in the oceans. (p. 125)

sarongs (sə·rongz′)   Skirtlike pieces of cloth worn by people in Samoa. (p. 300)

sashimi (säsh′ə·mē)   A Japanese dish of thinly sliced raw fish. (p. 294)

savings (sā′vingz)   The money people set aside for future use. (p. 158)

sawmill (sô′mil)   A factory in a logging area where big saws cut logs into boards. (p. 147)

scout (skout)   A person who finds out what is ahead and goes back to tell the group. (p. 238)

sculptures (skulp′chərz)   Works of art made from stone, clay, or metal. (p. 329)

sea level (sē lev′əl)   The level of the ocean. (p. 333)

services (sûr′vəs·əz)   Jobs people provide for us, such as car repairs or haircuts. (p. 157)

settlers (set′lərz)   People who come to a new place, especially to build houses and farms. (p. 257)

sewage (soo′əj)   Waste water from homes, businesses, and streets. (p. 202)

sewage treatment plants (soo′əj trēt′mənt plants)   Buildings where sewage is cleaned and treated. (p. 202)

shelters (shel′tərz)   Homes, stores, and other buildings. (p. 23)

shingles (shing′·gəlz)   Thin pieces of wood used to cover the sides of houses and roofs. (p. 306)

shish kebab (shish′ kə·bob)   Pieces of meat and vegetables cooked on a skewer. (p. 296)

skim milk (skim milk)   Milk that has had the cream taken off the top. (p. 92)

slaves (slāvz)   People who were owned by other people. (p. 259)

spur (spûr)   A short branch extending from the main line of a railroad. (p. 244)

suburb (sub′ərb)   A community close to a city. (p. 41)

subway (sub′wā)   A train that runs mostly underground. (p. 321)

Supreme Court (sə·prēm′ kôrt)   The most important court in the United States. (p. 183)

symbol (sim′bəl)   Something that stands for something else. (p. 6)

T

table (tā′bəl)   A special kind of list, often using lines or boxes to arrange facts. (p. 87)

taxes (tak′səz)   Money people pay to support their government and its services. (p. 212)

tepees (tē′pēz)   Cone-shaped tents in which some Indians lived. (p. 235)

Thanksgiving (thangks·giv′ing)   A special holiday in November, first celebrated by the Pilgrims. (p. 258)

thatched roofs (thatcht rōofs)   Roof coverings made from bundles of straw. (p. 307)

timeline (tīm′līn)   A line that shows a number of years and marks things in the order in which they happened. (p. 267)

tomato paste (tə·mā′tō pāst)   A thick, rich sauce made from ripe tomatoes. (p. 84)

town meeting (toun mē′ting)   A meeting in which all the people in a town take part in its government. (p. 176)

trade center (trād sen′tər)   A place where people buy and sell many goods. (p. 231)

transportation (trans·pər·tā′shən)   Moving people or things from one place to another. (p. 128)

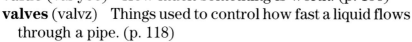

valley (val′ē)   Low land between hills or mountains. (p. 77)

value (val′yo͞o)   How much something is worth. (p. 156)

valves (valvz)   Things used to control how fast a liquid flows through a pipe. (p. 118)

volumes (vol′yo͞omz)   Separate books that are part of a set of encyclopedias. (p. 33)

volunteer (vol·ən·tir′)   A person who does something for free. (p. 214)

vote (vōt)   The way people in America decide what their choices will be. (p. 180)

well (wel)   A narrow, deep hole made in the ground to reach water, oil, or natural gas. (p. 97)

yogurt (yō′gərt)   A dairy product that is thicker than milk and has a slightly sour taste. (p. 88)

ZIP code (zip kōd)   A set of numbers that helps the Post Office find an address more quickly. (p. 49)

Page references for illustrations are set in boldfaced italics.

A

Address, 49
Advertisements, 187
Aerospace industry, *144,* 245
African Americans, 132, *132,* 135, *135*
Airplanes, 138, *138,* 144, *144,* 279
Alaska, 52, 56, *129,* 143, 232, *232,* 310
American Indians
    See Indians, American
American Revolution, 264, 268
"American's Creed, The," 166
Amish, 39–40, *39, 40*
Amsterdam, The Netherlands, 333, 334, *334*
Anasazi Indians, 72–73, *72, 73*
Appalachian Mountains, 104
Arapaho Indians, 235–237
Arizona, 253
Atlas, 3, *R22–R27*
Authors, 31
Auto mechanics, 158, *158, 160*
Aztec Indians, 332

B

Banks, 20, 99, 158
Bar graphs, 120, *120,* 121, *121, 241*
Beisbol, 319
Blimps, 46, *46*
Board of education, 204, *204*
Board of Selectmen, 177
Bobby, 328, *328*
Boonesboro, Kentucky, 47, 112
Borders, 51, 53
Boundaries, 51
British Columbia, Canada, 143
Brooks, Gwendolyn, 66
Brown, Molly, 110, *110*
Buffalo, *211,* 236–237
"Buffalo Dusk," 230
Business center, 20, *20, 308*
Butterfat, 91
By-products, 105

C

Cabot, John, 256, *256*
Calendar, 266, *266,* 267
California, 76–77, 82–83, 86–87, 93, 270, 315, 317
Canals, 134, 333, 334
Cannery, 81, 84–85, *85*
Cape Canaveral, Florida, 44–45, *45*
Capital, 44, 50, 318, 326, 331
Capitol, 50, *R5*
Caracas, Venuzuela, 318, *318,* 319
Cargo, 133, *133, 137, 138,* 143
Cascade Mountains, *127,* 141
Cattle, 75, *75,* 294, *294*
Celebrations
    of Christmas in Mexico, 340, *340*
    of Easter in Poland, 339, *339*
    of New Year's in China, 338, *338, 343*
    of Pesach in Israel, 339, *339*
    in the United States, *132,* 255, 258, *258,* 264, 272, 276, 340, *340*
    See also Holidays
Century, 278
Chain saws, 148, *148*
Chicago, Illinois, *38,* 130, *130,* 131–132, *132,* 133, 135, 136–138, 140, 315, 321
China, 93, 301, 315, 316, *316,* 317, *317,* 338, *338*
Chinese Americans, 93, *93,* 132, *340*
Choices, 179–181
Christmas
    in Mexico, 340, *340*
    in the United States, 340
"Christmas in April," 214, *214*
Cities, *38,* 41–44, 45, 125, *249, 308, 320*
    having fun in, 41, 43, *43, 113, 116,* 141–142, *142*
    jobs in, 42, 79, 114, 131–132, 144, *144*
    large, 42, *42,* 43, *249, 308, 318, 320*
    shelters in, 43, 308, *308*
    small, 44–45
    See also individual city names
Citizen, 1, 177, 184, 215, *216*
City council, 173, *173*
City manager, 173
Civil War, 271, *271,* 272, *272,* 274

Climate, 67, 69–71, 76, 82–83
Clinic, 203, *203*
Clothing
  of American Indians, 236, *236, 237, 254, 270*
  of Eskimos, 59–60
  materials used to make, 301, *301,* 304
  as a need, 23–24
  in Samoa, 300, *300*
  in Saudi Arabia, 300, *300*
  special kinds of, 300, *300,* 302, *302,* 304, *304*
  in Tibet, 299, *299*
Coal, 97, *97,* 99, 102, 105–109, *109*
  by-products of, *98,* 105
  at the factory, 109
  miners, 107, *107*
  mines, 97, 99, 105, *107, 108*
  mining and use of, 107–108
Coast, *124, 129,* 141
Coblentz, Catherine Cate, 252
Cody, "Buffalo Bill," 238, *238*
Colonies, 262, 263
Columbus, Christopher, 254, *255,* 256
Columbus Day, *132,* 255
Communities, 1, 4, *4,* 17, 18, *18*
  differences among, 36, *36,* 37–47, 317, 319
  farming, 66, *66,* 79, 88, 316, *316,* 317
  of the future, 233, *233*
  government in, 172–174, *174,* 175–178
  having fun in, 21, *21,* 41, 46, 207, *207*
  history of, 229–232
  laws in, 169, 215, 217
  meeting needs, 23, 24, *24,* 25, *25,* 26, *26,* 27,
    27
  mining, 96, *96,* 97–99, 104, *104,* 105–107,
    106, 107, 108–109, 113–119, *115, 234,*
    318–319, *318*
  port, 124–129, *129,* 130–133, 141–143, 320,
    320, 321
  rules in, 165–169, 215, *215,* 216, *216,* 217, *217*
  services in
    See Services
  similarities among, 18–21, 23, 308, 321
  as transportation centers, 130
  See also individual community names
Computers, 30, *109*
Congress, 183, *183*
Constitution, 265
Consumer, 159, 160, *160*

Containers, 133, *133, 137, 138,* 143, 149
Continent, *12, 14,* 15, 51, 52, *52,* 53, *53*
Cotton, *114,* 301, *301*
Courts, 174
Cows, 88, *88,* 89–90, *90*
Crater of Diamonds, 100–101, *100, 101*
Creamery, 91–92, *92*
Crew, 198, *198*
Crime, 194
Crops, 68–69, *69,* 70, *70,* 71, *71,* 74–75, 79, *80,*
  315, 316, *316,* 320
Crossroads, 232

Dairy farms, 88, *88,* 89–90
Dairy products, 88, 90, *90,* 91–92, *92*
Dam, 127, *127,* 150
Dar es Salaam, Tanzania, 326, *326,* 327
Declaration of Independence, 264, *264*
Denver, Colorado, 110, 235, 239–241, 242, 244,
  244, 245, *245,* 246, 247–248, *248,* 249, *249*
Denver Mint, 242–243, *242, 243*
Derrick, 117, *118, 319*
Deserts, 37, 70, 300
Detectives, 194, *194*
Detour, 168, *168*
Dictionary, 32, 33
Dikes, 333, *333,* 334
Directions, 10–13
  intermediate, 335
Distance scales, 7–9
Doctors, 26, 27, *27,* 203, *203*
Downtown, 1, 20
Drilling for oil, *98,* 114–115, *115,* 117, *117,*
  118, *118,* 119, 318–319, *319*
Du Sable, Jean Baptist Pointe, 135, *135*
Durham, North Carolina, 208–209, *209*

Earth, 12, 13, 65, 107, 116, 309–310, *310,* 311,
  311
Easter in Poland, 339, *339*

Economics, 160
Egypt, 307
Elections, 174, 180, *180, 181,* 182, 183
Electricity, 105, 109, 127
Emergencies, 187
Encyclopedias, 32–33, *33*
Energy, 99, 102
   from coal, 107
   electricity, 105, 127
   from oil, 116
   saving, 102, *102,* 103
England, 256, 257–259, 262–264, 328
English Colonies, 262–263
Equator, 13, 53, 311
Eskimos, 56–60
Explorers, 255, *255,* 256, *256,* 332

"Face to Face," 292
Factories, 74, *75,* 77
   cannery, 79–81, 84–85, *85*
   and coal, 108, 109, *109*
   creamery, 91–92, *92*
   refinery, 119, *119*
Family, 1, 19, 79, *79,* 89, 103, 132, 316
Farming, 66, 68–71
   in China, 316, *316,* 317
   dairy, 75, 88–90
   kinds of, 68, *68,* 69, *69*
   needs in, 67, 69–71, 83, 96, 127
   vegetable, *70, 71,* 76–78
Farragut, David, 273, *273*
Ferryboats, 143, *143*
Fertilizer, 70, 80, *98,* 116
Feta cheese, 294
Fiction, 31, *31*
Field, Rachel, 124
Finland, 295, *295*
Fire departments, 196–197, *197,* 198, *198,* 328
Fire fighters, 26, *26,* 173, 196–197, *197,* 198, *198*
First aid, 187
Fishing industry, 150, *150,* 151, *151,* 153
Flag, United States, R2, *R2*
Flow charts, 152, *152,* 153, *153*

"Folks Who Live in Backward Town, The," 36
Food
   of American Indians, 236, 253
   in Finland, 295, *295*
   in Greece, 294
   growing of, 66–68, *68,* 69, *69,* 70, *70,* 71, *71, 295,* 316, *316*
   in Italy, 296
   in Japan, 294, *294*
   as a need, 23–24, *292*
   packaging and processing, *85, 90, 92*
   from plants and animals, 68–71, *80, 81,* 293–295, *295*
   special kinds of, 296, *296*
   in Turkey, 296, *296*
   in Uruguay, 294, *294*
Fort, 329, *329*
Fourth of July, 264, R5
France, 256, 259, 328
Freedom, 263–264, 277
Fresh water, 125
Fuel, 107, 116, 119, 129

Gasoline, *98,* 116, 119
Ghost towns, 234, *234*
Giraffes, 220, 222, *222*
Globe, 12, *12,* 13–14, *14,* 15
Gold, 239, 270
   dust, 240
   mining, 239–241
   pan, 240, *240*
Golden Gate Park, 210–211, *210, 211*
Goodbye, My Island, 56–60, *56–60*
Goods, 67, *98,* 109
   shipping of, 136–138, 143
Governments
   around the world, 326, *326*
   in communities, 172–174, *174,* 175–178
   providing services, 190, *190,* 191, 197, 201, *201,* 203, *203,* 204, *204, 206,* 207
   in states, 182
   in the United States, 183, *183,* 184
   See also Lawmakers, Laws, Rules

Governor, 182
Grain, *69*, 293, 295, *295*
Graphs
    See Bar graphs
Great Lakes, 130, 134, *134*, *254*
Greece, 294
Greek Americans, 132
Greenhouse, 70, *70*
Grids, 199, *199*, 200, **200**, 226
Growing season, 71, 80

Haifa, Israel, 320, *320*, 321, *321*
Harbor, *124*, 129, *129*, 133, 141, 320, *320*
Harvest, *69*, 70, 81, *81*
Hawaiians, 298
Hazards, fire, 197, 216, *216*
Hemispheres, 53
Hendershot, Judith, 96
History, 231
    of Amsterdam, The Netherlands, 333–334
    of Denver, Colorado, 234–245, 247–249
    of Mexico City, Mexico, 331–332
    of the United States, 252–265, 268–276
Hoberman, Mary Ann, 36
Holidays, 132, 338–339
    Columbus Day, *132*, 255, R5
    Fourth of July, 264, R5
    Labor Day, 276, R5
    Lincoln's Birthday, 271, R5
    Memorial Day, 272, *272*, R5
    Presidents' Day, R5
    Thanksgiving, 258, *258*, R5
    Washington's Birthday, 265, R5
    See also Celebrations
"Home, Sweet Home," 18
Homogenized, 91, 92
Horses, 47, *47*, *75*, 236
Hospitals, 27, *27*, 203
House on Maple Street, The, 282–286,
House on Maple Street, The, 282–286,
    282–286
Houses
    See Shelters
Huff, Barbara, 190

In Coal Country, 96
Income, 157, 158, 159
Independence, Iowa, 88, 89
Indiana, 49–51
Indianapolis, Indiana, 49–51
Indians, American, 253, 254, *254*, *270*
    Anasazi, 72, *72*, 73, *73*
    Arapahos, 235–237
    and battles with settlers, 269
    history of, 253–254
    Navajos, 253
    Plains, 235–236, *236*, 237, *237*
    Wampanoag, 261, *261*
    women, 236–237
Industries, 147
    fishing, 150, 151, *151*, 153
    lumber, 147–148, *148*, 149, *149*
Ireland, 132, 275, 307
Irish Americans, 132
Irrigation, 71, *71*, 72–73, 80, *80*, 127, *295*
Island, 56, 300
Israel, 320–321, *320*, 339
Italian Americans, 132
Italy, 296

Jamestown, Virginia, 257
Japan, 143, 151, 294, 297, *302*, *303*
Japanese Americans, 132
Jefferson, Thomas, 264, *264*
Jobs
    in cities, 42
    in mining communities, 97, 99
    in Seattle, 144
    See also Work, Workers
John F. Kennedy Space Center, 45
Judges, 172, 174
    state, 182
    United States, 183
Jun Tan, China, 316, *316*, 317, *317*

Kansas, 74–75
Key, Francis Scott, R3
King, Martin Luther, Jr., R5, *R5*
King Island, 56–60

Labor Day, 276, R5
Lakes, 37, *38,* 126, 134, *195*
Lawmakers, 172, 173, *173*
  in England, 262
  in Newfane, Vermont, 178
  in Tanzania, 327
  See also Governments, Rules
Laws, 169, 172, 174, 177–178, 183, 265, 271
  about following, 215–217, *217*
  in the colonies, 170–171, 262–263
  in Tanzania, 327
  See also Governments, Rules
Levisa River, 106, *106*
Liberty Bell, R4
Librarian, 30, *30,* 205, *205,* 206, *206*
Libraries, 27, 30, *30,* 31, 190, *190,* 206, *206*
"Library, The," 190
Lighthouses, 145–146, *145, 146*
Lincoln, Abraham, 271, *271*
Lincoln's Birthday, 271, R5
Lists, 86, *86,* 87
Location, 136
London, England, 328, *328*
Louvre, the, 329, *329*
Lumber industry, 147–148, *148,* 149, *149*

Majority rule, 180
Mango, 32, *32*
Mankiller, Wilma, 185, *185*
Manufacturing, 245, *274*
Maps, 6–7, 199–200
  climate, 82, *82,* 83

keys, 6, *6,* 50
landform, 111, *111,* 112
population, 324–325, *325*
resource, 74, *74,* 75, *78, 89, 114, 131, 142*
route, 139–140, *139, 140,* 162, *162, 176, 196,*
  208, 235
symbols, 6, *6,* 7, 13, 50, *139,* 140, *140*
using intermediate directions, 335
Mayflower, 258
Mayflower II, 261, *261*
Mayor, 172, 173
Memorial Day, 272, *272,* R5
Merced, California, 77, *77,* 79, 80, 83, 315, 317
Mexican Americans, 132
Mexicans, 240–241
Mexico, 240, 331, 340, *340*
Mexico City, Mexico, 331–332, *332, 335*
Michigan, Lake, 130, *131, 134, 140*
Midland, Texas, 113, *113,* 114–115, *115,* 116–
  119, 121, 214, *214,* 319
Milking Machines, 88, 89, *90*
Mineral resources, 97, *97, 98,* 99, 114–117,
  274
Minerals, 97, *97,* 114
Miners, *96,* 106–107, *107,* 108–109, 239, 240,
  240, 304
Mines, 97, 105, 107, *107,* 108, *108*
Mining Communities, 96, 99
  coal, 104–107, *106, 107,* 108, *108,* 109
  gold and silver, 239–241
  oil drilling, 96, *96,* 113–119, 318–319
Mississippi River, 130, *131, 140*
Mitchell, Arthur, 22, *22*
Model, 4, *4,* 5, *5,* 6
Moore, Anne Carroll, 205, *205*
Mother Teresa, 330, *330*
Mount Carmel, 320, *320*
Mountains, 37, 104, 111–112, *112, 127,*
  320
Museums, 208–209, *209,* 260–261, *260,*
  261

Nairobi, Kenya, 308, *308*
Nation, 263, 264, 275

National Anthem, R3
Native Americans, 56–60
   See also Eskimos; Indians, American
Natural resources, 67, 96, 97, *97*, 102, 315
   minerals, 97, *97*, 114
   using mineral resources, 97–99
   water, 125–127, *126, 127*
   See Also Coal, Oil
Navajo Indians, 253, *253*
Needs, 23–25, 26, 292, 327
   See also Clothing, Food, Shelters, Water
Neighborhoods, 1, 43, 49, 132
Netherlands, The, 259, 333
New Year's in China, 338, *338*
New York City, New York, 42–43, *43*
Newfane, Vermont, 175, *175*, 176–178
News, 186, *186*
Nonfiction, 31
North America, *12*, 13, 14, 15, 51, 52, 53
**North Carolina Museum of Life and
   Science,** 208–209, *209*
Nova Scotia, 306, *306*
Nurses, 26, 27

Oceans, 13, 14–15, 37, 53, *277*
O'Hare International Airport, 138, *138*
Oil, 97
   beginnings of, 116
   drilling for, *115*, 117, *117*, 118, *118, 319*
   at the refinery, 119, *119*
   wells, 97, *98*, 114, *115*, 118
   and work, 114
Olympic Mountains, 141
Orangutans, 221–222, *221*
Orlando, Florida, 195–196, *195*, 198, *198*
"Our History," , 252

Page, William Tyler, 166
Paris, France, 328, 329
Parks and recreation department, *174*, 207

Passover
   See Pesach
Pasta, 296, *296*
Pasteurized, 91
Pastures, 47, *47, 88*, 90, *294, 327*
Payne, John Howard, 18
Pesach, 339, 340
Petroleum, 114
   See also Oil
Petroleum Museum, 115, *115*, 116, *116*
Pikeville, Kentucky, 104, *104*, 105–106, *106*,
   107–109, 111, 315
Pilgrims, 258, *258*, 260, *260*, 261, *261*
Piñata, 340, *340*
Plains, 111, 112, *112*, 245
Plains Indians, 235–237, *236, 237, 247*
Plateaus, 111, 112, *112*
Pledge of Allegiance, R2
Plimoth Plantation, 260–261, *260, 261*
Plot, 316
Plymouth, Massachusetts, 258
Poland, 339
Police department, 177, 191, 192–194, 328
Police officers, 26, *166*, 173, 192, 193, *193*,
   194, *194*, 328, *328*
   See also Bobby
Polish Americans, 132, *132*
Port communities, 124, *124*, 129
   Chicago, Illinois, *38*, 130, *130*, 131–133, 321
   Haifa, Israel, 320–321, *320, 321*
   Seattle, Washington, 141, *141*, 142, *142*, 143,
     143, 144, *144*, 145–146, 147–151, *151*
Posadas, 340
Posey, Anita, 292
Presidents, 44, 183, *183*, 265, *265*, 271, *271*
Producers, 158, 159, 160, *160*
Property, 192
   private, 192
   public, 192
Property tax, 212, *213*
Pryor, Bonnie, 282
Public school system, 27, 197, 204, *240*, 328
Public transportation, *143*, 203, *203*, 321, *321*
Public works, 201–202, *201, 202*
Puestos, 340, *340*
Puget Sound, Washington, 141, *142*, 143, 146
Pulp, 85
Pyramids, 331–332, *332*

Railroads, 109, *109,* 136, 137, *137,* 139–140, 231, 244, *244,* 245, 269, 278

Ranchers, *75,* 274

Recreation, *45, 128, 130, 142,* 207, *207, 246*

Recycling centers, 103, *103*

Refinery, 119, *119*

Reservations, 270

Reservoirs, 202, *202*

Resources
    mineral, 97, *97, 98,* 99, 274
    natural, 67, *148,* 315
    water, 124–126, *126,* 127–128, *127, 128, 240, 269*
    ways to save, 102, *102,* 103, *103*

Rice, 295, *295*

"Ring Around the World," 314

Rivers, 37, 106, *106,* 127, *127,* 128, *128,* 130, 134, 139, 147, 148, *240, 269*

Rocky Mountains, 235, *245,* 246, *246*

Rogers, Jean, 56

Routes, 139, *139,* 140, *140*

"Rudolph Is Tired of the City," 66

Rules, 44, 165, 166–167, 169, 215–217
    See also Governments, Lawmakers, Laws

Rural, 41

St. Lawrence Seaway, 130, 133, 134

Sales tax, 212, *212,* 213

Salmon ladders, 150, *150*

Salt box house, 306, *306*

Salt water, 125

Samoa, 300, *300*

San Diego Zoo, 220–221, *221,* 222, *222,* 223, *223,* 224, *224*

Sandburg, Carl, 230

Santa Rosa, California, 168, 173, *173,* 174

Sarongs, 300, *300*

Sashimi, 294, *294*

Saudi Arabia, 300, *300*

Savings, 158, 159

Sawmills, 147–148, 149, *149*

Sculptures, 329, *329*

Sea level, 333

Seattle, Washington, 141, *141,* 142, *142,* 143, *143,* 144, *144,* 146, 147–151, *151*

Seaweed, 297–298, *297, 298*

Second Harvest, 28–29, *28, 29*

Seder, 339, *339*

Serengeti National Park, 327

Services, 157, 190, *190,* 191
    around the world, 326, 328, *328*
    costing money, 212–213
    from the fire department, *26, 174, 190,* 196–197, *197,* 198, *198*
    for health care, 203, *203*
    from the parks and recreation department, 207, *207*
    from the police department, 192–193, *193,* 194, *194*
    public schools, 204, *204*
    public transportation, 203, *203, 321*
    from the public works department, 201–202, *201, 202*
    from volunteers, 214, *214*

Settlers, 257, *257,* 258, *258,* 259, *259,* 268, 269, *269,* 270, 275, *275,* 276

Sewage, 202, *202*

Shelters
    of American Indians, 236, 237, *237,* 253, *253*
    in cities, 43, 308, *308*
    in Egypt, 307, *307*
    of Eskimos, 58
    in Ireland, 307, *307*
    as a need, 23–24
    in Nova Scotia, 306, *306*
    in Sweden, 306, *306*
    in Thailand, 307, *307*
    of wood, *259,* 305–306, *306*

Shingles, 306, *306*

Shipping, 130, *133, 137, 138*
    in Chicago, Illinois, 132, 133, *133,* 136–137, *137,* 138, *138*
    of fish, 151
    in Haifa, Israel, 320, *320*
    in lumber industry, 149
    in Seattle, Washington, 143
    using containers for, 133, *133, 137, 138*

Shish kebab, 296, *296*

Silver mining, 240–241
Skim milk, 92
Skyscrapers, 43, *43*
Slaves, 259, 271
Smith, John, 257, *257*
Soil, 67, 69, 70, 76, 79, 80, *80*
Spanish Americans, 132
Spring, Texas, 45–46
Spurs, 244
Squanto, 258
"Star-Spangled Banner, The," R3
Statue of Liberty, R4
Strauss, Levi, 304, *304*
Submersibles, 277, *277*
Suburbs, 41, 45, *45*, 46
Subways, 321, *321*
Sun City, Arizona, 45
Supreme Court, 183
Sweden, 259, 276, 305–306, *306*
Symbols
    map, 6–7
    of the United States, R2–R5, *R2, R3, R4, R5*

Tables, 87, *87*
Tai, Chang Hong, 93, *93*
Tanzania, 326, *326*, 327, *327*
Taxes, 212–213, *212*, 214
Tepees, 235, 237, *237*
Thailand, 307, *307*
Thanksgiving, 258, *258*
Thatched roofs, 307, *307*
Tibet, 299, *299*
Time, 309, *309*, 310–311
Timelines, 267, *267*, 278, *278*, 279, *279*
Tomatoes
    at the cannery, 84–85, *85*
    harvesting of, 81, *81*
    paste, 84, 85, *85*
    planting of, 80, *80*
    pulp, 85
Topeka, Kansas, 74–75
Town crier, 177, *177*
Town meeting, *173*, 176, 177, 178

Towns, 41, 456, *175*
    See also individual town names
Trade centers, 231, 240
Transportation centers, 128–129, 130, 320–321
    See also Shipping
Trucking, 109, 137, *137*
Turkey, 296

United States
    celebrations in, 340
    freedom in, 263–264, 271, *275, 276,* 277
    government in, 44, 182–184
    history of, 252–264, *264,* 265, *265,* 268–276
    holidays of, R5
    symbols of, R2–R5, *R2, R3, R4, R5*
Uruguay, 294, *294*

Valley, 77
Value, 156–157
Valves, 118
Vegetable farming, 69, *70,* 76–77, 99–80, *80,* 81, *81*
Venezuela, 318, *318,* 319, *319*
Vespucci, Amerigo, 255, *255*
Volunteer services, 214, *214*
Voting, 178, 180, *180,* 264, *264,* 265

Wampanoag Indians, 261, *261*
Wampanoag Summer Campsite, 261, *261*
Wants, 158
Washington, D.C., 44, *44,* 182, 183
Washington, George, 44, 264, 265, *265*
Washington, state of, 141, *141,* 142, *142, 143, 144,* 253
Washington's Birthday, 265, R5

Water, *124,* 125–127, *126, 127,* 128–129, 231

Weather, 67, 76, 82, 311

Wells, 97, 114, 117–118

West, the, 268, *268,* 269–270

"Whistles," 124

Windmills, 333, *333*

Work, 20, 45, 46, 156–160, 276
   See also Jobs

Workers, *26, 70, 81, 96,* 97, *107,* 109, 114, *117, 144, 148, 201,* 206, *316, 317*
   See also Jobs

World's Fairs, 322–323, *322, 323*

Wright, Frank Lloyd, 48, *48*

Wynne, Annette, 314

Yogurt, 88

ZIP codes, 49

Key: (t) top, (b) bottom, (l) left, (r) right, (c) center.

Photographs

Front cover(t), Richard Hutchings/Photo Researchers; Front Cover(b), A. J. Hartman/Comstock; Back Cover, A. J. Hartman/Comstock; iv(t), John M. Roberts/The Stock Market; iv(b), Jane Latta/Photo Researchers; v(t), John M. Roberts/The Stock Market; v(b), Christopher Springmann Inc./The Stock Market; vi(t), HBJ Photo/Alec Duncan; vi(b), HBJ Photo; vii(t), Photri; vii(b), HBJ Photo; viii(l), Vance Henry/Taurus Photos; viii(r), Zoological Society of San Diego, Ron Garrison; ix(t), Historical Picture Service; ix(b), Historical Picture Service; x(t), Adam Woolfitt/Woodfin Camp & Assoc.; x(b), Larry Mulvehill/The Stock Shop; xi(l), Adam Woolfitt/Woodfin Camp & Assoc.; xi(b), Grant Heilman; xiv(l), HBJ Photo/Rob Downey; xiv(r), HBJ Photo/Rob Downey; 1(l), HBJ Photo/Rob Downey; 1(r), HBJ Photo/Rob Downey; 3, HBJ Photo/Terry Sinclair; 4, HBJ Photo/Rick Der; 5, HBJ Photo/Rick Der; 16-17, John M. Roberts/The Stock Market.

CHAPTER 1: 18, Peter Wong/Frozen Images; 20, Billy E. Barnes; 21, Tom Meyers; 22(t), Dominique Nabokov/Gamma-Liaison; 22(b), Jonathan Atkin; 26(l), HBJ Photo/Karen Rantzman; 26(r), HBJ Photo/Terry Sinclair; 27, HBJ Photo; 28, HBJ Photo; 29(t), Borland Photography; 29(b), Borland Photography; 30(l), HBJ Photo; 30(r), HBJ Photo/Karen Rantzman; 31, HBJ Photo/Rick Der; 32, Porterfield-Chickering/Photo Researchers.

CHAPTER 2: 36, J. Messerschmidt/The Stock Market; 38(t), Grant Heilman; 39, Mel Horst; 40(t), Blair Seitz/Photo Researchers; 40(b), Bill Coleman, Inc.; 40(inset), Jane Latta/Photo Researchers; 42, Jan Halaska/Photo Researchers; 43(t), Margaret Kois/The Stock Market; 43(b), Doris De Witt/TSW; 44, Leif Skoogfors/Woodfin Camp & Assoc.; 45(t), Ken Novak/TSW/Click, Chicago; 45(b), William L. Hamilton/Shostal Assoc.; 46, HBJ Photo/Dick Scott; 47, Anne Van Der Vaeren/The Image Bank; 48(t), Marvin Koner/Black Star; 48(b), Marvin Koner/Black Star; 64-65, Stephen R. Brown/The Stock Market.

CHAPTER 3: 66, Craig Aurness/Woodfin Camp & Assoc.; 68, Linda Dufurrena/Grant Heilman Photography; 69(t), Jim Merrithew/Picture Group; 69(b), Frederick D. Bodin/Picture Group; 70, Chuck O'Rear/Woodfin Camp & Assoc.; 71, U. S. Department of Agriculture; 72, John Elk III/Stock, Boston; 73(tl), Marc Gaede/Museum of North Arizona; 73(tc), Marc Gaede/Museum of North Arizona; 73(tr), Marc Gaede/Museum of North Arizona; 73(b), Dan Budnik/Woodfin Camp & Assoc.; 75(l), Photri; 75(r), Christopher Springmann Inc./The Stock Market; 77, HBJ Photo/Elliott Varner Smith; 79, HBJ Photo/Elliott Varner Smith; 80(l), HBJ Photo/Elliott Varner Smith; 80(r), Grant Heilman; 85, courtesy Contadina Foods/Carnation Co.; 88, Grant Heilman; 90, HBJ Photo/Alec Duncan; 92, Bryce Flynn/Picture Group; 93(t), Ruthanne Lum McCunn; 93(b), courtesy of The San Joaquin County Historical Museum.

CHAPTER 4: 96, Linda Bartlett; 97(t), E. R. Degginger; 97(b), E. R. Degginger; 100(t), Fred Ward/Black Star; 100(b), Tom Stolarz/Crater of Diamonds State Park; 101(t), Jerry Wilson/Crater of Diamonds State Park; 101(b), Tom Stolarz/Crater of Diamonds State Park; 103, HBJ Photo/Alec Duncan; 104, HBJ Photo/Alec Duncan; 106, Kentucky Department of Transportation; 107(t), HBJ Photo/Terry Sinclair; 107(b), Leo Touchet/Photo-Corp Services; 109(l), MSA, Pittsburgh, PA; 109(r), Bohdan Hrynewych/Picture Group; 110(t), Denver Public Library, Western History Department; 110(b), Denver Public Library, Western History Department; 112(tl), Grant Heilman; 112(tr), Doris DeWitt/TSW/Click, Chicago; 112(bl), HBJ Photo/Elliott Varner Smith; 112(br), Grant Heilman; 113, Pickwick Players, Midland Community Theatre, Michael Spicer; 115(t), James M. Blakemore; 115(b), J. Robert Williamson; 116(t), HBJ Photo/J. Robert Williamson; 116(b), HBJ Photo/J. Robert Williamson; 117, HBJ Photo/Rodney Jones; 119, courtesy of Chevron, USA.

CHAPTER 5: 124, Thaine Manske/The Stock Market; 126(l), Thomas Kitchin/Tom Stack & Assoc.; 126(r), Ronnie Kaufman/The Stock Market; 127, E. R. Degginger; 128, Bruce Roberts/Photo Researchers; 129, Grant Heilman Photography; 130, Kunio Owaki/The Stock Market; 132(l), John Sluis/Atoz Images; 132(r), Raymond F. Hillstrom; 133, HBJ Photo/Stephen Lewellyn (The Lewellyn Studio); 135(l), HBJ Photo/courtesy United States Postal Service; 135(b), HBJ Photo/courtesy United States Postal Service; 137, HBJ Photo/Stephen Lewellyn (The Lewellyn Studio); 138, HBJ Photo/Stephen Lewellyn (The Lewellyn Studio); 141, Richard Buettner/West Stock; 142, Wolfgang Kaehler; 143, Chuck O'Rear/West Light; 144, Eric Kroll/Taurus Photos; 145, Charles Krebs/The Stock Market; 146(l), Charles Krebs/The Stock Market; 146(r), Robert Frerck/Odyssey Productions; 147, HBJ Photo/Karen Rantzman; 148(bl), Robert Semeniuk/The Stock Market; 148(bl), Joan Menschenfreund/Taurus Photos; 149(l), Brian Payne/West Stock; 149(r), Frank Siteman/Stock, Boston; 150(t), HBJ Photo/Karen Rantzman; 150(b), William Cutsinger/Photo Researchers; 151, Terry Domico/West Stock; 164-165, Flip Chalfant/The Image Bank.

CHAPTER 6: 166, Stephen R. Brown/The Stock Market; 168, HBJ Photo; 169, HBJ Photo; 170, The Bettmann Archive; 171(t), The Bettmann Archive; 171(b), The Granger Collection; 173, HBJ Photo/Larry A. Brazil; 175, HBJ Photo/Alec Duncan; 177(t), Katherine Purinton, Office of the Town Clerk, Newfane, VT; 177(b), The Bettmann Archive; 179, HBJ Photo/Terry Sinclair; 180, Doug Wilson/West Stock; 181, HBJ Photo/Alec Duncan; 183, Brad Markel/Gamma-Liaison; 184, Angeles Girls Scout Council; 185(t), Dan Agent/Cherokee Nation Photo; 185(b), Marcy Nighswander/Wide World Photos; 186, Gregory Heisler/The Image Bank.

CHAPTER 7: 190, Elizabeth Crews/Stock, Boston; 192(l), HBJ Photo/courtesy Orange County, Florida Historical Museum, Orlando Loch Haven Park; 192(r), Alec Duncan/Taurus Photos; 193, HBJ Photo/Larry A. Brazil; 194(l), HBJ Photo/Karen Rantzman; 194(r), HBJ Photo/Karen Rantzman; 195, HBJ Photo/Earl Kogler; 196, Sea World of Florida, 1986; 198, HBJ Photo/Earl Kogler; 201, Vance Henry/Taurus Photos; 202, Tom Tracy; 203(l), HBJ Photo/Karen Rantzman; 203(r), HBJ Photo/Rodney Jones; 204, HBJ Photo/Karen Rantzman; 205(t), New York Public Library; 205(b), New York Public Library; 206, HBJ Photo/Karen Rantzman; 207, HBJ Photo/Frank Wing; 209, HBJ Photo/Billy E. Barnes; 210(t), Carol Simowitz; 210(b), Wells Fargo Bank; 211(t), Carol Simowitz; 211(b), Van D. Bucher/Photo Researchers; 212, HBJ Photo/Karen Rantzman; 214, courtesy Bobby Trimble & The "Christmas in April" Volunteers; 215, HBJ Photo/Karen Rantzman; 216(l), HBJ Photo/Karen Rantzman; 216(r), HBJ Photo/Karen Rantzman; 217, HBJ Photo/Karen Rantzman; 220, Zoological Society of San Diego, Ron Garrison; 221, Zoological Society of San Diego, Ron Garrison; 222, Zoological Society of San Diego, Ron Garrison; 223(l), Zoological Society of San Diego, Ron Garrison; 223(r), Zoological Society of San Diego, Ron Garrison; 224(t), Zoological Society of San Diego, 2 Ron Garrison; 224(b), Zoological Society of San Diego, Ron Garrison; 228,229, Keith Brofsky/The Stock Broker.

CHAPTER 8: 230, The Granger Collection; 232, Bill Gillette/Stock, Boston; 233, NASA; 234, The Bettmann Archive; 235, Historical Picture Service; 236, The Thomas Gilcrease Institute of American History & Art, Tulsa, OK; 237, courtesy Amon Carter Museum, Fort Worth, TX, "The Silk Robe," Charles M. Russell; 238(t), The Bettmann Archive; 238(b), The Granger Collection; 240(t), The Denver Public Library, Western History Department; 240(b), The Granger Collection; 242, Culver Pictures; 243(t), The Department of the Treasury; 243(b), HBJ Photo/Tom Stack; 244, The Denver Public Library, Western History Department; 245, Kunio Owaki/The Stock Market; 246, Jonathan T. Wright/Bruce Coleman, Inc.; 247, courtesy Amon Carter Museum, Fort Worth, TX, detail from "Indian Village," Alfred Jacob Miller; 248(t), Colorado Historical Society; 248(b), Colorado Historical Society; 249, HBJ Photo/Alec Duncan.

CHAPTER 9: 252, The Granger Collection; 253, Alan Pitcairn/Grant Heilman Photography; 254, Rochester Museum & Science Center, "Picking Wild Strawberries," Ernest Smith; 255(t), The Granger Collection; 255(b), New York Public Library; 256(l), Culver Pictures; 256(r), Historical Picture Service; 257, The Granger Collection; 258, The Bettmann Archive; 260, Brownie Harris/The Stock Market; 261(t), Barbara Kirk/The Stock Market; 261(b), Brownie Harris/The Stock Market; 264(t), Smithsonian Institution; 264(b), The Bettmann Archive; 265(t), Historical Picture Service; 265(b), courtesy of the Museum of Fine Arts, Boston, "George Washington," Gilbert Stuart; 268, The Granger Collection; 269, Museum of the City of New York; 270, The Granger Collection; 271, National 2 Archives; 272, The Granger Collection; 273(t), Culver Pictures; 273(b), The Granger Collection; 274, The Bettmann Archive; 275, Culver Pictures; 276, Paul Steve Proehl/The Image Bank; 277, Ron Church/Photo Researchers; 288, Historical Picture Service; 290-291, Wolfgang Kaehler.

CHAPTER 10: 292, E. R. Degginger; 294(t), HBJ Photo/Rick Der; 294(b), Tom Tracy; 295(t), Karen Rantzman; 295(b), Freelance Photographer's Guild; 296(l), HBJ Photo/Elliott Varner Smith; 296(r), HBJ Photo/Rick Der; 297, Lewis Trusty/Animals Animals; 298(t), Mike Yamashita/Woodfin Camp & Assoc.; 298(b), Ralph A. Lewin/Animals Animals; 299, Robert Frerck/TSW/Click, Chicago; 300(l), Elliott Varner Smith; 300(r), Walter Hodges/West Stock; 301(l), Cary Wolinsky/Stock, Boston; 301(r), Patricia Ward/Stock, Boston; 302(l), E. M. & A. Donner/Atoz Images; 302(r), Eli Heller/Picture Group; Charles Marden Fitch/Taurus Photos; 303(r), Vance Henry/Taurus Photos; 304(t), Levi Strauss Company; 304(b), Levi Strauss Company; 306(l), Hilding Mickelsson/Naturofotograferna; 306(r), Jim Merrithew/Picture Group; 307(tl), Simon Nathan/The Stock Market; 307(bl), Eli Heller/Picture Group; 307(r), D. Holman/West Stock; 308(l), Colour Library International; 308(r), Luis Villota/The Stock Market.

CHAPTER 11: 314, Richard Hutchings/Photo Researchers; 316, J. Alex Langley, Time Magazine; 317, Richard Bernstein, Time Magazine; 318, Venezuela Tourist Information Center, New York; 319, Vince Streano/TSW/Click, Chicago; 320, R. Gordon/Atoz Images; 321, Richard Pasley/Stock; 322(l), The Bettmann Archive; 322(c), Bettmann Newsphotos; 322(r), Culver Pictures; 323(l), The Bettmann Archive; 323(r), Chicago Historical Society; 326, Diane Rawson/Photo 2 Researchers; 327, M. Phillip Kahl/Photo Researchers; 328, Larry Mulvehill/The Stock Shop; 329(l), Adam Woolfitt/Woodfin Camp & Assoc.; 329(r), SEF/Art Resource; 330(t), A. Bhopal/Baldev-Sygma; 330(b), J. P. Laffont/Sygma; 332, AP/Wide World Photos; 333(t), Bullaty Lomeo/The Image Bank; 333(b), Tom McHugh/Photo Researchers; 338(t), George Holton/Photo Researchers; 338(b), Bjorn Klingwall; 339(t), HBJ Photo/Marilyn Gary-Mulkeen; 339(b), Hannah Schreiber/Photo Researchers; 340(t), Robert Frerck/Odyssey Productions; 340(b), Allen Russell.

FOR YOUR REFERENCE: 344-R1, Maggie Steber/Stock, Boston; R3(t), The Granger Collection; R3(b), HBJ Photo; R4(t), Norman D. Tomalin/Bruce Coleman, Inc.; R4(c), Steve Elmore/Tom Stack & Assoc.; R4(b), Leonard Lee Rue III/Bruce Coleman, Inc.; R5(t), Superstock; R5(b), Flip Schalke/Black Star; R6–R18(all), United States Postal Service.

Illustrations Dick Amundsen: 56-60. Ellen Beier: 156-160. Bill Colrus: 282-286. HBJ Art: 7, 8, 9, 10, 11, 162, 335, 342. Jane Heaphy: 33, 102. Intergraphics: 6, 11, 12, 49(tr), 49(br), 86, 87, 98, 108, 118, 120(r), 121, 139, 174, 199, 200, 202, 213, 220, 226, 241, 267, 278, 279, 310, 311. Kim Jacobs: 24, 25, 31, 152, 153. Charles Scogins: 81(t), 81(r), 259. Alan Watson: 14. Robert Williams: 7(r), 8, 50(l), 324, 325.

Maps R. R. Donnelley Cartographic Services: 50(t), 51, 52, 53, 74, 78, 82, 89, 105, 111, 114, 131, 134, 140, 142(t), 176, 196, 208, 235, 263, 334.